# Recognition, Conflict and the Problem of Global Ethical Community

*Edited by*
**Shannon Brincat**

First published 2015
by Routledge

2 Park Square, Milton Park, Abingdon, Oxon OX14 4RN
711 Third Avenue, New York, NY 10017, USA

*Routledge is an imprint of the Taylor & Francis Group, an informa business*

First issued in paperback 2017

Copyright © 2015 Taylor & Francis

All rights reserved. No part of this book may be reprinted or reproduced or utilised in any form or by any electronic, mechanical, or other means, now known or hereafter invented, including photocopying and recording, or in any information storage or retrieval system, without permission in writing from the publishers.

Notice:
Product or corporate names may be trademarks or registered trademarks, and are used only for identification and explanation without intent to infringe.

*British Library Cataloguing in Publication Data*
A catalogue record for this book is available from the British Library

ISBN 13: 978-0-415-73852-1 (hbk)
ISBN 13: 978-1-138-06041-8 (pbk)

Typeset in Times New Roman
by RefineCatch Limited, Bungay, Suffolk

**Publisher's Note**
The publisher accepts responsibility for any inconsistencies that may have arisen during the conversion of this book from journal articles to book chapters, namely the possible inclusion of journal terminology.

**Disclaimer**
Every effort has been made to contact copyright holders for their permission to reprint material in this book. The publishers would be grateful to hear from any copyright holder who is not here acknowledged and will undertake to rectify any errors or omissions in future editions of this book.

# Contents

| | |
|---|---|
| *Citation Information* | vii |
| 1. Introduction: Recognition, conflict and the problem of ethical community<br>*Shannon Brincat* | 1 |
| 2. Shame and recognition: the politics of disclosure and acknowledgement<br>*Julie Connolly* | 13 |
| 3. Reply: Shame and recognition: the politics of disclosure and acknowledgement: a reply to Julie Connolly<br>*Tony Castleman* | 30 |
| 4. Al-Muhajiroun in the United Kingdom: the role of international non-recognition in heightened radicalization dynamics<br>*Maéva Clément* | 32 |
| 5. Reply: Terrorism, discourse and analysis thereof: a reply to Clément<br>*Lee Jarvis* | 48 |
| 6. Recognition and the origins of international society<br>*Erik Ringmar* | 50 |
| 7. Reply: Recognition and the origins of international society: a reply to Erik Ringmar<br>*John M. Hobson* | 63 |
| 8. Treating Asian nations with respect: promises and pitfalls of status recognition<br>*Reinhard Wolf* | 66 |
| 9. Reply: Treating Asian nations with respect: promises and pitfalls of status recognition: a reply to Reinhard Wolf<br>*Michael Clarke* | 85 |
| 10. Interest, passion, (non)recognition, and wars: a conceptual essay<br>*Thomas Lindemann* | 87 |
| 11. Reply: Recognizing non-recognition: a reply to Lindemann<br>*Brent J. Steele* | 101 |
| 12. (Dis-)respect and (non-)recognition in world politics: the Anglo-Boer war and German policy at the turn of the nineteenth/twentieth century<br>*Lena Jaschob* | 103 |

CONTENTS

13. Reply: (Dis-)respect and (non-)recognition in world politics: the Anglo-Boer War and German policy at the turn of the nineteenth/twentieth century: a reply to Lena Jaschob  117
    *Bill Nasson*

14. Killing without hatred: the politics of (non)-recognition in contemporary Western wars  120
    *Mathias Delori*

15. Reply: Killing without hatred: the politics of (non)-recognition in contemporary Western wars: a reply to Mathias Delori  136
    *Kamil Shah*

    *Index*  139

# Citation Information

The chapters in this book were originally published in *Global Discourse*, volume 4, issue 4 (December 2014). When citing this material, please use the original page numbering for each article, as follows:

**Chapter 1**
*Introduction: Recognition, conflict and the problem of ethical community*
Shannon Brincat
*Global Discourse*, volume 4, issue 4 (December 2014) pp. 397–408

**Chapter 2**
*Shame and recognition: the politics of disclosure and acknowledgement*
Julie Connolly
*Global Discourse*, volume 4, issue 4 (December 2014) pp. 409–425

**Chapter 3**
*Shame and recognition: the politics of disclosure and acknowledgement: a reply to Julie Connolly*
Tony Castleman
*Global Discourse*, volume 4, issue 4 (December 2014) pp. 426–427

**Chapter 4**
*Al-Muhajiroun in the United Kingdom: the role of international non-recognition in heightened radicalization dynamics*
Maéva Clément
*Global Discourse*, volume 4, issue 4 (December 2014) pp. 428–443

**Chapter 5**
*Terrorism, discourse and analysis thereof: a reply to Clément*
Lee Jarvis
*Global Discourse*, volume 4, issue 4 (December 2014) pp. 444–445

**Chapter 6**
*Recognition and the origins of international society*
Erik Ringmar
*Global Discourse*, volume 4, issue 4 (December 2014) pp. 446–458

# CITATION INFORMATION

**Chapter 7**
*Recognition and the origins of international society: a reply to Erik Ringmar*
John M. Hobson
*Global Discourse*, volume 4, issue 4 (December 2014) pp. 459–461

**Chapter 8**
*Treating Asian nations with respect: promises and pitfalls of status recognition*
Reinhard Wolf
*Global Discourse*, volume 4, issue 4 (December 2014) pp. 462–480

**Chapter 9**
*Treating Asian nations with respect: promises and pitfalls of status recognition: a reply to Reinhard Wolf*
Michael Clarke
*Global Discourse*, volume 4, issue 4 (December 2014) pp. 481–482

**Chapter 10**
*Interest, passion, (non)recognition, and wars: a conceptual essay*
Thomas Lindemann
*Global Discourse*, volume 4, issue 4 (December 2014) pp. 483–496

**Chapter 11**
*Recognizing non-recognition: a reply to Lindemann*
Brent J. Steele
*Global Discourse*, volume 4, issue 4 (December 2014) pp. 497–498

**Chapter 12**
*(Dis-)respect and (non-)recognition in world politics: the Anglo-Boer war and German policy at the turn of the nineteenth/twentieth century*
Lena Jaschob
*Global Discourse*, volume 4, issue 4 (December 2014) pp. 499–512

**Chapter 13**
*(Dis-)respect and (non-)recognition in world politics: the Anglo-Boer War and German policy at the turn of the nineteenth/twentieth century: a reply to Lena Jaschob*
Bill Nasson
*Global Discourse*, volume 4, issue 4 (December 2014) pp. 513–515

**Chapter 14**
*Killing without hatred: the politics of (non)-recognition in contemporary Western wars*
Mathias Delori
*Global Discourse*, volume 4, issue 4 (December 2014) pp. 516–531

CITATION INFORMATION

**Chapter 15**
*Killing without hatred: the politics of (non)-recognition in contemporary Western wars: a reply to Mathias Delori*
Kamil Shah
*Global Discourse*, volume 4, issue 4 (December 2014) pp. 532–533

Please direct any queries you may have about the citations to
clsuk.permissions@cengage.com

# INTRODUCTION

## Recognition, conflict and the problem of ethical community

Recognition has become a key theme in contemporary political, social and international relations theory. Its centrality to social life appears almost self-evident given that how we recognise others and are recognised by others is fundamental to both the identity of individual subjects and the relations between self and other in ethical community. It follows that recognition is also central to political life: nominally, as a necessity in the formation of self-identity and therefore something properly basic to relations between self and other; expansively, as a normative foundation for ethico-political relations concerned with the mutual recognition of all members of society (both individuals and groups), the actualisation of their capacities, respect of their identity, and esteem of their social contribution.

It was Hegel (1977, §178) who first situated recognition as essential for self-consciousness, claiming famously that self-consciousness can exist only when it is recognised by another self-consciousness. In this way, recognition can be defined most simply as a relation between recogniser and recognisee, an intersubjective relation in which agents place value in the recogniser as capable of recognition and the recognisee as worthy of recognition (Ikäheimo 2002, 453–455). Recognition is both a responsive act, as in the recognition of pre-existing features of a subject or what it is to be recognised as a subject, and a generative notion that may confer specific characteristics or a certain status onto subjects. As such, recognition pertains to both individuals and groups/collectives and their respective identities, rights and value. Literature in the social sciences has been weighted towards the former, which is hardly surprising given that Hegel's phenomenology of the struggle for recognition in the Master/Slave dialectic became increasingly concerned with the formation of individual subjectivities or wills, leading to Kojève's existential reading of this relation, something taken up further by Sartre and others that have since overemphasised the individualised subject in the processes of recognition (Kojève 1969, 7; Sartre 1956, 471–534).[1] This is not to suggest, however, that group or collective recognition has not been accounted for. Hegel placed recognition as foundational to ethical life (*Sittlichkeit*) through formal expressions of right and in the ethical relations of the family, civil society and the state (Hegel 1980; see Smith 1989, 3–18). Similarly, Honneth's discussion of successful struggles for recognition and the social, practical and institutional forms of recognition in society (1995, Chapter 5) and Taylor's defence of multiculturalism and communitarian ethics (1994, 25–73) clearly articulate with the fundamentality of recognition in group/collective relations.

Developments in the theory and politics of recognition since the mid-1990s have been led by the pioneering work of both Taylor and Honneth, inspiring an ever-expanding list of supporting scholarship primarily focused on struggles for recognition within states and local communities.[2] This has been met with a growing interest, particularly in recent years, regarding the question of recognition in international relations with many scholars now concentrating on the processes of recognition between nation states.[3] What have yet remained under-theorised are the processes of recognition that are not framed by or within the state, that is, recognition processes between different individuals and groups *across, between* and *over* the state (Brincat 2013). Nevertheless, the primary thrust and analytical purchase of recognition theory is that it places intersubjectivity at the centre of ethical, sociopolitical life. This is far removed from the philosophy of the subject and atomistic/individualist doctrines that have dominated political philosophy in the modern period (see Macpherson 2010), just as it offers an alternative to the most common theories of justice (i.e. distributive, procedural, retributive or restorative models).[4] For recognition theory, such individualistic ontologies possess a sociopolitical naïvety, for rather than nominalism, atomism or rational choice, recognition theory holds that the individual subject – in both their identity and the articulation of their freedom – is a social achievement, something that can be formed only though successful acts of recognition in society. Hegel, Taylor and Honneth each show that intersubjectivity is a precondition for individual identity formation and, as such, look to the development of *genuine subjectivity* through, and with, others – or what Hegel cryptically referred to as 'being with oneself in one's other' (Hegel 1980, §7A). At the ontological level – and why recognition is deemed, by some, to possess a universally emancipatory character – is because all humans are believed to require recognition as a 'vital human need' (Taylor 1994, 26) at both psychological and sociological levels for the stable construction of identity. For Honneth, there is an inherent interest in all individuals for recognition, as he claims; 'the reason we should be interested in establishing a just social order is that it is only under these conditions that subjects can attain the most undamaged possible self-relation, and thus individual autonomy' (Honneth in Fraser and Honneth 2003, 259).

Offering one of the most systematic and fully developed accounts of a theory of recognition, Honneth explains its achievement through the tripartite social structures of recognition in 'love, rights and solidarity'. Here, subjects affirm essential aspects of their individual identity through three interrelated patterns of recognition, namely: *self-confidence* (in their primary relations through which subjects are socially recognised as the bearer of unique needs), *self-respect* (in society and formal relations where subjects are socially recognised as a person of equal responsibility and agency) and *self-esteem* (in sociocultural life where subjects are socially recognised as a bearer of something unique or something of social value). Expressed alternatively, it is through these social achievements that each individual is recognised in their *neediness*, their *equality* and *agency* and their *social contribution* to society (Honneth in Fraser and Honneth 2003, 170–171). While not presented in a systematic fashion as Honneth's theory, for Taylor, the centrality of recognition to identity is reflected in loving care, the politics for equal dignity *and* the politics of difference. While the first is not considered by Taylor as a matter of public contestation, the politics of equal dignity aims at the recognition of the common humanity in each individual. In contrast, the politics of difference focuses on the individual and specific uniqueness of each subject and group (1994, 37–39). While both hold an inherent universalism, it is the latter that is seen to express and preserve the particular. However, Taylor suggests that what is considered equal dignity is defined by the dominant social group and is therefore a form of hegemony (1994, 66) and he implores us to be open towards other cultures and see in these traditions something valuable (1994, 68–71). Honneth offers a different interpretation, one that is widely regarded as being more positive, even optimistic (see Connolly 2010). For him, disrespect is the experiential content from which social struggles for recognition are formulated and which offers the potential for either an expansion of the circle of those recognised in society or the qualities to be socially esteemed or valued (Honneth 1995, 110, 121–122).

This draws us directly to the optimistic or pessimistic appraisal of recognition processes, a question that pivots on the emancipatory potential of mutual recognition or the potential for domination within the established forms of recognition within a given society. What is a matter of extreme contention here is what can be best described as the *regulative* character of recognition, that is, does recognition serve to enable forms of self-identity or does it restrict these to established social patterns? Is there some almost transcendental quality to struggles of recognition by which individuals and groups may push against the status quo – a normative 'surplus of validity', as Honneth calls it, that may bring about 'an increase in the quality of social integration' (Honneth in Fraser and Honneth 2003, 184–185) – and which confirms an inherent emancipatory quality to recognition processes? Or is recognition a form of domination or cultural hegemony circumscribed by the structures (institutional and cultural) of ethical life *as it is*?

On the pessimistic side of this debate, what is at stake is what Levinas (1969) would have called the danger of reducing the other to a recognised form in our own subjective terms, thus negating the other's absolute difference. This problem can be traced as far back as the first articulation of the Master/Slave dialectic by Hegel in the *System of Ethical Life* where the relation is portrayed as a particular antagonism in which a 'living individual confronts a living individual' and because their power (*Potenz*) is 'unequal' 'one is might or power over the other' (Hegel 1979, 125). On this darkside of recognition, what is emphasised is the assimilationist tendency within recognition that works on at least two levels: the individual psychological and social. The first, as we have been introduced to, is where recognition takes place between two (or more) subjects and is regarded as a battle to dominant and normalise the other by reducing them to oneself. The second refers to the view of recognition as a form of social hegemony that privileges certain subjectivities and excludes or denigrates others.

Along the lines of the first critique, Judith Butler views the primary relation that constitutes every self-identity to be *exclusion*. For her, the Hegelian 'self-recognitive model' violently internalises the other as a unity with the 'I', thus leading to a permanent separation of subjects (see esp. Butler, Laclua, and Zizek, 2000, 172). This separation means that the Hegelian promise of *mutual* recognition is a false and unobtainable ideal. Hegel's notion that recognition cannot remain one sided (i.e. the domination of slave/ Bondsman as a form of misrecognition) but must be transcended through genuine reciprocity is a psychological impossibility for subjects. On a related point, Nancy Fraser has argued that because of the 'excessively personalised' injury that constitutes disrespect and denigration, that rather than an emancipatory struggle for recognition the subject may actually internalise the shame or disrespect, thus negating any emancipatory potential under an overarching hegemony of established recognition patterns (Fraser and Honneth 2003, 204).

In terms of the second critique regarding socially situated forms of recognition, Althusserian interpellation would suggest that subjects suffer preconscious definition of identity because they are caught within a fixed horizon of the forms of recognition that are socially possible. So too, Bourdeieu's notion of habitus suggests that we are framed by the forms of power through which the intersubjective relations of recognition take place. Any move beyond this social context of recognition would render the ideal of mutual recognition purely transcendental. Taking up this viewpoint in a sustained critique of recognition theory, Markell (2003) has posited that there is little space in either Taylor or Honneth's optimistic approaches for the individual to resist the dominant recognitive norms or institutionalised processes of one's ethical community. As such, demands for the recognition of one's identity are merely the reflection of the power and interests of the status quo rather than some authentic drive of selfhood towards actualisation. As shown by Butler, if forms of identity are governed by specific ethical norms, that is, processes and institutions that frame specific thought and actions in subjects, then there can be no ontology of identity but mere essentialised notions that are in fact exclusionary categories that cannot be used for solidarity (Butler 1992, 14–15). These are what Connolly, Leach, and Walsh describe as the 'circumstances that may corrupt our need for recognition, producing desires for forms of recognition that may well function to reproduce social inequalities' (2007, 3).

In distinction to these pessimistic interpretations of the possibilities of recognition, what lies at the centre of optimistic readings is the potential for *mutuality* and *struggle*. In regard to the former, mutuality is typically depicted as the ideal outcome of the recognition process in which neither party dominates the other but is recognised freely and equally by, and as, a unique subject. Indeed, mutuality forms both the normative and explanatory core of the recognition theoretic. As Hegel stressed, recognition is 'the double process of both self-consciousnesses... action from one side only would be useless, because what is to happen can only be brought about by means of both' (1977, 230–231). Without mutuality, recognition would be only partial, one sided, and thereby not only radically incomplete but a form of misrecognition: an error that not only harms or disrespects the misrecognised subject but also corresponds to a reduction in the possible freedom of the dominant subject. Mutuality, then, is nothing less than a 'precondition for self-realization' (Anderson, in Honneth 1995, x) in which it follows that 'legitimate recognition is *always mutual*' (emphasis added, Tully 2000, 474). This, in part, explains the 'vital necessity' of mutual recognition for all individuals and also its universally emancipatory quality for the social totality.

Borrowing from Honneth's framework once again, mutuality is premised as essential for each stage of stable identity formation, just as it is for the normative institutionalisation of a just and free social order. Initially, mutuality in the sphere of primary relations ('love') prepares the ground for the type of relationship-to-self of basic self-confidence that is considered 'conceptually and genetically prior to every other form of reciprocal recognition' (Honneth 1995, 107). Such individual self-confidence is indispensable for autonomous participation in public life and is therefore the foundation for institutionalised order of 'rights' that secures mutual recognition in the negative sense of the formal equality of citizen-subjects, their agency and responsibility (on this see Hegel [1979, 101–110, 1980, Section One]; Williams [1997, 59–68]; Honneth [1995, 92ff]). In turn, the mutual esteem of the specific properties of individuals and groups serves to define the difference of each subject – their unique personality, interests and abilities – and to register these 'goals and desires' as something of social contribution and worth (Honneth 1995, 122, 169). However, there is contestation over what should count as an achievement or quality of social value (Honneth 1995, 126), and some have indicated the problematic nature of esteem that may intensify group competition and be inconsistent with egalitarianism (see McBride [2009]).

Nevertheless, taken together, mutuality across these three social spheres is seen to eschew any lesser forms of 'mere' recognition and create institutions necessary for the diversity and difference to flourish. As Taylor suggests, the politics of difference may secure the unique specificities and cultural features of all individuals and groups (1994, 37). Or as expressed by Appiah (1994, 149), through these social achievements can be secured the conditions for recognising someone as he *really is*. Others, like Ricoeur (2005), actually envision social change through pure ethics of recognition. It is this fundamental aspect of the Hegelian tradition of mutual recognition that offers the empirical basis for mediating the particular and universal in society, and which thus offers a unique response to the vexatious question of ethical prioritising between insider/outsider or citizen/human – a relation that is typically portrayed as an antagonistic and exclusionary dualism (see Linklater 1990; Walker 1993). While this radical potentiality in recognition is perhaps expressed in an overly idealised rather than actualised manner, it is the second element of the optimistic interpretation – its focus on *struggle* – that gives recognition theory purchase on lived social relations that may bring such mutuality about.

As explained by Tully, struggles for recognition are both a challenge to a prevailing rule or norm of intersubjective recognition and a demand for a new rule or norm, thereby altering in complex ways the unjust relations of power that these established rules/norms have legitimised (2000, 470). Such struggles are more than Hegel's (1977, 232ff) encounter between two self-consciousnesses and involve multilateral webs of relations (and their affect) throughout society (Tully 2000, 474). In this context, to assert monological notions of identity is to overlook the intersubjective basis of the self and the social context of struggles for recognition. For Honneth, experiences of distorted recognition, disrespect or denigration generate the impetus for new social struggles. That is, the violation of our moral expectation to be recognised and the perception of such injustices of disrespect or denigration – that includes, but is not limited to, humiliation, degradation, insult, disenfranchisement and physical abuse (Anderson in Honneth 1995, viii) – provides Honneth with a model of social struggle towards the establishment of ideal processes of mutual recognition. Such experiences provide the motivational basis, the reasons and emotional responses, against distorted processes of recognition. However, this does not mean that such struggles will be successful or even take place – rather this tension informs a dialectic in which the potential for the emergence of mutuality is ever present. The actualisation of mutuality is a contingent and political question of struggle and power. Optimism emerges from the belief that given the fundamentality of recognition for individual subjectivity and social flourishing, transgressions will spur political action. However, even Ricoeur (2005, 218) who is perhaps the most optimistic of all recognition theorists, admits that demands for recognition may never end and may even result in what Hegel called the 'unhappy consciousness', in which the self remains alienated from others. As such, rather than a telos or endpoint, struggles for recognition are best described as open-ended, or what Tully (2000, 477) labels 'continuous processes'.

Turning now to lived struggles, we can see that while these overlap with different socioeconomic contexts and distributional demands (Fraser in Fraser and Honneth 2003, 50–54), anticolonial and apartheid struggles, first wave feminism, the Civil Rights movement and the international workers movement can all be seen as unique forms of struggles for recognition. That is, they can be seen to share an affinity with the so-called struggles in the politics of difference or identity – i.e. ethnic, religious, lesbian, gay, bisexual, transgender, queer and intersexed community, disabled and indigenous, to name some of the more prominent social struggles that seek to affirm recognition of the needs, equality and contribution of these individuals and groups. Even struggles between nation states, while typically seen as merely instrumental conflicts for power, have been shown to include struggles for recognition, prestige and honour (see Lindemann and Ringmar 2012). As such, it is by mutuality and struggle that contemporary political conflicts can not only be understood but also be justified.

This tension between pessimistic and optimistic accounts of recognition has been the guiding problematic animating this Special Issue of *Global Discourse*. While not aiming at resolution, *Recognition, Conflict and the Problem of Ethical Community* was based around exploring these themes in a truly transdisciplinary manner across social, political and international theory by examining recognition processes between individuals, groups and states. The Special Issue canvasses a broad array of different research on recognition:

from conceptual pieces as offered by Lindemann (2014a) and Ringmar's (2014a) contributions to historical and practical examinations of recognition as advanced in Jaschob (2014) and Delori (2014); from policy prescriptions for foreign relations (Wolf 2014) and recognition processes between individuals (Connolly 2014) to pathologies of recognition in violent groups (Clément 2014).

*Recognition, Conflict and the Problem of Ethical Community* begins with Julie Connolly's (2014) exploration of the phenomenology of shame in struggles for recognition. Connolly argues that without some kind of disclosure, the formulation of the relevant claim, the struggle for recognition cannot get started and that without acknowledgement, recognition will remain incomplete. This suggests a refinement of Axel Honneth's critical theory of social recognition that Connolly considers optimistic regarding the possibilities of the experience of misrecognition. For Connolly, things are not so straightforward regarding resolution through just institutional innovations. This is not only because recognition may fix identity, reproducing the limitations on agency via hegemonic social standards but also because the lack of an emotional response may make it unlikely that the injustice will be exposed and solidarity will be formed in social struggles for recognition. Quite simply, Connolly suggests that not all struggles for recognition may be emancipatory. Turning to Agnes Heller and Martha Nussbaum, Connolly reveals a more complex phenomenology of shame, guilt and moral conscience in their work that shows the need for mediation between ethics and negative feelings. Similarly, Morrison's novel *The Bluest Eye* (1999) depicts how the consequences of shame are difficult to predict and may have a destructive impact. The question for struggles for recognition is how solidarity can be formed through disclosure and acknowledgement rather than negative emotional power. Turning to Hannah Arendt, Connolly argues that the politics of recognition rests on the politics of disclosure and acknowledgement through which we appear to each other and that may problematise the very structure of interpretation of self-realisation and human agency in society. Castleman (2014) replies that the next step may be to explore what conditions, contexts and other factors influence responses to these phenomena and to identify factors that influence agency and disclosure and acknowledgement processes.

Continuing with the critical interrogation of recognition theory, Clément (2014) examines the problem of misrecognition – those cases in which, far from an emancipatory change in social life towards mutuality, leads to discourses of supremacy and an increase in violence. Focusing on the radical Islamist group Al-Muhajiroun (that operated from 1996 to 2004 principally within the UK), Clément explores the dynamics between the alleged experience of non-recognition of this group and the reorientation of the group's preferences towards violent practices. Viewing misrecognition as a mismatch between self-image and the image reflected by others, groups facing denials of recognition can either accept demeaning/disrespectful images imposed by others or they may challenge these. Clément shows that the representations with Al-Muhajiroun's discourses about the 9/11 attacks and the war in Afghanistan orientated the group towards increased radicalism and violence. Specifically, as Al-Muhajiroun's world view was rooted in prestige, seeking recognition as an Islamist group, the Islamic Emirate of Afghanistan, and the transnational community of Muslims or Ummah, it was not concerned with contesting hegemony or domination, but wished to replace Western hegemony with an Islamic world state. Adopting a poststructuralist discursive epistemology, Clément analyses an array of Al-Muhajiroun's discourses showing the gradual transformation of the nature of its struggle for recognition, how it transfigured the West to a lesser subjectivity, disqualifying its capacity as an intersubjective recognition partner. In turn, Al-Muhajiroun sought unilateral recognition of its dominance in a new hegemony, removing the case far from the ideal of mutuality. However, as Jarvis (2014) notes in his reply, such radicalisation has a particular history that needs to be acknowledged. That is, analysis should take into account how Al-Muhajiroun has been itself discursively constructed by other interested parties, thus opening up the reconstruction of the intentions/purposes behind discursive acts by asking why Al-Muhajiroun sought to construct its struggle as it did and deconstructing Al-Muhajiroun's struggle in its own terms.

Turning to international relations, Ringmar's (2014a) groundbreaking article offers nothing less than an alternate history of the origins of international society. On the one hand, he finds that international society was formed through practices of recognition that affirmed the similarities between European states, and, on the other, through practices of non-recognition that affirmed differences between Europeans and non-Europeans. This contradicts not only liberal and English School accounts of the historical narrative of world politics that remains deeply embedded in the disciplinary mainstream of international relations, but also the assumption of acculturation, the idea that international society was formed when a core of like-minded European states realised how much they had in common and extended this outward to other nations. As Ringmar shows through examples taken from diplomacy, trade, warfare and his case study on cultural artefacts, international society was formed by a sharp distinction drawn between Europeans and all others. That is, practices of mutual recognition amongst Europeans existed alongside practices of non-recognition for non-Europeans. Whereas European states enjoyed full sovereignty, 'savages' had no standing in international law and 'barbarians' were international subjects only in certain respects. Such practices of non-recognition established differences and inequalities into the very structure of international society; European states were made alike and non-Europeans were made different. The latter process was not some aberration but was constitutive of international society and continues to exist at the heart of the paradoxical nature of sovereignty, despite the rhetoric regarding equality and universal rights. For Hobson (2014), this begs the question as to how we can move beyond this hierarchical Eurocentric conception of recognition or indeed the very foundation of international society. For Hobson, if this is possible it must be to first recognise the mutually co-constitutive influences of East and West that have driven development of international society and, secondly, a process of mutual dialogue in which all peoples can sit down at the table of global humanity and mutually recognise each other.

Offering a practical engagement with status recognition in foreign relations, Wolf (2014) formulates a ten-point policy recommendation aimed at facilitating international cooperation through respect and recognition. For Wolf, research has demonstrated that meeting claims for recognition can foster international understanding while status misrecognition can fuel conflict. So whilst international recognition is more nuanced and variable, its importance is acute. Respect increases the chances of cooperative behaviour, allows for an open and thorough exchange of ideas and helps avoid status conflicts. In turn, disrespect can aggravate ongoing conflicts, harm an actor's reputation, intensify resistance, incite resentment and ruin prospects for long-term cooperation. Looking to demands for respectful treatment by China, Iran and India – who have experienced 'status mismatches' through colonial subjugation and other infringements by the West – Wolf offers clear examples of how calls for respect are not just a desire for better treatment but for moral consideration of the social importance and worth of these nation states (including recognition of their ideas and values, physical needs and interests, achievements, efforts, qualities and virtues, and rights). Despite the modest costs of respect (time, materials, opening up to external influences, conflation, competition and domestic standing), Wolf is resolute in his advice regarding how Western policies and gestures should convey greater respect and thus promote international progress, or at least minimise the damaging effects of disrespect. Along similar lines Clarke (2014) views respect as a cognate of honour, highlighting the benefits of Wolf's approach in conceiving recognition as a socially constituted and dynamic factor shaping international relations. However, Clarke also notes the problem presented by those situations in which parties in conflict may have irreconcilable interests and contradictory status-oriented goals.

Lindemann's (2014a) conceptual essay makes the strong claim that behind conflict and war always lies hidden conceptions of non-recognition between self and other. This thesis forms part of a larger research project on non-recognition, war and the 'minimization of the other' as a motivation for conflict – an approach that contends with the far more popular explanations for war as based on security, power or profit. For Lindeman, by contrast, conflicts arise when the self holds minimised presentations of the other and it is this tension that forms the basis – or condition of possibility – for wars of interest. That is, wars for 'cold interests' are only possible when emotions of compassion are neutralised by the non-recognition of the other. Lindeman offers compelling empirical evidence that even wars most commonly interpreted in terms of material interest actually entail a 'minimizing' or non-recognition of the other. When the other is perceived as a threat, or as inanimate, or at an effective distance, the propensity for violence is increased by justifying war and paralyzing compassion. However, the claim that material interests can only lead to war if the other is minimised (or misrecognised), is queried by Steele (2014) on epistemic grounds. Steele asks whether we have knowledge of such a process, suggesting that conflict may not occur only when correct recognition is negated or in error, but where one recognises the other but seeks to destroy them.

Turning to history, Jaschob (2014) provides an account of the impact of disrespect and non-recognition through an analysis of Anglo-German interactions during the Anglo-Boer War (1899–1901). For Jaschob, respect can be seen as the adequate recognition of one's subjectively deserved status and yet such status, unlike material capabilities, cannot be gained unilaterally. Consequently, a status mismatch can occur when another party does not adequately express or reflect this status through practices of respect, increasing the antagonism and potentially leading to serious conflict (Wolf 2011). Jaschob finds that the Anglo-German relationship was characterised by misunderstandings, feelings of non-recognition and disrespectful behaviour on both sides. Focusing on the political consequences of the 'Bundesrath-Affäre', Jaschob argues that while the diplomatic crisis was quickly resolved, the underlying perceptions of disrespect and non-recognition had a persistent and negative effect on the Anglo-German relationship. Moreover, it was these subjective experiences that dominated the political actions on the German side who sought compensations, both symbolically and materially. The desire for respect even overshadowed power-political interests that are typically seen as most important in conflicts regarding competing foreign policy objectives, a finding complementary to both Lindemann (2014a) and Wolf's (2014) arguments, presented above. Jaschob thereby highlights the importance of status as a structural phenomenon in the international system, something typically downplayed in classical accounts of international relations and realpolitik. This signifies that greater concern with practices of recognition may help explain – and indeed mediate – foreign relations. Jaschob provides rich and detailed historical account of the ensuing diplomatic and relational crisis, and the residual status mismatch between the German Kaiserreich and Great Britain remained. In the long run, burdened by these incidents, the Anglo-German relationship would threaten the entire system. However, Nasson (2014) replies that this was not the only flashpoint in many concerning recognition and respect between Germany and Britain. While he agrees that status seeking left simmering attitudes that infected the relationship, this should not be pressed too far as not only were there still unilateral material considerations at play, but the UK was ascendant in the region and globally, and Germany was seeking to revise this order. As such, it is important to not lose sight of the convergence of political, strategic and economic imperatives alongside these status or recognitive dimensions of struggle.

Concluding the Special Issue, Delori (2014) offers sociological and ethnographic insights into the processes of recognition in contemporary Western wars through a case study of French pilots who participated in the war in Libya in 2011. Delori's empirical work provides a unique engagement with the conceptual aspect of recognition and killing, a subject area rarely engaged. For Delori, military consent for killing is mediated by powerful discursive structures that frame those lives that are recognised as liveable and those excluded from the ethics of compassion. He goes further however, through findings from his interviews with 40 French pilots/soldiers involved in the military action, that those killed were 'ungrievable lives' (Butler 2010, xix), signifying a spectacular case of misrecognition – a phenomena he suggests that may increase in the context of contemporary humanitarian and technological wars. This contests sharply with those that see in modern technologies of war not the reification and dehumanisation of the enemy, but a trend towards human representation resulting in a greater control of violence and decrease in number of people killed. Given this highly contested area, Delori's empirical research offers some insights into how ideas and materialities co-constitute each other in the discourse of wars that are inseparable from power. He shows that both the pilots and the vast majority of media outlets reporting on the conflict had no account of the number of Libyan loyalist combatants killed in their bombing runs, or the conflict as a whole. Even in the pilot's celebration of their missions, the enemy remained complexly absent. Both of these seem to confirm Delori's thesis that misrecognition has contributed to the ideational framing of humanitarian war on the one hand, and new technologies on the other, into a discourse in which some lives have become invisible and ungrievable. Shah (2014) responds, however, that such contemporary Western wars have been built upon the incredible insecurity of the West whose list of perceived threats and enemies has proliferated. The war in Libya was buttressed by discourses of humanitarianism and it invoked the *Responsibility to Protect*, conflating the West with the international community and privileging its discourses on humanitarian and military intervention to decide who could live or die.

Finally, we have two Review Symposium on seminal texts focused on recognition in international relations and social theory, respectively. The first engages with Lindemann and Ringmar's (2012) edited volume *The International Politics of Recognition*. This book contains a number of chapters that apply recognition to the problems of international conflict, offering an alternative to mainstream approaches in international relations and security studies. Providing reviews are Zuo (2014), Duncombe (2014) and Olsson (2014) with individual responses from both Lindemann (2014b) and Ringmar (2014b). The second is Axel Honneth's (2012) *The I in We*, a collection of essays that develop Honneth's theory of recognition in terms of a theory of justice, social reproduction and individual identity formation. Reviews are given by Weber (2014), Murray (2014) and Heins (2014), and a detailed response is provided by Honneth (2014).

In closing, I would like to sincerely thank the authors who participated in the Review Symposia, Axel Honneth, Thomas Lindemann and Erik Ringmar, and those reviewers who offered an array of critical viewpoints on these texts. I would also like to thank all of the authors in the Special Issue for their rich and thought-provoking articles and who have offered a genuinely transdisciplinary engagement with the problem of recognition, violence and ethical community. Finally, a special mention of gratitude must be given to both the anonymous referees and those reviewers who wrote replies to the articles and who make this journal unique.

## Notes

1. On this transition between Hegel's Jena Period and the *Phenomenology* see Honneth (1995).
2. For some key examples see Banting and Kymlicka (2001), Tully (2004, 84–106), Thompson (2006), Connolly (2007), Van Den Brink and Owen (2007). For a general introduction to recognition theory see McQueen (2011).
3. For some key examples see Wendt (2003, 491–542), Haacke (2005, 181–194), Heins (2008, 141–153), Kochi (2009), Lindemann and Ringmar (2012).
4. Arguably, there is some overlap between all four models and recognition. However, recognition has been shown to articulate with a capabilities-based approach and to be highly useful in a variety of contexts (see e.g. Schlosberg [2012, 445–461]).

## References

Appiah, K. A. 1994. "Identity, Authenticity, Survival: Multicultural Societies and Social Reproduction." In *Multiculturalism: Examining the Politics of Recognition*, edited by A. Gutmann. Princeton, NJ: Princeton University Press.

Banting, K., and W. Kymlicka. 2001. *Multiculturalism and the Welfare State: Recognition and Redistribution in Contemporary Democracies*. Oxford: Oxford University Press.

Brincat, S. 2013. "Cosmopolitanism: The Fourth Dimension of Recognition?" Paper presented at the International Studies Association (ISA) Annual Convention, San Francisco, CA, April 2–6.

Butler, J. 1992. "Contingent Foundations: Feminism and the Question of 'Postmodernism'." In *Feminists Theorize the Political*, edited by J. Butler and J. W. Scott. London: Routledge.

Butler, J. 2010. *Frames of War. When is Life Grievable?* London: Verso.

Butler, J., E. Laclau, and S. Zizek. 2000. *Contingency, Hegemony, Universality*. London: Verso.

Castleman, T. 2014. "Shame and Recognition: The Politics of Disclosure and Acknowledgement: A Reply to Julie Connolly." *Global Discourse* 4 (4): 426–427. doi:10.1080/23269995.2014.933056.

Clarke, M. 2014. "Treating Asian Nations with Respect: Promises and Pitfalls of Status Recognition: A Reply to Reinhard Wolf." *Global Discourse* 4 (4): 481–482. doi:10.1080/23269995.2014.939903.

Clément, M. 2014. "Al-Muhajiroun in the United Kingdom: The Role of International Non-Recognition in Heightened Radicalization Dynamics." *Global Discourse* 4 (4): 428–443. doi:10.1080/23269995.2014.918306.

Connolly, J. 2007. "Risks and Vulnerabilities in the Struggle for Recognition." In *Recognition in Politics: Theory, Policy and Practice*, edited by J. Connolly, M. Leach and L. Walsh. Newcastle: Cambridge Scholars.

Connolly, J. 2010. "Recognition and the Politics of Disclosure." Paper presented at Australian Political Studies Association Conference 2010 Connected Globe: Conflicting Worlds, School of Social and Political Sciences, University of Melbourne, September 27–29 (unpublished).

Connolly, J. 2014. "Shame and Recognition: The Politics of Disclosure and Acknowledgement." *Global Discourse* 4 (4): 409–425. doi:10.1080/23269995.2014.926733.

Connolly, J., M. Leach, and L. Walsh. 2007. "Introduction." In *Recognition in Politics: Theory, Policy and Practice*, edited by M. Leach and L. Walsh. Newcastle: Cambridge Scholars.

Delori, M. 2014. "Killing without Hatred: The Politics of (Non)-Recognition in Contemporary Western Wars." *Global Discourse* 4 (4): 516–531. doi:10.1080/23269995.2014.935102.

Duncombe, C. 2014. "*The International Politics of Recognition*, by Thomas Lindemann and Erik Ringmar. Non-Recognition in International Relations: Developing New Approaches to Political Problems." *Global Discourse* 4 (4): 536–538. doi:10.1080/23269995.2014.917036.

Fraser, N., and A. Honneth. 2003. *Redistribution or Recognition? A Political-Philosophical Exchange*. London: Verso.

Haacke, J. 2005. "The Frankfurt School and International Relations' on the Centrality of Recognition." *Review of International Studies* 31 (1): 181–194. doi:10.1017/S0260210505006376.

Hegel, G. W. F. 1977. *Phenomenology of Spirit*. Translated by A. V. Miller. Oxford: Oxford University Press.
Hegel, G. W. F. 1979. *System of Ethical Life*. Translated and edited by T. M. Knox. Albany: SUNY.
Hegel, G. W. F. 1980. *The Philosophy of Right*. Translated by T. M. Knox. New York: Oxford University Press.
Heins, V. 2008. "Realizing Honneth: Redistribution, Recognition, and Global Justice." *Journal of Global Ethics* 4 (2): 141–153. doi:10.1080/17449620802194025.
Heins, V. M. 2014. "*The I in We: Studies in the Theory of Recognition*, by Axel Honneth. Survival through Recognition?" *Global Discourse* 4 (4): 560–562. doi:10.1080/23269995.2014.919789.
Hobson, J. 2014. "Recognition and the Origins of International Society: A Reply to Erik Ringmar." *Global Discourse* 4 (4): 459–461. doi:10.1080/23269995.2014.917033.
Honneth, A. 1995. *The Struggle for Recognition*. Cambridge, MA: MIT Press.
Honneth, A. 2012. *The I in We*. Cambridge: Polity.
Honneth, A. 2014. "*The I in We: Studies in the Theory of Recognition*, by Axel Honneth. Rejoinder." *Global Discourse* 4 (4): 562–566. doi:10.1080/23269995.2014.952075.
Ikäheimo, H. 2002. "On the Genus and Species of Recognition." *Inquiry* 45 (4): 447–462. doi:10.1080/002017402320947540.
Jarvis, L. 2014. "Terrorism, Discourse and Analysis Thereof: A Reply to Clément." *Global Discourse* 4 (4): 444–445. doi:10.1080/23269995.2014.930599.
Jaschob, L. 2014. "(Dis-)Respect and (Non-)Recognition in World Politics: The Anglo Boer War and German Policy at the Turn of the Nineteenth/Twentieth Century." *Global Discourse* 4 (4): 499–512. doi:10.1080/23269995.2014.917028.
Kochi, T. 2009. *The Other's War: Recognition and the Violence of Ethics*. Abingdon: Birkbeck law Press.
Kojève, A. 1969. *Introduction to the Reading of Hegel: Lectures on the "Phenomenology of Spirit"*. Translated and edited by A. Bloom and J. H. Nichols. New York: Basic Books.
Levinas, E. 1969. *Totality and Infinity: An Essay on Exteriority*. Pittsburgh, PA: Duquesne University Press.
Lindemann, T. 2014a. "Interest, Passion, (Non)Recognition, and Wars: A Conceptual Essay." *Global Discourse* 4 (4): 483–496. doi:10.1080/23269995.2014.926734.
Lindemann, T. 2014b. "*The International Politics of Recognition*, by Thomas Lindemann and Erik Ringmar. Recognizing (Mis)Recognition from the inside and the Outside. Some Criteria for "Seizing" a Slippery Concept." *Global Discourse* 4 (4): 542–549. doi:10.1080/23269995.2014.919791.
Lindemann, T., and E. Ringmar Eds. 2012. *The International Politics of Recognition*. Boulder, CO: Paradigm.
Linklater, A. 1990. *Men and Citizens in the Theory of International Relations*. 2nd ed. London: MacMillan Press.
Macpherson, C. B. 2010. *The Political Theory of Possessive Individualism*. Oxford: Oxford University Press.
Markell, P. 2003. *Bound by Recognition*. Princeton, NJ: Princeton University Press.
McBride, C. 2009. "Demanding Recognition: Equality, Respect, and Esteem." *European Journal of Political Theory* 8 (1): 96–108. doi:10.1177/1474885108096962.
McQueen, P. 2011. "Social and Political Recognition." *Internet Encyclopedia of Philosophy*. Accessed July 20, 2014. http://www.iep.utm.edu/recog_sp/
Morrison, T. 1999. *The Bluest Eye*. London: Vintage.
Murray, M. 2014. "*The I in We: Studies in the Theory of Recognition*, by Axel Honneth. Differentiating Recognition in International Politics." *Global Discourse* 4 (4): 558–560. doi:10.1080/23269995.2014.919788.
Nasson, B. 2014. "(Dis-)Respect and (Non-)Recognition in World Politics: The Anglo-Boer War and German Policy at the Turn of the Nineteenth/Twentieth Century: A Reply to Lena Jaschob." *Global Discourse* 4 (4): 513–515. doi:10.1080/23269995.2014.917032.
Olsson, C. 2014. "*The International Politics of Recognition*, by Thomas Lindemann and Erik Ringmar. Warfare and Recognition in IR: On the Potential Inputs of the Historical Sociology of the State." *Global Discourse* 4 (4): 539–542. doi:10.1080/23269995.2014.917037.
Ricoeur, P. 2005. *The Course of Recognition*. Translated by David Pellauer. Cambridge, MA: Harvard University Press.

Ringmar, E. 2014a. "Recognition and the Origins of International Society." *Global Discourse* 4 (4): 446–458. doi:10.1080/23269995.2014.917031.

Ringmar, E. 2014b. "*The International Politics of Recognition*, by Thomas Lindemann and Erik Ringmar. On the Reality of Mental Constructs." *Global Discourse* 4 (4): 549–555. doi:10.1080/23269995.2014.947069.

Sartre, J. P. 1956. *Being and Nothingness*. London: Philosophical Library.

Schlosberg, D. 2012. "Climate Justice and Capabilities: A Framework for Adaptation Policy." *Ethics & International Affairs* 26 (4): 445–461. doi:10.1017/S0892679412000615.

Shah, K. 2014. "Killing without Hatred: The Politics of (Non)-Recognition in Contemporary Western Wars: A Reply to Mathias Delori." *Global Discourse* 4 (4): 532–533. doi:10.1080/23269995.2014.940782.

Smith, S. B. 1989. "What is 'Right' in Hegel's *Philosophy of Right*?" *The American Political Science Review* 83 (1): 3–18. doi:10.2307/1956431.

Steele, B. J. 2014. "Recognizing Non-Recognition: A Reply to Lindemann." *Global Discourse* 4 (4): 497–498. doi:10.1080/23269995.2014.928134.

Taylor, C. 1994. "The Politics of Recognition." In *Multiculturalism: Examining the Politics of Recognition*, edited by A. Gutmann, 25–73. Princeton, NJ: Princeton University Press.

Thompson, S. 2006. *The Political Theory of Recognition: A Critical Introduction*. Cambridge: Polity Press.

Tully, J. 2000. "Struggles over Recognition and Distribution." *Constellations* 7 (4): 469–482. doi:10.1111/1467-8675.00203.

Tully, J. 2004. "Recognition and Dialogue: The Emergence of a New Field." *Critical Review of International Social and Political Philosophy* 7 (3): 84–106. doi:10.1080/1369823042000269401.

Van Den Brink, B., and D. Owen. 2007. *Recognition and Power*. Cambridge: Cambridge University Press.

Walker, R. B. J. 1993. *Inside/Outside*. Cambridge: Cambridge University Press.

Weber, M. 2014. "*The I in We: Studies in the Theory of Recognition*, by Axel Honneth. Pushing the Constellations of Recognition." *Global Discourse* 4 (4): 556–558. doi:10.1080/23269995.2014.919790.

Wendt, A. 2003. "Why a World State is Inevitable." *European Journal of International Relations* 9 (4): 491–542. doi:10.1177/135406610394001.

Williams, R. R. 1997. *Hegel's Ethics of Recognition*. Berkeley: University of California Press.

Wolf, R. 2011. "Respect and Disrespect in International Politics: The Significance of Status Recognition." *International Theory* 3 (1): 105–142. doi:10.1017/S1752971910000308.

Wolf, R. 2014. "Treating Asian Nations with Respect: Promises and Pitfalls of Status Recognition." *Global Discourse* 4 (4): 462–480. doi:10.1080/23269995.2014.947064.

Zuo, Y. 2014. "*The International Politics of Recognition*, by Thomas Lindemann and Erik Ringmar. On the Empirical Study of International Recognition." *Global Discourse* 4 (4): 462–480. doi:10.1080/23269995.2014.917035.

Shannon Brincat
*July 2014*

# Shame and recognition: the politics of disclosure and acknowledgement

Julie Connolly

*School of Political Science and International Studies, University of Queensland, St Lucia, QLD, Australia*

> Alongside his critical theory of social recognition, Axel Honneth develops a phenomenology of shame. He suggests that the harms of misrecognition are registered in feelings of shame, which in turn prompt struggles with, for and over recognition: struggles that he variously describes as emancipatory or progressive. In effect, Honneth suggests that shame is a resource for politics. The first part of the article examines the rhetorically compelling concepts of shame and suffering that structure Honneth's critique of misrecognition. Drawing on the work of Agnes Heller, Martha Nussbaum and Toni Morrison, I offer an alternative analysis of the politics of shame, which has implications for Honneth's analysis of emotions and selfhood. More importantly, however, this analysis suggests that Honneth does not explain how the struggle for recognition can become political. With recourse to Hannah Arendt, I argue that the politics of recognition rests on the politics of disclosure and acknowledgement.

## Introduction

The activities of disclosure and acknowledgement are integral to the politics of recognition. Something must first be disclosed if it is to be recognised, even if that disclosure is theoretical and takes places outside a dyadic context. The capacity of women to share in humanity, and the political rights associated with which, is a case in point. This was and is a general argument levelled at both individuals and institutions. The point is without some kind of disclosure, the formulation of the relevant claim, the struggle for recognition cannot get started. Moreover, in the absence of acknowledgement, recognition remains incomplete. Acknowledgement can be simple: an 'aha' moment, when you catch sight of the reflection of a friend in the coffee shop window. Or it can be more complicated, mediated by institutions rather than just realised in interpersonal relationships. One of the great strengths of Axel Honneth's contribution to the debate about the utility of our struggles for recognition, for both politics and critical theory, is his analysis of the nexus of individual desire, interpersonal experience and institutional formations, which structures the realisation of mutual recognition in generalised forms that nonetheless remain the subject of debate and renovation. His analysis traverses our intimate and public experiences of recognition. His account is distinguished by his attempt to draw out the normative kernel of our mutual vulnerability to misrecognition, and on this basis, he reconstructs an ethical order in late modernity. Accordingly, different forms of social organisation provide the basic forms of recognition requisite for human flourishing. This is an ambitious project. In his most recent book, *Freedom's Right*, Honneth has extended his argument asserting that different forms of recognition promote aspects of human freedom, providing the basis for not only an account of ethical life in modernity but also for a theory of justice. This, however, is not the concern of this article. Instead, I am interested in exploring moments of disclosure and acknowledgement in the struggle for recognition, moments that have received little attention from Honneth.

The first part of the article examines the rhetorically compelling ideas of suffering and shame that animate Honneth's early analysis of our vulnerability to misrecognition. Honneth's concern with moral injury and its relationship to social movement activism is consistent throughout his work on recognition. In his analysis, such experiences prompt social struggle. He is cognisant of the limits of political theories, including some forms of Marxism, that cite economic interest as the sole or even primary factor that compels political agency, including that of social movements. Critical of such crude materialism, Honneth offers a more complicated analysis of human emotions. He argues that our vulnerability to moral injury explains why the struggle for recognition is an enduring feature of politics: misrecognition causes forms of suffering that we are predisposed to mitigate. The intersubjectivity of his analysis vitiates the Hobbesian (or perhaps Freudian) conclusion that such struggle is likely to be unending in the absence of an external authority to regulate our desires for recognition. Honneth argues instead the mutual recognition pacifies struggle. In his rather optimistic analysis, our struggles for recognition can and do resolve themselves in institutional innovations, like the extension of suffrage. This article, however, contends that matters are not so straightforward.

Towards the end of *The Struggle for Recognition*, Honneth comments that 'social shame is a moral emotion that expresses the diminished self-respect typically accompanying the passive endurance of humiliation and degradation' (1995, 164). Leaving aside Honneth's description of 'social shame' as a 'moral emotion', this contention raises the interesting possibility that active resistance to violence and exploitation can engender self-worth. This possibility is not explored by Honneth. Indeed, it is somewhat at odds with the general thrust of Honneth's argument in *The Struggle for Recognition*. In this text, Honneth seeks to demonstrate our constitutive dependence on social recognition for the formation of a sense of ourselves as individuals, with unique biographies and shared identities. Most often, Honneth suggests that self-worth is a consequence of social recognition, not of social agency. This argument serves to ground his claims about the normative significance of recognition. It also suggests why suffering and shame, terms that appear as shorthand for our mutual vulnerability to moral rather than physiological injury, are experiences worthy of interrogation for Honneth.

The link Honneth posits between emotion and agency as catalyst for the struggle for recognition, however, deserves greater scrutiny than has been the case till now. Honneth's optimism regarding the outcomes of our struggles for recognition relies on a somewhat truncated account of our experience of misrecognition. Although not fatal for his theory, this leaves Honneth more vulnerable than he needs to be to pessimistic reconstructions of the struggle for recognition, which variously contend that our psychological vulnerability to recognition may remedy us for domination rather than freedom. That the politics of recognition may be animated by desire to fix identities in advance of interrogating whether or not they reproduce expectations that are implicated in limiting agency and imagination, without examining whether the politics of recognition appeals to hegemonic standards that might be better disputed by radical politics (Markell 2003). Whether the struggle for recognition gives rise to a kind of *ressentiment*, in which protagonists seek to invert rather than transcend marginalisation (Brown 1995). This article argues that to get a handle on the pessimistic critique, Honneth would do well to distinguish and interrogate moments of disclosure and acknowledgement in the struggle for recognition. Some of the resources for this engagement are implicit in Honneth's thinking but not well articulated as yet.

To this end, the article explores the politics of shame drawing on Agnes Heller, Martha Nussbaum and Toni Morrison's first novel *The Bluest Eye*: the story of a little black girl who 'yearns for the blue eyes of a little white girl' (1970/1999, 162). My analysis works to substantiate the criticisms articulated in my reconstruction of Honneth's account of emotions and agency, regarding the complex relationship between moral injury, emotional discontent and political activism. The choice of thinkers is not disinterested. Heller and Nussbaum share in the intersubjectivity of Honneth's analysis of shame. Like Honneth, Nussbaum is deeply indebted to John Dewey and Donald Winnicott in this regard. However, both Heller and Nussbaum develop a more internally complex phenomenology of shame and its relationship to the cognate experience of guilt and the activation of moral conscience. Morrison's novel provides a type of case study in which to explore Honneth's claim that negative experiences of social recognition predispose us to struggle for recognition. Here, my methodology derives from Honneth's reading of Ralph Ellison's *The Invisible Man*. Honneth (2001) analyses Ellison's novel to consider the question of recognition epistemologically. His reading provides a reasonably straightforward confirmation of the concepts under analysis. I do not wish to revisit this analysis, my focus is shame not invisibility, and the results are more complicated. Morrison's novel entails a confirmation of the centrality of recognition to the development of human subjectivity. In the 1993 Afterward to *The Bluest Eye*, Morrison comments that she was spurred to investigate 'racial self-loathing' in the aftermath of the civil rights movement's attempt to reclaim racial beauty (1999, 162). But even as the novel aptly illustrates Honneth's arguments that our sense of selves depends on forms of recognition, it also suggests that Honneth underestimates the destructive impact of shame on both our desires and struggles for recognition, leaving him vulnerable to the pessimistic critique articulated earlier.

This discussion confirms my suspicion that while Honneth is correct to identify the negative emotional experiences that attend misrecognition, such experiences are attributed too much agency in his account of the emergence of the struggle for recognition. In the final part of the article, I argue that it is important to explore how solidarity can be fostered by practices of disclosure and acknowledgment that are internal to the struggle for recognition, rather than rely on the negative emotional power of misrecognition to prompt critique and transformation. My analysis does not entail an attempt to empirically redeem this claim. Rather, I look to the development of the conceptual distinctions required to understand the struggle for recognition as distinctly political action, not simply reliant on the vicissitudes of human emotion, without derogating from the intersubjectivity of Honneth's account of human agency. To this end, I draw upon Hannah Arendt's analysis of the conscious pariahs of Jewish modernity. Although not a theorist of recognition, the concept is not foreign to her thinking. Arendt is alert to the moment at which a struggle for recognition crosses a threshold to become political. Applied to Honneth's version of the struggle for recognition, this analysis opens up new avenues for critique and inoculates his approach against the more pessimistic rejoinders that suggest the struggle for recognition is less emancipatory than Honneth supposes.

## Honneth's theory of recognition

Axel Honneth works out of a tradition known as the Frankfurt School of Critical Theory. It is difficult to construct a single thread that links together the corpus and thinkers associated with the Frankfurt School. Indeed, any attempt to suggest more continuity than rupture between Theodor Adorno and Jürgen Habermas, for example, is bound to fail or at least misrepresent the complexity of their thinking. It is not just that Habermas' trenchant defence of democracy separates him from Adorno's pessimistic account of modernity, but more fundamentally, each thinker develops an alternative methodology with which to approach social critique, which Honneth might describe as world disclosure and rational reconstruction respectively. Each thinker is also equipped with a well-articulated epistemological justification for their choice. As Honneth (2007) has argued, the distinctive and shared feature of their contributions, and other thinkers associated with the Frankfurt School, is a commitment to epistemological reflexivity that does not back-slide into either relativism or narcissism.

All share in a philosophical tradition that extends at least back to Immanuel Kant. Following Kant, their work is inflected with an awareness of the individual's active role in constructing knowledge of the world around them. In addition, however, and loyal to a tradition that extends back through Marx and Rousseau, that same individual is understood to exist in circumstances marred by inequality and structural injustice that penetrate thought, potentially compromising judgement. The task of critical theory is thus complicated by an anterior understanding that knowledge is the product of fallible creatures caught in webs of understanding and social relationships that may in fact obscure insight in favour of extant power relations. Traditional theory, a term coined by Max Horkheimer, to designate more orthodox approaches to social analysis, is not burdened with this peculiar form of epistemological reflexivity (Honneth 1991). By contrast, critical theory must pierce forms of understanding, perhaps ideologies, that either maliciously or inadvertently buttresses exploitation in its various manifestations.

The task assumed by critical theorists is further complicated by certain normative commitments: to explore the possibility for substantive justice that will alleviate unnecessary suffering and undermine the oppressive structures that perpetuate such unhappiness. This is the second characteristic that distinguishes critical theory. Marx's eleventh thesis, which enjoins thinkers to consider the practical implications of their thought, indeed to write to change the world, thus permeates critical theory. Scholars associated with the Frankfurt School do not share in Marx's seemingly naïve faith in the working class as the standard bearer of history. Nonetheless, some hope that their analyses will provide assistance and direction, perhaps voice the concerns of social movements, motivates critical theorists. Moreover, critical theorists locate the normative standards for critique in extant social practices. Antagonism to alternatives, such as employing transcendental or a priori criteria with which to interrogate social forms, has been associated with a post-metaphysical or deflationary understanding of philosophy (Benhabib 1986). However, a commitment to immanent critique is also evident in metaphysicians such as Hegel. The particular understanding shared by scholars associated with Frankfurt School is that while social forms reflect the understandings and intentions of social actors, such expectations are, for a variety of reasons, unevenly realised. The ensuing tensions and, in some cases, outright contradictions are implicated in crisis and resistance, which provide further impetus for critical theorists: confidence that their standards for social criticism are indeed immanent to praxis, even if poorly realised therein, and that social transformation is possible.

This is particularly true of Axel Honneth who has consistently argued that analysing social recognition will provide means to analyse the as yet poorly articulated, or 'pre-theoretical' demands for justice that characterise today's underprivileged groups. In Honneth's discussion, recognition is invariably, if sometimes implicitly, preceded by the term 'social'. The import of this term resides in its connotations of intersubjectivity. The term 'social' immediately locates recognition in a space of shared imaginaries, narratives and experiences. The philosophical and later critical significance of recognition thus adheres to its contribution to understanding how and why we acknowledge the singular subjectivity of others as something particular for ethics and politics. Honneth's analysis recognition begins with our lived experience of recognising and being recognised by others. Honneth (2001, 120) argues that social recognition begins with a number of performative gestures with which we acknowledge one another, such as a smile or a verbal greeting. This means that social recognition is a communicative exchange (Honneth 1994, 265). It is also a thoughtful process and can be withheld or modulated according to the circumstances in which we find ourselves. According to Honneth (2002, 508), social recognition takes place within a space of 'historically alterable' reasons. In a positive formulation, however, individuals strive to mutually affirm each other through reciprocal acts of recognition. In other words, social recognition involves a type of attentive responsiveness to another person. Honneth (2001, 45) is primarily concerned with respect but allows that social recognition takes place in circumstances that are not regulated by norms of mutuality. Recognition between adults and children, for example, involves other types of attentiveness in addition to respect (Honneth 1995, 96).

Honneth (2001, 51) argues that social recognition in the sense just discussed is integral to personal integrity, requisite for self-realisation and the practice of freedom. Only by distinguishing between our general desire for recognition and specific historical struggles for recognition, however, is it possible to analyse which claims for recognition ought to be acknowledged as the basis for an emancipatory politics. To this end, Honneth (1995, 129) differentiates between three orders of recognition in modernity: love-based, rights-based and merit-based recognition. In love-based recognition, individuals known to each other through close affective ties respond to the emotional and corporeal vulnerability of specific others. Rights-based recognition acknowledges the moral equivalence of individuals as subjects of positive law. In modern society, individuals are also recognised on the basis of characteristics and attributes shared with solidary social groups. Honneth (1995, 2003) refers to this type of recognition as solidarity and, in more recent publications, merit-based recognition. Each pattern of recognition corresponds to a different aspect of personal integrity, which Honneth calls 'practical relations to self' (1995, 128–129). These are self-reflexive attitudes that signify different ways of understanding oneself and one's capacity for agency. Honneth argues that when all three types of recognition are available, we are able to experience self-confidence, self-respect and self-esteem.

Additionally, Honneth locates each form of social recognition in a separate social domain: the family, the state and civil society. On this basis, Honneth makes two arguments of significance. First, the ethical particularity of love-based recognition, which is associated with the intimate sphere of the family, militates against its usefulness for emancipatory social change. Second, and by contrast, Honneth locates the progressive impetus of modernity in the separation of rights-based from merit-based recognition. He contends that further elaboration of these forms of recognition supplies us with some hope that further emancipation from domination is possible. Moreover, Honneth uses this threefold categorisation to identify deficits in recognitive practices. He distinguishes between three forms of disrespect that represent the inverse of social recognition so differentiated. In the absence of recognition, Honneth suggests we may experience 'the violation of the body, the denial of rights, and denigration of ways of life' (1995, 131). Honneth uses the examples of torture and rape to indicate the types of disrespect that disrupts a person's self-confidence, otherwise engendered by love-based recognition. Systematic exclusion from political rights suggests an inequality that reflects a failure to recognise the moral equivalence of persons and thereby undermines self-respect. For Honneth, 'insult' is the inverse of solidarity; it is manifest in forms of exclusion and denigration that arise in no small part from distributive inequities. For Honneth, the harm entailed in misrecognition involves coupling impediments to action with damage to personal integrity and identity. In other words, and *inter alia*, misrecognition produces feelings of shame. From this, however, he derives an impetus to struggle for recognition and a basis from which to critique the social relations characteristic of late modernity. He argues that misrecognition prompts political action: the moral grammar of social movements.

Part of the strength of Honneth's arguments derives from his analysis of intersubjective structure of human emotions. In Honneth's view, misrecognition gives rise to negative emotions: 'experience of moral injustice is necessarily accompanied by a mental shock', which 'cognitively inform the person in question of his or her social situation' (1995, 135). By this, Honneth means that the feelings for which misrecognition is a catalyst lets us know that a boundary has been crossed. Honneth employs John Dewey's psychology of emotions to explain why this is the case. According to Dewey, emotions are thoughtful and evaluative responses; they contain some cognitive content. He links emotion, both positive and negative, to the realisation of intentions through action and the types of behaviour this elicits in others. Pleasure and satisfaction then refer to emotional states that are not simply derived from intrapsychic machinations. Instead, they are related to the successful conduct of behaviour in accordance with personal intentions and social expectations. By contrast, negative emotional responses are correlated with failures to achieve desired results. In other words, a job well done is more satisfying in light of the approval of others. Equally, failures are more painful when they attract the disapprobation of others. In all, the emotions that arise in recollection of an event involve an evaluation of its success or failure against social standards that have most likely been internalised. Of course, not all misrecognition is experienced as a disappointment, catalysing the negative emotions that he mentions: whilst a cold reception from a friend would almost certainly cause concern, a similar reception from a colleague or a customer may well be disregarded. Honneth is primarily concerned with forms of misrecognition that produce suffering and are related to social power: people, practices and institutions that either indirectly or purposively interfere with our capacity to flourish. Important to Honneth's theory then is a distinction between forms of misrecognition that are trivial or tragic and forms of misrecognition that arise from the unjust application of laws or the oppressive structure of social relations that subordinate some social groups. Although this distinction is not clearly articulated by Honneth's theory, it is central to the coherence of his approach.

In my view, Honneth is correct to suggest that injustice will produce an emotional response and that this ought to be a factor in developing an adequate account of the impact of oppression, including the reasons for political activism. His argument, however, requires further qualification. Honneth's analysis of our emotional response to injustice is premised on the fact that the associated injury affects the individual who is treated unfairly, it is she who is prompted to struggle for recognition. With this argument,

Honneth sidelines the moral relevance of emotions like compassion, that is, the emotional response of a witness to injustice, who nonetheless is not personally harmed by the unjust act. The average citizen of the first world who witnesses the starving masses of Africa or orphans in Afghanistan is a good example of such a witness. Exposure to information about the suffering of others may produce fatigue, anger, disgust or compassion. Although in the absence of an emotional response it is unlikely that exposure to injustice will produce solidarity at all, whether any of these emotions prompts action that might contribute to alleviating this suffering is likely to be affected by factors other than the experience of the emotion itself. My point is that these types of emotional response, which are central to understanding the impact of oppression and injustice, are not accounted for by Honneth's theory.

Moreover, Honneth says little about whether our emotional responses to injustice are reliable. Our emotional responses to misrecognition can be unreliable in three ways. First, experiencing oppression might not produce an emotional response. This is particularly the case if the source or structure of oppression is not evident. Take, for example, an individual entering a casualised workforce unaware that previous generations of employees had been the recipients of better working conditions and greater job stability. The casualisation of this particular workforce was a consequence of policies designed to minimise the cost of labour and diminish the influence of the union. But the newest member of the workforce had been unemployed for some months and was deeply relieved at the prospect of paid employment. Even though the conditions of employment signify the disempowerment of workers in labour markets where there is little effective representation or regulation of working conditions, she feels little emotion about the conditions according to which she will be employed and a lot of emotion about the fact of employment. Second, even if there is an emotional response to circumstances such as those described earlier, this response may not be directed at the relevant unjust conditions. Even if our hypothetical employee felt anger about her working conditions, there is a possibility that this emotion could turn inwards into self-blame, guilt, despair or self-loathing for not finishing school or for leaving her husband. Third, the types of emotional responses that may signify oppression can also be felt in other circumstances. Moral outrage and indignation can be unjustified as in the case of a misperceived insult, or the reasons for such feelings may be odious. Both miscegenation and same-sex marriage, for example, have produced moral outrage and indignation. It is not clear, however, that such feelings correspond to extant injustices.

For Honneth, such complications suggest a role for social theorists to provide a 'categorical framework' with which to supplement the experience of felt injustice. However, if my arguments are correct and emotions are an unreliable guide to oppression, and even injury to personal integrity, then Honneth's argument about the relationship between misrecognition and emotion needs to be supplemented by other considerations. Some criteria are necessary to determine whether circumstances of misrecognition that produce negative emotions are unjust: whether these emotions can withstand the test of reflection. Feeling compassion for the plight of others, feeling indignation in the face of injustice and not feeling outrage at minor slights are examples of emotional reactions that must be learnt and supported. The final reason that Honneth's argument about the experience of misrecognition and the emotions it elicits requires further qualification is that emotions can prompt very different types of action. The hypothetical employee mentioned earlier could decide to join a union and attempt to recruit and organise her co-workers. Alternatively, feelings of despair or anger could be displaced or sublimated, leading to effective political acquiescence.

## The politics of shame

In the light of the above analysis, Honneth's assertion that shame is an experience that may be indicative of injustice or oppression is of interest. So too his argument that such negative emotional reactions may prompt resistance and struggle, or more particularly the struggle for recognition. Shame is divisive within moral philosophy (Nussbaum 2004, 22; Williams 1993). Shame that is experienced as discomfort and embarrassment may be considered too trivial to pretend at properly philosophical analysis: a more appropriate subject for ironists and satirists of the human condition. Nonetheless, shame is a powerful emotion, not easily dismissed. Apologists variously suggest that shame coupled with humour, as ridicule that is, can puncture pretensions and provoke reflections on the adequacy of social norms, or that the sense of shame, particularly when consequent to a transgression of sorts, can precipitate restitution (Metcalfe 2004, 432). Any defence of shame assumes that we feel it for good reason, either because we have indeed transgressed or perhaps in anticipation of the judgement of those that we respect (Calhoun 2004, 128). This means that shame may have a positive function in anticipating conscience (Manion 2003, 31). In this way, shame or humiliation has a disciplinary logic, which if not always righteous nonetheless produces social cohesion (Saurette 2002, 67).

Agnes Heller (1980, 5) notes that shame 'is a social affect par excellence'. Despite its near ubiquity as human experience, shame is intelligible following the internalisation of ethical standards of the community of which one is a part. In other words, we learn to be ashamed. For this reason, shame is an exemplary tool for socialisation. Indeed, it is exactly the type of emotional response that lends support to Dewey's argument that our emotions bear both cognitive content and the weight of social expectations. The experience and the expression of shame can tell us much about our perceptions of the world and vulnerability to the judgements of others (Probyn 2005). Drawing on Winnicott's work, Martha Nussbaum provides reasons why this is the case. She explains that shame accompanies us from infancy as we are forced to rescind the type of hallucinatory omnipotence attributed to the infant psyche by psychoanalytic thinkers (2004, 178–179). Nussbaum argues that our sense of shame is related to our experience of vulnerability and dependence. These experiences loom large in the life of an infant. Shame is thus a primary emotional experience. In fact, our early experiences of it threaten to swamp the entire, but not yet fully formed person. Even in later life, this is the impact of 'primary shame' (2004, 184). It is registered in pervasive feelings of inadequacy, which seem to lack focus on a particular experience or attribute – instead shame is linked to our very humanness. For this reason, Nussbaum is critical of communitarian thinkers who link a decline in social standards and social solidarity to the failure to experience shame. This is because the shaming penalties they advocate are animated by 'an intent to degrade and humiliate', not to reconstitute social bonds (2004, 24). She suggests that guilt is a better partner for solidarity. Her distinction between guilt and shame is also based on an object relations approach to infancy. The primitive nature of shame, particularly its relevance to our nascent and easily wounded narcissism, means that it is experienced before we start to relate to others as whole persons who, like ourselves, may be wounded by acts of aggression. Guilt, however, is a more complicated achievement (2004, 186). It requires cognisance of the vulnerability of others to our actions and arises in congruence with a desire to make reparations for real or imagined slights. While shame threatens to engulf the individual in self-loathing, guilt functions to reconnect people to one another.

None of Nussbaum's discussion of shame contradicts Heller's assertion that it functions as a 'social affect'. Quite to the contrary, Nussbaum also examines particular examples of social groups that are stigmatised. The process of social stigmatisation takes place not when individuals are simply physically or socially ostracised, but when they are made to feel shame for characteristics that are deemed inadequate and mark the whole person for separate treatment. For example, Nussbaum suggests that disability functions in this way in contemporary US society (2004, 204). In other words, it is possible to reconstruct which types of attributes and experiences are constitutively excluded from the band of normalised experiences and attributes (Young 1990). This means that the association of shame with particular social groupings, like the disabled, has a particular genealogy. Nussbaum argues that this process of constructing normality and stigmatising difference functions to preserve us from being overwhelmed by our ambiguous, perhaps hostile, feelings about our own 'mortality and animality' (2004, 322). This process protects us from our vulnerability by localising and stigmatising reminders of it in social groups who are subsequently ostracised and victimised.

To account for the mutability of shame, both its cultural specificity and its ignorance of guilt, Heller too distinguishes between shame and conscience (1980, 1). Whilst the former may be a pinprick for the latter, it is not a reliable guide. Not, that is, if shame is common to the criminal and the victim – the often remarked upon experience of shame by victims of crime is Heller's implicit example here. Nussbaum's distinction between shame and guilt, like Heller's distinction between shame and conscience, serves to highlight that the link between shame and ethics requires greater mediation than the negative feelings to which it gives rise. Nussbaum argues that our infantile experiences of shame and the concomitant experience of vulnerability, readies us for the power of shame in our adult lives (2004, 218). She also argues that unleashing its power is likely to sever our links to one another. Shame militates against care, justice and solidarity because it fosters a fear of degradation. Its power derives from the archaic layers of the psyche, which retain unconscious memories of vulnerability and dependence. Nussbaum's critique of shame presupposes its potency; in her analysis, guilt is a more rational experience that retains the significance of emotional bonds for social cohesion, while preserving the sense of self simultaneously required to sustain these bonds. Nussbaum concludes that shame is not a resource for either moralists or lawmakers. Nonetheless, her analysis also points towards the politics of shame. The propensity of marginalised social groups, like the disabled, to feel the shame rather than, or in step with, the injustice of their circumstances warrants political analysis (see Bartky 1991; Sennett 2003).

In a plaintive and political evocation of shame in *The Bluest Eye*, Toni Morrison suggests that shame infects marginalised groups where standards of beauty and moral worth are conflated at the expense of humanity. In this novel, Morrison traces 12-year-old Pecola Breedlove's descent into madness following the stillbirth of the child she conceived after being raped by her father. This crime occurs in the last section of the book, and although it precipitates Pecola's disintegration, the bulk of the novel is devoted to an explanation of how and why this crime, and its consequence, could occur. The novel's power lies not only in its depiction of the racially motivated and domestic violence that encircles the lives of the characters. Rather, throughout the novel, Pecola's growing isolation, her ever deepening belief in her own ugliness, is juxtaposed to her slightly younger companion and the novel's erstwhile narrator, Claudia MacTeer's, emerging sense of herself. Unlike Pecola, Claudia is protected from self-loathing by the care of her mother, who is not without faults but nonetheless loves her with a love that is 'as thick and dark as Alage syrup' (Morrison 1999, 7).

Morrison's novel confounds analyses that link shame to guilt and innocence. This is not only because the chief protagonists of the novel are children and somehow too morally or emotionally immature to warrant either judgement. Both Pecola and Claudia actively participate in deriving meaning from their experiences, even if their analysis is poor this hardly distinguishes them from adults. Morrison's book, however, invites empathy rather than judgement from readers. Even Cholly, Pecola's father, is presented sympathetically. Morrison recounts that his first sexual experience is interrupted by two white men, who command 'Get on wid it nigger' (1999, 116). His humiliation quickly turns to hate and is directed at the unfortunate Darlene. To the extent that there is condemnation in the novel, it is of bankrupt ideas, physical beauty and romantic love, which Morrison describes as 'probably the most destructive ideas in the history of human thought' (1999, 95). The sentimental subterfuge completed by each is ideological and yet somehow sidesteps political analysis. In the novel, ideology is encapsulated by movies, the heroines of the silver screen. The unattainable ideal is white, while reality is embodied by poverty.

Morrison comments that the extreme violence to which Pecola is exposed is exceptional. Nonetheless, it also resounds as the apogee of the types of alienation that afflict the poor black community, which in the words of Claudia existed as 'a minority in both caste and class, [moving] about anyway on the hem of life, struggling to consolidate our weaknesses and hang on' (1999, 11). The novel forcefully demonstrates Honneth's contention that our sense of selves is contingent on forms of recognition. Examples of misrecognition punctuate the novel. When Pecola goes to buy candy, for example, she is struck by the 'total absence of human recognition' in the eyes of Mr Yacobowski, the store-owner: 'somewhere between retina and object, between vision and view, his eyes draw back, hesitate and hover' (1999, 36). On leaving the store, Pecola's shame is almost replaced by anger, but instead is sublimated into a desire for blue eyes. Claudia's only defence against similar humiliations is hate. This is made possible by love. Nonetheless, love is not impervious and Claudia comments that later she too learns to love Shirley Temple: an almost religious 'conversion from pristine sadism to fabricated hatred, to fraudulent love' (1999, 16).

Morrison traces the destructive impact of shame on a community and individual lives. In her analysis, the impact of shame on individuals is variable; in my analysis, the impact of shame on politics is variable. Shame may lead to acquiescence, however, personally destructive, to social norms or withdrawal into subcultures (Heller 1980, 2; Honneth 1995, 124). When linked to a social group, shame may motivate moral panic (Nussbaum 2004, 250). It may lead to resentment, the politics of which are more likely to see a perhaps 'imaginary' inversion of the regimes of recognition to punish the powerful (Brown 1995, 44). All these responses are evident in Morrison's novel. The Breedloves too readily accept their shame; in Morrison's words, they 'wore their ugliness, put it on so to speak, although it did not belong to them' (1999, 28). And Claudia takes delight in dismembering little white dolls. She comments, 'I destroyed little white baby dolls. But the dismembering of dolls was not the true horror. The truly horrifying thing was the transference of this same impulse to little white girls' (Morrison 1999, 15).

All such responses signify a struggle that arises out of a negative experience of social recognition. Not all signify a struggle *for* recognition and those that do may not aim at expanding the social relations of recognition in an emancipatory direction. Honneth, however, is centrally concerned with movements and campaigns that struggle to expand the social relations of recognition towards greater inclusiveness and tolerance or rights and solidarity. Albeit he does not examine such movements directly, his theory aims at understanding the precursors to social struggle. He argues that it is our very vulnerability to moral injury that often prompts social struggle. Morrison's description of shame, however, suggests that while this vulnerability is very real, its consequences are difficult to predict. By the end of Morrison's novel, Pecola believes that by virtue of some miraculous plastic surgery, she has attained the blue eyes she so longed for. Her struggle for recognition was stillborn, much like the child she conceived, and she withdraws into psychosis. Pecola's story is a devastating indictment on shame that so thoroughly infects the lives and subjectivities of marginalised groups. By integrating the symbolism of 'whiteness' and beauty into her understanding of self, Pecola suggests that shame does not necessarily precipitate an awareness of injustice, nor that it catalyses agency.

This suggests that Honneth's theory demands more clarity about the conditions under which our experiences of recognition become meaningful prior to revealing guideposts for ethics or politics. This may seem obvious. The translation that takes place between experience and ethics, or from phenomenology to critical theory, is an interpretative feat: Honneth mentions a 'semantic bridge' (1995, 31). My argument is that this semantic bridge is not simply constructed by the intersubjective structure of emotions and identity. Instead, we must actively deconstruct and reinterpret, deliberate and debate our experiences. Honneth is right to suggest that our emotions have an intersubjective structure. He is also right to suggest that misrecognition has an emotional impact on us. While both premises are defensible, they do not add up as Honneth suggests. Misrecognition plus emotion does not give rise to ethics or politics directly. Honneth concedes that the link is not automatic, but does not explicate the intervening processes.

The analytical distinction, between shame and guilt or conscience, proposed by Heller and Nussbaum, suggests some of the reconstructive work that needs to happen to reveal both the moral and political significance of shame. In their analysis, shame is too primal to result in a predictable politics and the analyst requires additional tools with which to specify injustice. However, Morrison's novel contains another lesson. She does not simply ask us to witness the destructive impact of shame or share in Pecola's sense of hopelessness. Her novel itself is an act of solidarity, which articulates both sympathy and critique. In the final pages of the novel, as Claudia and her sister become aware of Pecola's plight, without quite understanding the implications, they come to feel a 'defensive shame' towards Pecola and her unborn child (Morrison 1999, 149). Sympathy leads to a small and poignant act of solidarity: Claudia and Freida sacrifice their dream of a new bicycle and plant the marigold seeds they planned to sell in the hope that both Pecola and the child survive. Magic and prayer do not suffice. Nonetheless, Morrison's novel accomplishes a more effective act of solidarity. Morrison creates a *res publica* of readers perhaps readied to identify with or condemn the politics of shame she depicts. Perhaps, the novel is an example of the semantic bridge to which Honneth refers and which functions to link misrecognition to struggle via deliberation, narrative and imagination. At the very least, Morrison's novel demands some kind of acknowledgement.

## Arendt and the politics of disclosure

The implications of the earlier analysis are manifold. The point I wish to make, however, is that shame is not necessarily a resource for politics. Our mutual vulnerability to moral injury, beautifully rendered in Morrison's novel, supports the ethics of Honneth's theory but not the politics. Without further investigation into how, when and why struggles for recognition can support an emancipatory politics, the critical edge of Honneth's theory is blunted, and his theory is vulnerable to analyses of the struggle for recognition that suggest it functions to mitigate angst rather than extend justice. Patchen Markell's work is a good example. Like Honneth, he is alert to our vulnerability to misrecognition, arguing this reveals an ontological insecurity, the ultimate contingency of our identifications and investments. In Markell's analysis, recognition functions to certify and consolidate some of these investments and identifications but by way of appeal to a dominant authority: this is the path available to ethnic minorities, for example, who look to the state for the kinds of recognition that will facilitate political and economic inclusion. Markell's analysis of the 'double binds' of this strategy, however, suggests that such struggles are motivated by existential uncertainties and recognition functions to shield us from acknowledging these. I am not sure that Markell's argument is ultimately convincing. But he is correct to identify that any struggle for recognition motivated by vulnerability may tend to hubris rather than solidarity. It is of interest that Markell draws inspiration from Hannah Arendt. I too think Arendt's analysis contains insights of relevance to Honneth's project.

Arendt was an unapologetic advocate for the 'right to have rights', precisely that which the victims of twentieth-century totalitarianism lacked (Bernstein 2005). This entails a fundamental form of recognition which Honneth has theorised as one of three forms of recognitive practice that is integral to the normative coherence of modernity. Arendt argued that the death of the 'juridical and moral subject' of rights-based recognition preceded the actual physical annihilation of Jews during the Second World War (Benhabib 2000). She carefully deconstructed the attitudes and events that precipitated the final solution and concluded that it was not insignificant that the Jews were stripped of legal and moral personhood before they were murdered. When it comes to understanding Arendt's analysis of political action, however, recognition is less of a consideration that the activity of disclosure. According to Arendt (1958), political acts are revelatory of 'who' not 'what' we are. The revelatory and agonistic character of political action as theorised by Arendt has caused commentators some disquiet. Kateb (1977), for example, articulates this succinctly when he argues that Arendtian politics is disdainful of practical matters and specific political outcomes. He takes exception to her suggestion that moral virtues such as compassion can be divorced from politics as secondary or irrelevant analytical considerations. Likewise, Benhabib (2000, 23) worries that Arendt's project harbours elitist and antidemocratic tendencies. Both thinkers, and others besides, seek an accommodation with her thought, not to domesticate her insights but to supplement them with greater sensitivity to existing injustices. Leaving aside such investigations into the limits of Arendt's philosophy, I wish to reconstruct her analysis of disclosure as rejoinder to Honneth, providing a political foundation for the struggle for recognition.

In my analysis, it is useful to interpret Arendt's description of political activity in *The Human Condition* alongside her examination of the conscious pariahs of Jewish modernity (Arendt 1978a). The distinction between pariah and parvenu, borrowed from Bernard Lazare, is present in Arendt's work from her early biography of Rahel Varnhagen (Ring 1991, 434). To summarise, both the pariah and the parvenu are refused equal recognition on the basis of an ascriptive but not necessarily elective identity category, the Jew, in conditions of oppression. Both must negotiate the contradictions of assimilation into a culture, European modernity, which insists upon a difference it is unwilling to accommodate. The parvenu accepts the terms of assimilation: partial recognition on the basis of some sacrifice of integrity. The pariah, without becoming a social recluse, does not. The conscious pariah externalises the contradictions through actions that simultaneously expose the parvenu's invidious condition, but more importantly work to critique mainstream society and the choice it imposes.

Arendt argues that pariahs essentially contest the terms of recognition offered to them. Their alienation from hegemonic norms is completed by reflexive analysis that attends to the structure of the outcast category to which they belong. Arendt's discussion of Charlie Chaplin and Franz Kafka is a case in point. As pariahs, Chaplin and Kafka assert their rights to recognition, 'the admission of Jews as *Jews* to the ranks of humanity' through public, although not specifically political, acts that entail social critique, including of the position of outcast (Arendt 1978a, 68, emphasis in original). Chaplin and Kafka are two of four pariahs that Arendt identifies as part of a 'tacit and latent' tradition (Arendt 1978a, 68). She is concerned with Chaplin's 'grotesque portrayal of the suspect' and Kafka's 'poetic vision of the fate of the man of goodwill' (1978a, 69). Chaplin's characters' insistence on the invidious position of the under-class whose spontaneity is always suspect to the force of law suggests for Arendt the position of European Jewry up to the middle of the twentieth century and subsequently the life of refugees. Chaplin's comedy belies the structure of surveillance practiced by the guardians of monocultural states. In Kafka's *Castle*, Arendt detects the impossibilities of assimilation that attempts to eradicate differences. The struggle of the protagonist, K, for moral and intellectual autonomy is thwarted by the opportunity costs of assimilation, which K understands work to maintain his status as exceptional. K's struggle for ordinary acceptance coincides with a growing isolation as he asserts independence from the norms imposed by the 'castle'. For K, to be ordinary, to participate in the basic structure of rights shared by his fellow villagers, is to be extraordinary. In Arendt's analysis, Chaplin and Kafka create characters that struggle with the limitations imposed by inadequate social recognition; they are variously excluded and isolated for reasons over which they have little control. Arendt concludes her essay with the opinion that the Second World War has rendered the distinction between pariah and parvenu irrelevant – both can be murdered. The tone of the essay suggests that collective political action might better remedy these contradictions. These exemplary pariahs, however, are not strictly speaking political actors, not that is, until they attain political consciousness as rebels. Ultimately, this is Arendt's recommendation, for pariahs and European Jews. Her analysis is instructive with regard to both the practical and existential toll exacted by social exclusion and the cost of resistance. K faces isolation, the lack of a common world to inhabit and in which to disclose who he is to others. For Arendt, such a life is unsustainable: K becomes increasingly unintelligible in the life of the village; so too Chaplin's heroes as the Great Depression altered the fate of the every man.

The distinction Arendt proposes between parvenu and pariah dovetails with her later analysis of the difference between a conscientious objector, who acts in accordance with the dictates of personal conscience, and the civil disobedient, who acts to expose suffering and the contradictoriness of legal norms (Arendt 1972). The action of the first pertains to private well-being, the other is public, deliberately addressed to others, is demanding of recognition and therefore political. The implicit normative analysis Arendt maps onto such distinctions receives greater clarity by considering her theory of political action elaborated in the *Human Condition*. Accordingly, politics takes place in public spaces for appearance, the conditions of which include plurality, that is, the presence of multiple distinct individuals, and disclosure (1958, 198). The normative force of her analysis relies on an association between freedom, action and the capacity for new beginnings in a world of remarkable social complexity. The rights of citizenship, whose extension she attributes to the 'enormous political productivity' of the working class, comprise a means to appear in public and acquire freedom. The depreciation of public action and the diminution of public space thus provide the core of Arendt's critique of modernity and indeed the history of western political philosophy.

Arendt's argument that we reveal ourselves through speech and action provides an interesting contrast to Honneth whose emphasis remains on our responsiveness, if not dependence on recognition. Of course, she recognises that public disclosure may be inauthentic. The very word 'disclose' suggests our capacity to conceal aspects of our identity and even withdraw into 'spectatorship'. Arendt's point is that we 'insert' ourselves into the human world through speech and action; we may be 'stimulated' by others but we are certainly not 'conditioned' by them (1958, 175). In other words, self-realisation, whatever this means, is something we achieve by disclosing aspects of ourselves to others. Arendt's contention is in stark contrast to Honneth's argument that self-realisation depends on the social relations of recognition. Honneth's argument seems somewhat one-dimensional because he links self-realisation to recognition alone. Self-realisation, however, must also be about human agency. In Arendt's analysis of the active self chooses how they appear, 'up to a point' (1958, 176).

Arendt's analysis of the active self is complemented by her ruminations on the contemplative self in *The Life of the Mind*. The counterpart to the individual, who inserts themselves into the human world of experience, is the self who 'withdraws' into thought (1978b, 34). For Arendt, thinking is a truly speculative activity that requires 'solitude' (1978b, 69). This she distinguishes from loneliness, which is an existential condition that arises when human company departs (and also a political condition under totalitarianism). In her analysis, the thinking self withdraws from activity. There is an intuitive plausibility to her argument. Thinking does not coincide with active engagement with the world because the process of representing the world to ourselves in thought requires that it not be present to us directly. Each of us understands that to be lost in thought implies that our attention is not fixed on any immediate task whether that be conversation or chopping vegetables; in this way, we are 'absent-minded' (1978b, 72).

Like Honneth, Arendt is finely tuned to the fact that we come to know and understand ourselves, to the extent that we can, in the presence of others. She does not fall prey to the solipsistic illusion that we create ourselves *ex nihilo*. Her analysis suggests that our identities are both revealed and camouflaged by creative disclosure in the realm of appearance and speculative withdrawal into the solitude of thinking. This means that even if the self is in part a product of the intersubjective environment, the self is also an emergent property that cannot be reduced to the conditions of her emergence. The emergent self remains dependent on others, not least as she learns to ascribe meaning to her emotions and content to her identity. The quality of reflexivity that also characterises human consciousness, however, unleashes creative potential that is independent of although informed by relations of recognition. The activity of disclosure must take place within an extant recognitive order according to which that which is meant, cited, performed or submitted can be interpreted. But disclosure also threatens or promises to disrupt such structures of recognition.

For Arendt, disclosure exhibits freedom, not identity, precisely because it enjoins people (note the plural) to address, that is, to acknowledge and recognise, the meaning of that which is exposed. In Arendt's analysis of politics, neither the self nor the public is interpellated by demands for recognition; rather, the public is constituted by acts of disclosure through which people appear to each other and which may in turn problematise the very structure of interpretation on which the intelligibility of such acts is reliant. Therein, for Arendt, resides the possibility for political freedom; the definition of which is irreducible to liberal concerns for freedom of choice. The politics of disclosure certainly takes place within contingent circumstances, such as those Markell describes. Nonetheless, disclosure disrupts the political certainty and structural determination of interpretation, opening spaces for freedom occasioned by said disclosure. Moreover, disclosure remains incomplete unless it is also acknowledged and narrated.

Forms of acknowledgement are not subjected to the same level of detailed analysis by Arendt. Benhabib argues that although Arendt did not expend ink explaining her methodology, the practice of storytelling was central to her craft (1990, 186). Storytelling, or the development of narratives, entails recall or observation, interpretation and deliberation, and then telling or some other kind of representation. For Arendt, storytelling complements and completes the activity of disclosure. This process is analogous to what is meant by acknowledgement here. When such acknowledgement is public, it is likely to also involve contestation at each and every stage and may be humble of hubristic. For Arendt, the activity of storytelling is an appropriate activity for political philosophers, which is consistent with the ontological structure of action she describes in *The Human Condition*. For my purposes, storytelling thus described works to explain the structure of acknowledgement that is responsive to disclosure and thus liminal to the politics of recognition. Acknowledgement as storytelling is deliberative and narrative and subject to the same constraints of interpretation that function to make disclosure possible and political.

Storytelling is also largely a retrospective, reconstructive activity. In the realm of aesthetics, its purpose is less to establish truth than meaning – an attribute Arendt suggests is shared by politics, the exploration of *doxa* (Arendt 1990). The terms on which disclosure and acknowledgement proceed are not equivalent. They are, however, mutually imbricated and brought together by recognition. Indeed, recognition intercedes at the point of disjuncture between disclosure and acknowledgement, enabling us to breach the interpretative divide and thereby establish new forms of relationality and understanding. To this end, Arendt's analysis is instructive. Forms of public disclosure, like Morrison's novel, initiate politics, entail struggle and demand acknowledgement. The analysis supplements Honneth's insights into the impact of the shame and suffering caused by misrecognition. Such experiences may well motivate struggle, but are not necessarily political.

## Conclusion

This article has argued that differentiating the struggle for recognition into moments of disclosure and acknowledgement opens up new avenues for critique. Disclosure and acknowledgement are integral to recognitive practice. There is no need to disclose that which already known, unless the purpose is cliché. To remain intelligible, that which is disclosed must always remain partially or potentially digestible given extant orders of recognition. However, this does not mean that the meaning of what is disclosed is easily understood or assimilated, particularly if the latter relates to experience of suffering and shame. Instead, disclosure risks incomprehension and reconfigures possibilities for understanding. Disclosure can initiate a struggle for recognition, but it is not without risks. The activity of disclosing who one is, what one believes or wants, through specifically public action, transforms the expression of discontent from subterranean dismay to that which demands recognition. This is the lesson learnt from Arendt's conscious pariahs and civil disobedients. Each engages in a struggle for recognition precisely by contesting the terms of recognition, of identity and action. This analysis does not need to derogate from Honneth's emphasis on the intersubjectivity of the human condition, nor his analysis of the normative content of contemporary, institutionalised, recognitive practices. Instead, it can explain how the struggle for recognition becomes political without relying on suffering and shame as a catalyst for political action.

## References

Arendt, H. 1958. *The Human Condition*. Chicago, IL: University of Chicago Press.
Arendt, H. 1972. *Crises of the Republic: Lying in Politics, Civil Disobedience, on Violence, Thoughts on Politics and Revolution*. New York: Brace Jovanovich Harcourt.
Arendt, H. 1978a. "We Refugees." In *The Jew as Pariah: Jewish Identity and Politics in the Modern Age*, edited by Ron H. Feldman. New York: Grove Press.
Arendt, H. 1978b. *The Life of the Mind*, edited by Mary McCarthy. San Diego, CA: A Harvest Book.
Arendt, H. 1990. "Philosophy and Politics." *Social Research* 57 (1): 73–103.
Bartky, S.-L. 1991. *Femininity and Domination: Studies in the Phenomenology of Oppression*. New York: Routledge.
Bauman, Z. 1993. *Postmodern Ethics*. Oxford: Blackwell.
Benhabib, S. 1986. *Critique, Norm and Utopia: A Study in the Foundations of Critical Theory*. New York: Columbia University Press.
Benhabib, S. 1990. "Hannah Arendt and the Redemptive Power of Narrative." *Social Research* 57 (1): 167–196.
Benhabib, S. 2000. *The Reluctant Modernism of Hannah Arendt*. Lanham, MD: Rowman and Littlefield.
Bernstein, J. M. 2005. "Suffering Injustice: Misrecognition as Moral Injury in Critical Theory." *International Journal of Philosophical Studies* 13 (3): 303–324. doi:10.1080/0967255 0500169117.
Brown, W. 1995. *States of Injury: Power and Freedom in Late Modernity*. Princeton, NJ: Princeton University Press.
Calhoun, C. 2004. "An Apology for Moral Shame." *The Journal of Political Philosophy* 12 (2): 127–146. doi:10.1111/j.1467-9760.2004.00194.x.
Heller, A. 1980. *The Power of Shame*. Melbourne: Latrobe Working Papers in Sociology.
Heller, A. 1990. *A Philosophy of Morals*. Oxford: Blackwell.
Honneth, A. 1991. *The Critique of Power: Reflective Stages in a Critical Social Theory*. Translated by Kenneth Baynes. Cambridge: MIT Press.
Honneth, A. 1994. "The Social Dynamics of Disrespect: On the Location of Critical Theory Today." *Constellations an International Journal of Critical and Democratic Theory* 1 (2): 255–269.
Honneth, A. 1995. *The Struggle for Recognition: The Moral Grammar of Social Conflicts*. Translated by Joel Anderson. Cambridge: MIT Press.
Honneth, A. 1999. "Postmodern Identity and Object-Relations Theory: On the Seeming Obsolescence of Psychoanalysis." *Philosophical Explorations* 2: 225–242. doi:10.1080/ 10001999098538708.
Honneth, A. 2000. *Suffering from Indeterminacy: An Attempt at a Reactualisation of Hegel's Philosophy of Right, Two Lectures*. Amsterdam: Van Gorcum.
Honneth, A. 2001. "Recognition: Invisibility: On the Epistemology of 'Recognition': Axel Honneth." *Aristotelian Society Supplementary Volume* 75: 111–126. doi:10.1111/1467-8349.00081.
Honneth, A. 2002. "Grounding Recognition: A Rejoinder to Critical Questions." *Inquiry: An Interdisciplinary Journal of Philosophy* 45 (4): 499–519. doi:10.1080/002017402320947577.
Honneth, A. 2003. "Redistribution as Recognition: A Response to Nancy Fraser." In *Redistribution or Recognition? A Political-Philosophical Exchange*, edited by N. Fraser and A. Honneth. London: Verso.
Honneth, A. 2007. *Disrespect: The Normative Foundations of Critical Theory*. Cambridge: Polity Press.
Honneth, A. 2014. *Freedom's Right: The Social Democratic Foundations of Democratic Life*. Cambridge: Polity Press.
Kateb, G. 1977. "Freedom and Worldliness in the Thought of Hannah Arendt." *Political Theory* 5: 141–182.
Manion, J. C. 2003. "Girls Blush, Sometimes: Gender, Moral Agency and the Problem of Shame." *Hypatia* 18 (3): 21–41. doi:10.1111/j.1527-2001.2003.tb00820.x.
Markell, P. 2003. *Bound by Recognition*. Princeton, NJ: Princeton University Press.
Metcalf, R. 2004. "Balancing the Senses of Shame and Humor." *Journal of Social Philosophy* 35 (3): 432–447. doi:10.1111/j.1467-9833.2004.00243.x.
Morrison, T. 1999 (1970). *The Bluest Eye*. London: Vintage.

Nussbaum, M. 2004. *Hiding from Humanity: Disgust, Shame and the Law.* Princeton, NJ: Princeton University Press.
Probyn, E. 2005. *Blush: The Faces of Shame.* Sydney: UNSW Press.
Ring, J. 1991. "The Pariah as Hero: Hannah Arendt's Political Actor." *Political Theory* 19: 433–452.
Saurette, P. 2002. "Kant's Culture of Humiliation: Politics and Ethical Cultivation." *Philosophy and Social Criticism* 28 (1): 59–90. doi:10.1177/0191453702028001589.
Sennett, R. 2003. *Respect: The Formation of Character in an Age of Inequality.* London: Penguin Books.
Williams, B. 1993. *Shame and Necessity.* Berkeley: University of California Press.
Young, I. M. 1990. *Throwing Like a Girl and Other Essays in Feminist Philosophy.* Bloomington: Indiana University Press.

# REPLY

## Shame and recognition: the politics of disclosure and acknowledgement: a reply to Julie Connolly

Tony Castleman

*George Washington University, Washington DC, USA*

This is a reply to:

Connolly, Julie. 2014. "Shame and recognition: the politics of disclosure and acknowledgement." *Global Discourse.* 4 (4): 409–425. http://dx.doi.org/10.1080/23269995.2014.926733.

It is often interesting, enlightening, and even humbling to read work by scholars in other fields about subjects that one studies with one's own disciplinary lens. I certainly found this to be the case reading Julie Connolly's 'Shame and Recognition: The Politics of Disclosure and Acknowledgement', which I thoroughly enjoyed and from which I learned a lot. Dr Connolly offers an engaging and insightful analysis of social recognition, shame, and their roles in politics. She identifies and addresses the need to increase the granularity with which we examine the relationships among shame, the struggle for social recognition, and politics. In particular, she points to the value in distinguishing the roles that disclosure and acknowledgement play in the process of seeking recognition and in the implications this process has for politics.

In developing her analysis, Dr Connolly draws from multiple disciplines and even from literature. This is a valuable and refreshing approach, given that the topic is inherently multidisciplinary. In particular, the author's interpretation of Toni Morrison's first novel, *The Bluest Eye*, offers a moving and concrete example of manifestations and responses to shame. While this novel is a different genre than the other sources cited in the article, Dr Connolly's discussion of *The Bluest Eye* serves as an engaging way to advance the paper's analysis.

The author makes a persuasive argument that responses to shame vary and that shame and the struggle for recognition do not necessarily generate political responses. Given this, a valuable next step may be to explore what conditions, contexts, and other factors influence responses to these phenomena. This would both deepen understanding and help guide efforts at improving responses in various contexts. Characteristics of the individuals involved, social norms, power structures, environmental factors, economic and other material conditions, and external sources of discontent may be among the relevant factors. Based on the author's perspective of breaking down the steps in the struggle for recognition, one approach to take to this question would be to identify factors that influence agency and the disclosure and acknowledgement processes. This in turn will inform understanding of the factors affecting responses to shame and the struggle for recognition. Though beyond the scope of this paper, it may be a useful topic for future work.

As someone who has been looking at a particular type of recognition in different contexts, I found that having recognition and misrecognition defined early in the article (or at least some parameters identified) would have been helpful, especially because the various works referenced seem to refer to somewhat different forms of recognition. Similarly, greater specificity on what the term 'politics' encompasses in the context of shame and recognition would be valuable.

Related to the definitions, an issue the paper raises in my mind is the nature of miscrecognition, and in particular the distinction between (a) simply withholding social recognition and (b) actively, deliberately dehumanizing, as manifested in some of the more extreme examples in the article such as rape and genocide. Questions that could benefit from greater clarity about the spectrum – if it is a spectrum – of misrecognition from non-acknowledgement to dehumanization include: whether the difference between neutral, non-acknowledgement, and active dehumanization is qualitative, quantitative, or both; whether and under what conditions non-acknowledgement leads to dehumanization; and what the conditions, determinants, and outcomes are of various points along the spectrum of misrecognition.

In examining the roles that related issues of respect and dehumanization play in poverty and public health, I find that in these contexts we generally do not explore the nature and dynamics of shame and social recognition as deeply as this paper does. To the extent that we do include these issues, they are often taken as components of social capital or as fixed outcomes of the behavior of health care workers. Thus, in addition to providing interesting insights, the paper's analysis of the dynamics of, and responses to, shame and social recognition also offers a helpful model of a deep, critical examination of these issues.

# Al-Muhajiroun in the United Kingdom: the role of international non-recognition in heightened radicalization dynamics

Maéva Clément[a,b]

[a]Department of Political Science, Goethe University, Frankfurt am Main, Germany; [b]Department of Law and Political Science, Versailles Saint-Quentin University, Versailles, France

> This article aims at uncovering the dynamics between non-recognition – real or perceived – and increasingly violent practices, with a case study focusing on the representations of the violent radical Islamist group Al-Muhajiroun following the 9/11 attacks and the outbreak of the war in Afghanistan in 2001. The article argues that these two events were considered salient by the group in terms of both 'Muslims' social value and self-esteem and were presented, on behalf of the *Ummah*, as instances of non-recognition. From this interpretation, the group's discourse became increasingly political, structured and violence-endorsing. The article concludes by showing that Al-Muhajiroun's distorted claims for recognition translated into policy prescriptions advocating an all-out Jihad to try and establish a world caliphate as an alternative, superior hegemony.

While research on violent Islamic radicalization from an organizational-operational perspective is quite advanced, the intersubjective as well as psychosocial dimensions of Islamic radicalization processes have been largely ignored by political science. Few studies have explored the role that misrecognition can play in political violence by radical Islamic groups. In this respect, worth mentioning is the article by Fattah and Fierke (2009; see also Fierke 2014) on the political dimension of experiences of humiliation and betrayal in the Middle East. Despite their call to pay greater attention to these dynamics, few studies have theoretically extended or methodologically systematized the analysis. Also, the misrecognition theme has yet to be steered towards European Islamist groups' practices. Analysis on European Islamist groups' specificities might have seemed unnecessary until the 1990s, when most radical Islamist groups operating in Europe had largely been imported from Egypt, Algeria or Syria and focused on the 'struggle back home'. The appearance of two phenomena should have revealed the relevancy of the subject matter at hand. The 'old' radical Islamist groups have increasingly focused their attention on Europe as part of a more global agenda (Pew Forum on Religion and Public Life 2010). In addition, new 'home-grown' radical groups have emerged, particularly in the United Kingdom, and have explicitly targeted a European audience (Vidino 2007).

In this article, I explore the use of the misrecognition problematic in discursive practices by Al-Muhajiroun ('the emigrants', hereafter AM) and how it led to an increase in radical behaviour from the end of 2001. AM was a violent Islamist group that operated from 1996 to 2004[1] principally within the United Kingdom and to a lesser extent in other

European countries, in the United States and in Pakistan. This case study was confined to international politics and more precisely to two political events that were particularly important for the group: the attacks on New York on 1 September 2001 and the following US-led war in Afghanistan. The purpose of this article is not to argue that international politics is the primary bone of contention of radicalized Islamist groups, but merely to give a plausible account of the gradual transformation of AM's practices towards increased radicalism. Thus, the following questions are to be addressed: What were AM's discursive representations of the 9/11 attacks and the declaration of war against Afghanistan and to what extent did they refer to misrecognition theme? To what discourse (s) did these representations belong? What kind of practices did they make possible? Central to this study is thus to trace the variations in meanings and representations within the group's discourse(s) and to analyse what kind of discursive practices and action-related options they made possible.

After highlighting the theoretical background and methodological choices of my research design, I show that not only were these two events salient for AM's identity, but they also impacted the group's discourse on several levels, starting with the re-presentation[2] of 9/11 and the war in Afghanistan as instances of non-recognition, followed by AM's contestation of the dominant discourses on the 'war on terror' and 'world hegemony'. The last part of the article shows how AM's evolving discursive practices and distorted struggle for recognition orientated the group towards deeper engagement for the Jihadist cause that, in turn, further radicalized its action-related practices.

## Identity, international recognition and violence

Drawing on the increasingly sophisticated literature on recognition in political science, sociology and philosophy (Taylor 1994; Honneth 1995, 2010; Lindemann 2010; Lindemann and Ringmar 2012; O'Neill and Smith 2012; Wendt 1999; Wolf 2011a, 2012), this article tries to uncover the potential dynamics between AM's alleged experience of non-recognition and the reorientation of the group's preferences towards increasingly violent practices. Non-recognition, as per a differentialist conception, is conceptualized here as the mismatch between the (real or imaginary) self-image that one actor claims in social interactions and its image as reflected by other actors. The bigger the gap between the claimed self-image and the image reflected by others, the stronger the feeling of being denied recognition (Lindemann and Saada 2012). This definition allows me to stress two important points. First, following the Hegelian tradition, non-recognition – as is recognition – is construed here as a *relational* concept, e.g. it only exists in social interaction. Second, (non-)recognition cannot be separated from identity reproduction: if recognition matters so much, it is because it participates in the maintenance of an actor's identity (Taylor 1994; Honneth 1995). When recognition is partially or wholly denied, an individual or social group perceives its identity as threatened, menacing its emotional balance, sense of self-worth and agency.[3] In short, non-recognition can inflict harm. It 'can be a form of oppression, imprisoning someone in a false, distorted, and reduced mode of being' (Taylor 1994, 25). Beyond the emotional pain, a denial of recognition may thus carry important consequences in terms of cognition: it can bring the non-recognized party to forcibly change its identity or foster violent behaviour (Mead 1934). Yet, it would be inaccurate to conclude that non-recognition always leads to violence. First, non-recognition has varying effects on subjects, depending on their differing *need* to be recognized. Some political entities may lend more weight than others to have the 'sufferings, achievements, or self-image' of their people 'recognized by foreigners' (Heins 2012). Second, the articulation of an experience as a denial of recognition cannot be understood if we fail to consider how the entity's identity might have been shaped by previous interactions (e.g. relation resting on stigma). The interpretation of an event as an experience of non-recognition is not elaborated in a void; it passes through identity-based filters and often firmly anchored belief systems. These in turn add up to shift reality, either by downplaying or by amplifying the experience of non-recognition. In the case study at hand, AM shows signs of a 'hubristic identity' (Lindemann 2010) well before the events under scrutiny and reproduces a belief system and worldview rooted on prestige, which oriented the group towards increased sensitivity to the experience of non-recognition.

To better appreciate AM's (alleged) experience of international non-recognition, let us first assess the forms non-recognition may take. It often occurs under the form of *disrespect*,[4] which can be defined as the 'inacceptable[sic] mismatch between the social position one is assigned by the Other and the position one expects to deserve according to prevailing standards and norms' (Wolf 2011a, 106). Disrespect targets the social status and/or social value of the disrespected party, which is primarily concerned with its threatened social position in relation to other entities. A subcategory of disrespect, *humiliation*, is also relevant to our case study. Compared to disrespect, humiliation is at the same time more public and more restrictive. Fattah and Fierke (2009, 72) point out that humiliated is the individual, community or nation, whose status or value has been publicly 'lower[ed]', whereas this entity 'expect[ed] a higher status' or an acknowledgement of its value. Humiliation is less relational than disrespect in the sense that the referential for the recognition gap is less the humiliating entity's relative position but the humiliated entity's previous position in the system.

Entities facing denials of recognition either accept the demeaning self-image imposed by the Other or they challenge this image. At the actor's level, passivity often leads to a diminished sense of self-esteem. At the intersubjective level, the humiliated entity often sees its authority vanish on the international scene (Mercer 1996). A denial of recognition may even be regarded as a security threat, since other political entities may interpret it as a license to dispose of an unwanted entity.[5] An actor's decision to take action due to the non-recognition of its self-image may lead to two different kinds of struggles for recognition. An authentic struggle is characterized by the demand for reciprocal, egalitarian recognition and may be designated as a 'struggle for dignity' (Lindemann and Ringmar 2012). Conversely, a distorted claim to recognition defines the situation in which social actor A purports claims to recognition, which imply social actor B's unilateral recognition of A's superior force, superior status or higher accomplishments (social value). In this case, the struggle for recognition departs from a universal and egalitarian demand for dignity in that actor A seeks to requisition prestige for itself. This 'struggle for prestige' is even more distorted when it contradicts existing international norms and standards. In either case, there are two ideal type strategies to push forward a claim to recognition: a pacific one, which often amounts to the non-recognized party complying with international expectations, and a violent one, which implies that the non-recognized party is ready to consider armed violence to force – often unilateral – recognition. As highlighted earlier, the emotional, cognitive and political consequences of non-recognition can be perceived so costly that political entities may decide to resort to violence against all odds; be it to 'save face' (Lindemann 2010), to regain respect (Saurette 2006; Wolf 2008), to promote a 'stable identity' (Mitzen 2006) or even just to cease being considered as a passive object (Wolf 2008).

Analysing AM's 'struggle for recognition' does not stretch recognition theory too far, since group identity may be considered the prolongation – the 'pendant' – at a higher level, of one's relation to oneself (Honneth 2010, 184). This is even more relevant in the case of sectarian or radical violent groups organized around selective membership, where people are chosen on the basis of their adequacy with the group's values, aims and means. The affective and identity-based value of the collective for the construction and reproduction of the Self explains that a social group can – as a collective – experience a denial of recognition (Taylor 1994; Honneth 1995). But what about social groups or movements that experience a denial of recognition vicariously? For instance, AM does not merely seek recognition for itself as an Islamist group but for a larger entity, the Islamic Emirate of Afghanistan (IEA)[6] and beyond that for the (imagined) transnational community of Muslims or *Ummah*.[7] Recognition theory has little to say on the denials of recognition experienced on behalf of *another* entity. The first theoretical prolongation of recognition theory would be to argue that the logic of recognition does not have to be limited to self-worth, but can be bridged to the question of justice (Lindemann and Saada 2012). In this regard, some entities might struggle to achieve justice and recognition on behalf of other entities towards which they feel empathy or even responsibility. A second possibility would consist in arguing that some entities may put forth recognition claims on behalf of other (larger) entities to ultimately gain control over them. At that point, a theoretical bridge to Laclau and Mouffe's (1985) concept of hegemony can be useful to analyse critically AM's distorted claims to recognition and the group's own interests in the international recognition of the *Ummah*.

## A pluralistic approach to discourse analysis

The proposed interactional analytical framework has led me to adopt a post-structuralist discursive epistemology. The discourse analysis developed here is a cross between several and, in my opinion, complementary, methodological approaches. It combines elements of the Foucauldian tradition of discourse analysis – and notably its German developments in the 'sociology of knowledge' – with the Copenhagen school's methodological focus on foreign policy and identity.

The present analysis focuses mainly on written and spoken language. The corpus consists of (1) communiqués, official statements and articles published on AM's official websites[8]; (2) interviews and (3) official statements of the organization's leaders[9] in the English-speaking press and television between September 2001 and September 2002. Only sources that contained a direct or indirect reference to the 9/11 attacks or the war in Afghanistan were introduced into the corpus. Secondary attention was given to the group's 'body language' (Hansen 2006, 23), such as violent public demonstrations or the organization of military training workshops, which were also included in the discourse analysis.

There are generally two types of discourse analysis: one type that 'aims at specifying the bandwidth of possible outcomes' and one that takes into scrutiny a specific outcome and 'demonstrate[s] the preconditions for it happening' (Neumann 2009, 62–63). The present discourse analysis corresponds to the second type since I start with the increase in radicalism of the group's practices and try to give a plausible account of *how* this may have happened. Discourse analysis has known many developments in the past 40 years (Paveau and Rosier 2005; Keller 2011), with each 'strand' advocating a slightly different version of it. First, with regard to the research problem addressed here, I chose to focus on a little known variant outside of the German academia. The *Wissenssoziologische*

*Diskursanalyse* (best translated as 'Discourse analysis based on the sociology of knowledge'; Keller 2005, 2011), inspired by the Frankfurt critical school and drawing upon a quasi literal rereading of the Foucauldian tradition, contributes to the epistemological refining of the methodology proposed here. An important consequence of incorporating this approach was the careful examination of the re-production of knowledge and especially the 'struggles for truth' (Keller 2005) as part of AM's larger struggle for recognition.

Second, the Copenhagen school's focus on the interplay between identity and foreign policy within securitization practices (Wæver 1989; Hansen 2006) has been a great source of inspiration. Though the analysis is concerned here with a different type of political actor, I argue that AM's policy prescriptions in terms of Islamic foreign affairs share many similarities with 'those particular foreign policies that are constructed in terms of security' (Hansen 2006, 33). Evidently, it is provocative to treat a terrorist organization's political discourses as foreign policy discourses; yet, there are a few empirical examples of terrorist organizations that political activities compare to that of states, such as the Hezbollah claiming state prerogatives in the south of Lebanon, or the coming to power of the Hamas, internationally blacklisted as a terrorist organization, in 2007 in the Gaza Strip. Furthermore, from a theoretical point of view, nothing bars the analysis of AM's policy prescriptions in terms of security policy. As Hansen points out, security has been traditionally associated with the state, 'not because the state is an immortal entity or because security is objectively provided by the state' (2006, 34). As Buzan, Wæver, and de Wilde (1997, 25) point out, constructing something as a threat to security is to present it as 'an existential threat to a designated object (traditionally, but not necessarily, the state, incorporating government, territory and society)'. As such, the 'designated object' need not be a state or even a nation but could be, for instance, a transnational community. I shall argue that AM's claims to recognition, on behalf of the *Ummah*, are indeed formulated in terms of security. The group presents itself as acting as a legitimate representative of the *Ummah* in the absence of proper representation. I thus argue that the analysis of AM's prescriptions following the 9/11 attacks and the war in Afghanistan in terms of foreign policy can provide many an insight into the workings and evolution of the group's discourse and claims to recognition.

## The re-presentation of 9/11 and the war in Afghanistan as instances of non-recognition

The 9/11 attacks and, even more so, the declaration of war against Afghanistan are salient for the group, particularly in terms of social status (self-respect) and social value (self-esteem). For a radical group that praised the 1998 attacks against American embassies in Dar es Salaam and Nairobi, AM's position towards the 9/11 attacks was at first surprisingly ambiguous. On the one hand, its leaders praised the event as a punishment of America's 'arrogance', but on the other hand, they regarded it as yet another chance to 'victimize Muslims'.[10] In the days following the attacks, the organization issued many statements in which it rejected quite vehemently the accusations according to which the attacks were perpetrated by an Islamist group. In an interview on 12 September 2001, Omar Bakri Mohammed (hereafter: OBM), spiritual leader and head of the organization, argued that hijacking a civilian airplane is 'a Sin' because 'the civilians onboard have sanctity and it is prohibited to use them as a weapon against a military target'. Thus to accuse 'Muslims' of the 9/11 attacks would be to challenge their religious identity. Condemning the attacks 'as a crime as far as Islam is concerned', OBM stressed that there was 'no proof' that a terrorist Islamic organization was behind the attacks. A month later, OBM, asked who was responsible for the attacks, contemplated conspiracy theories and answered that it was probably 'the MI6' or 'the political elite in America'. In an AM press release entitled 'USA at War with Islam', American leaders were indeed presupposed not to be above such crimes to point 'the accusing finger' at 'Muslims'. The attack was thus seen as a negative event in terms of 'Muslims' worldwide image, an attempt to lower 'their' status and social value as a community.

Worth stressing here was the attempt by the group to frame the event as an opposition between 'the West' and 'Muslims/the Muslim world' as naturalized, homogeneous categories. Antagonistic predication is indeed the most striking feature of the corpus. In AM's ideology, 'the West' encompasses the United States, its allies and more generally all Western powers (Israel included), described as unbelievers or 'kuffaar', as well as the 'coward leaders of the Muslim world'. Conversely, the category 'Muslim world' includes all true believers, the Taliban and bin Laden's organization included. Though encompassing highly heterogeneous religious and political items, these two categories were nevertheless presented by AM as monolithic ones. The group's leaders thus conveniently argued that when a component of the 'Muslim world' category is wrongly accused of a crime, all Muslims are being victimized and, conversely, the whole 'West' is being oppressive.

OBM considered that the United States lacked proof that individuals of Muslim faith committed the 9/11 attacks and was orchestrating a 'witch hunt' to 'demonis[e] Muslims' and lower their image worldwide. In a communiqué dated 21 September 2001, the group furthermore argued that Muslim individuals were being prosecuted in the United States for the 9/11 attacks merely on the basis of their religious convictions. OBM was quick to reassert AM's difference with 'the West' by stressing that 'Islam forbid[s] us to fight people because of their Nationality, Color [sic], etc …'. The social category 'Muslim world' was thus displayed as possessing a higher morality. AM's extensive use of predication indeed tells us a lot about how the group ordered the world and what positions the different subjects of its discourse occupied in it. While the predicates 'victims', 'survivors', 'oppressed', 'peaceful', 'gentle', 'accused wrongly', 'innocent civilians', 'believer' and 'solidarity' were used repeatedly to refer to the socially constructed category 'Muslim World', the qualifiers 'oppressors', 'crusader', 'guilty', 'murderers', 'terrorists', 'coward', 'disbeliever', 'perverse', 'sadistic' and 'barbaric' served to exemplify 'the West' and its allies. To use Doty's (1993) wording, these categories imply that there were *superior* and *inferior* kinds of subjects in AM's social world. While militarily advantaged, 'the West' was considered fairly low in terms of morality, whereas the 'Muslim world' was deemed morally and spiritually superior. In this worldview, being collectively falsely accused of a crime while the 'guilty' (i.e. 'the West') roamed free and 'rush[ed] quickly to accuse [its] own victims' was perceived as an intolerable injustice.

Though framing the 9/11 and its consequences as part of a Western powers' move to persecute Muslims, the group regarded nevertheless this event positively. AM condemned the attacks from a *technical* point of view and because of the negative effects in terms of worldwide 'Muslim' image, yet it praised the results from a *tactical* point of view. The group welcomed what the 9/11 represented, from OBM's half-veiled references – directly after the attacks – to the 'lessons we could derived[sic] out of it', such as 'shak[ing] the arrogance of the Western Government[s] and undermin[ing] their claims to be invulnerable', to the group's celebration of the 9/11's anniversary a year later with a rally entitled 'A towering day in history' in reference to the destruction of the twin towers. According to OBM, the 9/11 attacks were 'the consequences of the atrocities and the aggression committed by the US Government and its forces against the Third World in general and the Muslim World [...] in Particular[sic]', which is to say that the 9/11 was considered both an act of revenge *and* a warning to refrain from further alienating the rest of the world. This is puzzling in so far that the group concurrently pretended that American or British intelligence services were probably behind the attacks. This apparent incoherence may be explained by the fact that AM widely believed in direct divine intervention. This explanation is corroborated by an AM leaflet, distributed around British campuses directly after 9/11, which stated that 'Allah has responded once again to the cries and supplications of the Muslims worldwide'. In terms of recognition, the 9/11 attacks thus represented a relative lowering of the US's status as a superpower, a downgrading that yet did not seem to compensate, in AM's eyes, the unjust lowering of the 'Muslim world's' image, nor its multiple experiences of non-recognition as highlighted by the group's recurring litany of grievances associated with past and present conflicts in Chechnya, Kashmir, Palestine, Kuwait, Saudi Arabia, Iraq, Egypt, Turkey, Somalia, Sudan, Afghanistan, Bosnia and Kosovo.

In this context, the declaration of war against Afghanistan was perceived by AM's leaders as a renewed, aggravated experience of non-recognition. The group argued that the attacks in New York served as an excuse to wage a long-prepared war. In a communiqué dated 21 September, AM contended that 'the western world seems intent on using the destruction of the World Trade Center as a precursor to attack Muslims [sic]'. Already in the immediate aftermath of the 9/11 attacks were there talks of a military intervention against Afghanistan; AM uses this timing to support its argument that the war was not waged for the alleged purpose – rooting terrorism out – but to destroy a regime perceived as an enemy to 'the West'. Afghanistan under the Taliban did not enjoy the international recognition it expected, a state of affairs not lost by AM that argued that 'the decision to bomb Afghanistan is a blatant violation of sovereignty for the State of Afghanistan [sic]'. Generalizing from this, AM contended that the goal of the war against Afghanistan consisted in the destruction of 'Muslim's way of life', thus strongly referring to disrespect. 'The West''s assumed intent to destroy Muslims' way of life was constructed by the group's leaders as a self-evident threat to 'Muslims'' identity and, defined in broad terms, to their security. First, empirical proof is inscribed discursively in AM's recurring narrative of conflicts involving 'the West' and Muslim countries. Second, AM's leaders use ambiguous, taken out of context Islamic scriptures to stake their claim: 'they will praise you by their tongues but their hearts reject you' (English Maariful Quran 9:8) and 'never will the Jews and Christians be satisfied with you unless the[sic] take you away from your Islamic way of life' (English Maariful Quran, Surah al Baqaraa, 120). AM's line of argument indeed recurrently involved 'cherry-picking'[11] Islamic scriptures, through which the group's claims acquired a teleological dimension and hence both an irrevocable character and a timeless quality. Thus, according to AM, the IEA was not granted recognition *because* of its Islamic character, with the implication that the then current international order differentiated between subjects (states) on the basis of prejudice. The group claimed to experience such a denial of recognition on behalf of the IEA and more generally on behalf of all Muslims, because of what it saw as the absence of proper Islamic representation, denouncing 'the so-called coward leaders of the Muslim world [who] remain[ed] silent at these crimes'.

AM indeed claimed to be nothing less than 'The Voice, The Eyes & The Ears of The Muslims', in short, to represent all Muslims. From an intertextual point of view, this is not all too surprising in so far that the group's discursive practices extensively referred to the Wahhabi tradition.[12] First, AM considered its religious doctrine not as a school of thought but as Islam itself. To drive this point home, the group stressed that 'the Taleban ARE Afghanistan, who ARE Muslims, and the definition of Terrorism by the Bush and Blair regimes IS the actions of MUSLIMS fulfilling the Islamic obligation [sic]'. Indeed, the group considered Muslims who belonged to other schools of thought as *muharib* (i.e. those who combat society) and, as such, as legitimate targets of violence. Second, AM directly imported Wahhabism's attachment to egalitarianism. One of its main features, in terms of religious and political legitimacy, is that it 'deconstructs any notions of established authority within Islam' (El Fadl 2001). In this tradition, in case of an endangerment of the Muslim community, every Imam[13] has the authority to declare *Jihad*, even more so when the political authorities in charge are deemed failing (Commins 2007). Third, in a similar manner, to claim that 'the West' wants to see *the* Muslim way of life destroyed, AM argued that there is only *one* Muslim way of life, consisting in the example given by the Prophet, a literarist interpretation also consistent with Qutbism.[14] AM's claim to represent all Muslims clearly refers to an old strategy of domination within Islam itself. For those revering these references, AM's self-presentation bestowed the group with legitimacy to speak for the *Ummah* and power to prescribe and undertake action. More subtly, AM targeted thereby the competition as well, i.e. UK-based as well as global Jihadi groups, which were expected to recognize AM's legitimacy (and maybe, leadership) in calling to *Jihad*.

Yet why was the war against the IEA so important for AM as an Islamist radical group? The short answer may be that it constituted the newest addition on the group's list of grievances. AM's leaders were probably trying to ride the wave of indignation while it lasted to increase publicity for the group's ideology. But a more in-depth answer would have to pay greater attention to intertextuality. I argue that the US-led attack on Afghanistan was interpreted not only as a denigration of ways of life but also as an attempt by 'the West' to prevent the rise of the *Khilafah* or world Islamic state. As already emphasized, AM's ideology borrowed from both Wahhabism and Qutbism, which, among other things, share an emphasis on the necessity of re-establishing the *Khilafah* to ensure 'God's sole right to sovereignty' (Commins 2007). Its main feature would be the strict application of *Shari'ah* law, as was the case in the IEA according to AM: 'the Taleban are Muslims working for the establishment of the Shari'ah'. On these grounds, the group regarded the IEA as the sole, truly Islamic state on the planet, from which the *Khilafah* should have been extended. A defeat of the IEA would have represented both a strong humiliation and a major setback in the struggle to ensure security for the 'Muslim world' through a world Islamic state. This interpretation gives a more plausible account of why a group such as AM cared so much about the international non-recognition of and war against the IEA.

## The contestation of dominant international discourses as a struggle for 'truth'

AM's interpretation and articulation of these two events as strong denials of recognition brought about important changes within the group's discourse. AM newly took position within two international discourses – what I identified as the 'war on terror' and 'world hegemony' discourses – to convince a world audience of the injustice constituted by the non-recognition of the *Ummah*'s physical integrity, status and social value. AM's contestation of these two dominant discourses referred to a struggle for 'truth' as part of its larger struggle for recognition.

Within the 'war on terror' discourse, the dominant position at the time was occupied by the United States' American representations of terrorism in the aftermath of 9/11, since

US President Bush himself coined the term.[15] Within this discourse, AM acted as the representative of an imagined, homogeneous Islamic community and defended a marginal, antagonistic position that could be roughly summarized as follows: 'the USA and its allies are quick to accuse innocent Muslims because they despise us and want to destroy our Muslims' way of life; they are the real terrorist'. To prove its point, AM made extensive use of 'the West's' own normative and legal concepts to argue that the United States and its allies disrespected the rule of law they pretended to fight for. On one occasion, AM quoted, for instance, the Collins dictionary's definition of terrorism – 'the systematic use of violence and intimidation to achieve political ends' – to denounce 'the West's' hypocrisy. Drawing a parallel between 'the West's' foreign policies and acts of terror, the group thereby stressed the existence of double standards in the international system. According to the group, 'the West's' actions fitted 'the description of the terrorists much more readily than those Muslims struggling to liberate Muslim land under occupation'. As part of its struggle for 'truth', AM thus rebranded the 'war on terror' discourse as a 'war on Islam and Muslims'. According to AM, the non-recognition of the 'Muslim world' was even more unjust considering that 'Islam is the fastest growing ideology in the world'. This alternative discourse was addressed to a world audience to clear Muslim's name and to Muslims worldwide to empower and mobilize the *Ummah*.

The other international discourse in which AM newly took position, albeit a very marginal one, was the discourse on what I called 'world hegemony'. This discourse is to be understood as the set of practices pointing to a normative definition of the kind of international system and hegemon that is deemed best for the world. The dominant position at the time was exemplified by the Western power's 'democratic club' discourse, whose main characteristic was to consider that the then current international order, while imperfect, ensured justice, equality and free trade and was, as such, the best possible system to organize the world. Conversely, the group argued that the international system equalled injustice, exploitation and insecurity because it only served the West's interests at the expense of the rest of the world. The group's newly formed discourse on 'world hegemony' appeared in the wake of the 9/11 attacks and the war in Afghanistan. It was composed of a Wahhabi-inspired, anti-hierarchical, legal and social mode of organization, combined with a Trotskyist worldview. Yet, AM's position shared some similarities with the dominant position in so far as the group did not question the assumed necessity of having a hegemon regulate the international system. AM's leaders merely contested 'the West's' definition of a 'good' hegemon. The group thus aimed at exposing the international order as the deceptive reproduction of 'the West's' 'hegemony' over the world. It further identified the nature of the current hegemony as the cause of Muslims' non-recognition. The 'Muslim world' and the 'third World in general [sic]' were denied proper recognition because 'the West' could not have 'exploit[ed]' them if there was to be mutual, egalitarian recognition. To the international order under 'Western hegemony', AM opposed an 'Islamic State[sic] in order to end the malaise of capitalism'. Such an order would have allegedly guaranteed the moral character of the new hegemony. Thus, far from contesting the *principle* of a world hegemon, AM offered to replace the current one with an Islamic world state. Worth stressing is the fact that AM's proposed hegemony was matched with only vague normative prescriptions.[16]

AM quite easily incorporated these discursive developments into its Jihadi ideology, based on a synthesis between the Wahhabi and Qutbist traditions. In their contemporary versions, merged into the modern Salafism defended by radical violent Islamist groups, both traditions agree on the necessity of *Jihad* to eliminate the 'submission to human authority' and to restore the *Shari'ah* or divine law (Commins 2007). AM reproduced this interpretation, arguing throughout the corpus that the circumstances in which the 'Muslim world' finds itself are the product of the 'corruption of man made law[sic]', as opposed to divine law. As such, if the 'Muslim world's' physical integrity, social status and value are constantly disrespected, 'Western' international laws are to blame. AM's marginal positions within the 'war on terror' and 'world hegemony' discourses thus gained increased coherence when gradually merged into a 'war on the war on terror'[17] discourse – a transformation echoed globally by most Jihadi groups. From September 2001 onwards, the discursive practices of the group transformed into an increasingly radical, more clearly articulated, globalized discourse. While previously denounced rather on a case-by-case basis, the occupation of Muslim lands became systematically put into a larger political, economic and religious context and considered one of the many features of the dysfunctional international system under 'Western' hegemony.

Considering that the Islamist field is highly competitive, the group's needs in terms of legitimacy were consistent with the reproduction of the dominant Jihadi discourse. Yet, to distinguish itself from other radical groups, AM had to be able to add its own flavour. What differentiated AM from other Jihadi groups is its gradual re-presentation of 'the West' as key to the success of an Islamic world state. This is where AM's newly taken position within the discourse on 'world hegemony' is so crucial to understanding its radicalization. AM's new developments on the necessity of an Islamic world state targeted a world audience and primarily the group's (potential) followers in non-Muslim countries, encouraged by OBM to 'constitute a 5th column' in 'the West'.

Unsurprisingly though, AM's discursive practices were not exempt from contradictions. For instance, within the discourse on the 'war on terror', AM's marginal position consisted in arguing that the United States and its allies were terrorists according to their own definition. Yet, arguing from the same definition, AM contended that attacks perpetrated by Muslim individuals to achieve political ends were not to be viewed as terrorism but as 'acts of war, a war started by America'. Similarly, in terms of predication, the 'Muslim world' was depicted as the pious, innocent victim of the perverse 'West'. Yet, this candid representation was in conflict with AM's insistence on Muslim's determination, courage and capacity to 'give the US-led forces a shock', as well as at odds with the violent, missionary character of its 'world hegemony' and Jihadi discourses.[18]

## From a distorted struggle to unjustified claims to recognition

Around the re-presentation of 9/11 and the war against Afghanistan as instances of non-recognition, AM's discourse acquired two new features. First, AM constructed the 'war on terror' as a threat to the 'Muslim world's' security, social status and ways of life, thus explicitly referring to non-recognition. Second, the group contested the international discourses on the 'war on terror' and 'world hegemony' and stressed the necessity of replacing the current international order with an Islamic world state to put an end to this threat. Yet, the gradual transformation of AM's discursive practices transformed the nature of its struggle for recognition.

By re-presenting the United States and its allies as possessing a lesser kind of subjectivity, closer to that of a beast than that of a human being, AM disqualified their capacity at intersubjective recognition. No longer is 'the West' considered a potential recognition partner. Indeed, as a result of 'reifying typifications' – exemplified by AM's use of radically negative predication – and a belief system rooted in a particularly cleaving ideology, AM denied 'the West' the qualities normally attributed to an Other in the process of recognition (autonomy and consciousness of its particularity). As a forgetting of recognition (Honneth 2007), it could further be argued that the group's practices towards 'the West' entered a process of reification. 'The West' gradually *disappeared* as a significant Other when AM ceased acknowledging its capacity to recognize the *Ummah*. In short, AM, by considering that 'the West' would not recognize the *Ummah*, seemed to abandon the struggle for mutual recognition and to even dispute that it ever recognized 'the West' as a significant Other.

Yet, individuals and groups need some source of recognition to be able to maintain a sense of ethical life. From where did AM draw recognition if intersubjective recognition was disqualified? As its practices gradually transformed into a discourse on the necessity to replace the current 'evil' world order by an Islamic world state, AM provided itself and the *Ummah* with two alternative sources of recognition: *self-recognition* and *divine recognition*. In terms of subject positioning, AM's leaders re-presented the group and, by extension, 'the Muslim world' as a subject with a worldview, assessing problems and solutions, offering spiritual guidance and initiating actions. Since the present 'evil' world order was not considered irreversible, uncritical, positive self-predication was aimed at empowering the imagined *Ummah* into overthrowing it. Stressing the virtuousness and superiority of the 'Muslim way of life' implied on AM's part that self-recognition could and should suffice to itself. The 'religious obligation' of contributing to the *Jihad* and beyond that to the establishment of a new world caliphate furthermore provided the group with a sense of purpose and social value backed up by a teleological vision of history. AM's *Ummah*, as a community of values with a specific destiny, was on a divine mission. Indeed, in the group's view, the harder the task, the better, since being given a 'test' by God equals being on the right 'path'. Following what AM saw as God's will, the *Ummah* thus cannot fail to enjoy divine recognition. Indeed, AM's presentation of itself, its mission and that of the *Ummah* implied that the Self ceased to be a meaning-conferring, autonomous subject. Here again, AM developed a reified conception of the *Ummah* and itself, both only existing through their engagement and exclusively in the future as instruments towards the *Khilafah*.

Does this mean that AM renounced all claims to intersubjective recognition though? The group's insistence on the necessity of an Islamic world order to preserve humanity from 'exploitation' and to restore its 'dignity' as well as its targeting a world audience seemed to point to the contrary. It is my interpretation that the group *indirectly* struggled for intersubjective recognition, on behalf of a socially constructed *Ummah*, by *implicitly* requesting the recognition of a future world caliphate as a better system to organize the international order. This claim to recognition was particularly distorted since (1) it implied unilateral recognition as opposed to reciprocal recognition, (2) it concerned future potential accomplishments and (3) it strived to establish a new hegemony to replace the contested one. This struggle for prestige raises problematic questions: How can a group that does not mutually recognize the autonomous and fundamentally moral character of others be itself a subject of recognition? Who in the reified 'West' was supposed to *unilaterally* give this recognition? And to whom, the *Ummah* or maybe to AM as the forefront of the coming *Khilafah*? Apart from the questionable moral character of a struggle for prestige, there was a fundamental inconsistency in AM's claims to unilateral recognition. AM would have found itself in the same impasse as Hegel's 'master' confronted to the 'mere slave'; discarded as an autonomous and competent judge, the slave is hence unable to provide adequate recognition (Hegel 2010 [1807]). Conversely, if AM would have reintroduced 'the West' as a potential recognition partner – if not an equal then at least an autonomous one – intersubjective recognition would still have been problematic. Since AM's discursive practices suggested that the criterion for recognition is the Other's self-image, then the recognition of the *Ummah*'s (alleged) moral superiority would have equally implied the recognition of 'the West's' (alleged) superior self-image.

AM's case study has significant implications for recognition theory, since it suggests that mutual recognition does *not* always suffice to overcome violence. If we define adequate intersubjective recognition as the authentic process by which mutually affirming subjects come to recognize the Other's moral character as well as his capacity to provide recognition, then AM, in its self-appointed role to prepare for the *Khilafah*, would probably not have had much interest. Indeed, it seems that only unilateral recognition might satisfy the group's demands on behalf of the *Ummah*. Yet even that is questionable: As Heins (2012) points out, social groups that have felt disrespected for decades might be 'deaf' to 'reconciliatory messages' and not even come to realize when signs of respect are genuinely offered. The case study also suggests that not all struggles for recognition can and should be satisfied, for instance, when one actor's prestige claims imply that the Other renounces his 'right to be an autonomous source of authentic appraisals' or even impede third parties' recognition claims (Wolf 2011b). In terms of action-related prescriptions, what would be the 'natural thing to do' (Neumann 2009) for AM to bring its distorted claim to superiority forward? It seems logical that the radicalization of AM's discursive practices would be followed by the radicalization of the group's action-related prescriptions. Even more so when one considers that accepting that activism stagnates implies interrupting the moral gratifications attached to what is seen as a just struggle as well as risking to lose its followers (Hirschman 1982). All the more so since the group presents its claim on behalf of the *Ummah* as part of a disinterested struggle. AM's leaders often sought to pass as mere 'Muslim scholars', fulfilling the emancipatory role of guiding the *Ummah* towards 'the truth'. AM's large definition of 'security' – including, for instance, the protection of Muslims' way of life – also implied a specific kind or responsibility. Hansen indeed points out that a security discourse 'bestows power as well as responsibility on those speaking within it'; if it gives a 'particular legitimacy', it also demands 'decisive' action (2006, 34). AM's discourse on the necessity to achieve the *Khilafah* to protect Muslims' life, status and social value thus demanded that the group takes 'decisive' action.

Since the international order was re-presented as a self-help system and 'the West' as irremediably belligerent, the possibilities of practice were narrowed down to violence, which was presented by the group as both necessary and justified.[19] Yet, it seemed ludicrous for such a small group as AM to pretend to be able to take on the United States and its allies in a traditional war. Guerilla war within Western states was also not an option; in the United Kingdom, for example, the number of AM 'activists' (official members and 'students') did not exceed 900 individuals at any given time, while the group's 'contacts', occasionally joining in AM's events, amounted to less than 7000 individuals[20] (Wiktorowicz and Kaltenthaler 2006). To further engage into the asymmetric type of warfare that terrorism represents was the obvious choice, especially since the reified *Ummah* had the obligation to 'sacrifice' everything to 'fight the enemies of Allah'.

AM's call to *Jihad* indeed followed the transformation of its discursive practices. First, while previously focusing on the United States, AM's leaders started condoning the use of *Jihad* wherever Muslim 'lives' and wherever their 'properties' and 'honour' were at stake. Second, they gradually softened the rules governing the practice of *Jihad*, especially concerning the status of innocent civilians' deaths, regarded with more leniency. For instance, AM began recruiting *en masse* for global *Jihad*, sending increasing numbers of British recruits to its office in Lahore, Pakistan, from where they were to join in the fight in Afghanistan. Third, and perhaps most significantly, AM started calling its followers to greater activism *within* Western countries. This is an important change, since before 9/11 and the war in Afghanistan, AM's prescription was to 'either b[ear] the persecution or migrat[e]'. Though still mostly refusing to directly advocate terrorist attacks in the countries in which it operated,[21] AM started encouraging its followers to constitute Islamic 'fifth columns' in Western states to destabilize their governments from within and bring about a worldwide Islamic state. The group began expanding, opening, for instance, a new branch in Ireland in October 2003. AM engaged increasingly in seditious violence within the United Kingdom, with actions ranging from the distribution of violent leaflets welcoming the 9/11 attacks on university campuses to the aggressive recruiting and fund-raising for Jihad, and all the way to the organization of military training camps within the United Kingdom (also known as the 'Sakina affair'). The group became known as well for organizing yearly 'commemorations' of the 9/11 attacks, in which it regularly showed graphic videos of planes crashing on potential Western targets. Muslims in 'the West' were thereby called to be 'the front line of the coming Khilafah' since 'bonding the Muslim community in the West with the Muslims globally' was the key to bringing about a 'worldwide Islamic revolution'.

## Conclusion

Beyond the question whether the accusations following the 9/11 attacks and the declaration of war against Afghanistan constitute objective denials of recognition of the *Ummah* that AM pretends to represent, this article has tried to provide an account of how the group discursively constructed them as such. AM's discursive practices revolving around the theme of recognition proved to be particularly dense: (1) AM perceived the two international events as 'the West's' attempt to lower the 'Muslim world's' image and depreciate its social status and value; (2) the group constructed 'the West's' 'exploitation' of foreign peoples, particularly of the 'Muslim world', as characteristic of an evil hegemony; (3) on those grounds, AM disqualified the possibility of intersubjective recognition and in turn denied 'the West' recognition and (4) the group turned instead to self-recognition and divine recognition and, in doing so, reified itself and the *Ummah* to a large extent. These discursive transformations allowed for the further radicalization of AM's Jihadi ideology and action-related practices. While previously consistently advocating *Jihad* merely against the United States, the group turned to calling for an all-out *Jihad* against the whole 'West' and its international order as well as for the constitution of 'fifth columns' within 'the West' to bring about an Islamic revolution supposed to lead to the establishment of an Islamic world state. By the end of 2001, AM's claims to recognition had thus gradually transformed into distorted claims to superiority, precluding the possibility of being satisfied by authentic, mutual recognition.

## Acknowledgements

The author would like to thank Thomas Lindemann, Reinhard Wolf, Jean-Vincent Holeindre and Justin Cook for helpful discussions and comments. Thanks are also due to Shannon Brincat as well as the two anonymous reviewers for their valuable feedback on an earlier draft of this article.

## Notes

1. The group reappeared under different names in 2005, 2006 and 2009 and was subsequently banned (Neumann 2008; Zara Raymond 2010).

2. Term borrowed from Neumann (2009), which better captures the idea of gradual *change* in the presentation of reality.
3. Maslow (1954) already argued in 1954 that self-esteem is a fundamental psychological need of the individual. More recently, Mitzen (2006) contends that 'ontological security', i.e. the need for a stable 'Self', is at the core of states' decision-making process. Wolf (2011a) writes about a 'self-protective urge to reestablish one's "rightful position"' to regain self-respect and thus a positive relationship to oneself.
4. On the scope of non-recognition and disrespect, see Wolf (2011a).
5. Lindemann and Saada (2012, 16) share a similar point of view. Realist theorists go as far as to argue that an entity with a reputation for weakness encourages other actors to aggression, see Alt, Calvert, and Humes (1988).
6. The IEA may be considered a de facto state from 1996 on, when the Taliban seized Kabul and proclaimed the Emirate – or, more restrictively, from 2000 on, when they achieved control over 90% of the territory. Yet, the IEA did not enjoy the *thicker* recognition – to use Wendt's term – of being accepted as part of the international community of states. The overwhelming majority of states decided *collectively* not to grant the IEA equal sovereignty. The main reason put forward was the violent conditions of the Taliban's access to power – a fact contested by AM – which violates widely accepted international norms. On the international community's tendency to condemn violent access to power, see Shannon et al. (2014).
7. AM's definition of the term *Ummah* implies that the group denies the very existence of multiple tendencies and schools of thought within Islam.
8. At the time of the events, the organization was maintaining two official websites: www.muhajiroun.com, the official platform of the group, and www.obm.clara.net, the website of Omar Bakri Mohammed, spiritual leader of the organization. Since both websites were shut down after AM's dissolution, I used the Wayback Machine (www.archive.org) to search for archived versions of AM's web pages.
9. Those are Omar Bakri Mohammed, spiritual leader; Anjem Choudary, leader of AM UK; Irfan Rasool, leader of AM's Scottish branch; Adeel Shahid and Hassan Butt, spokesmen of AM.
10. The quotes that follow are taken from the following texts of the corpus: Interview of Omar Bakri Mohammed, *OBM's website*, September 12, 2001; 'USA at war with Islam', AM press release, *OBM's website*, September 16, 2001; AM communiqué, *OBM's website*, September 21, 2001; Interview of OBM, *Sunday Business Post*, October 6, 2001; 'A war against Afghanistan is a war on Islam', AM press release, *OBM's website*, October 7, 2001; Interview of OBM, *The Providence Journal*, October 7, 2001; Press statement of Adeel Shahid, spokesman of AM, *Pakistan Press International*, October 8, 2001; Interview of OBM, *The Globe and Mail*, October 15, 2001; Interview of Irfan Rasool, spokesman of the Scottish branch of AM, *Sunday Herald*, November 4, 2001; Interview of OBM, *Calgary Herald*, November 17, 2001; Interview of Hassan Butt, *BBC News*, January 7, 2002; Press statement of OBM, *The Wall Street Journal Europe*, August 16, 2002; Press statement of OBM, *London Telegraph*, September 9, 2002.
11. Expression borrowed from El Fadl (2001).
12. As based on the works written by Mohammed Abd Al-Wahhab (1703–1792), notably his book *Kitab at-Tawhid*.
13. Not only was Omar Bakri Mohammed AM's spiritual leader at the time, he was also 'Judge of the Shariah Court of the UK', through which he claimed religious authority.
14. As based on the later works written by Sayyid Qutb (1906–1966), notably his book *Ma'alim fi'l-Tariq*.
15. The expression was first used by US President G.W. Bush in a televised address to a joint session of Congress on 20 September 2001.
16. The only explicit delimitation ruled on by AM at the time is that the Khilafah should be governed by 'Islamic clerics'.
17. Expression borrowed from Mazid (2008).
18. For an example of the tension between the 'hero' and the 'innocent victim' in the case Al-Qaeda's narratives, see Lindemann (2013).
19. AM draws here extensively on the 'just war' discourse as a means to legitimize Jihad. On the relationship between Western (Christian-inspired) and Islamic 'just war' discourses, see Hashmi (1996), El Fadl (2003) and Kelsay (2007).

20. These figures should be treated with caution, yet they seem plausible. As Wiktorowicz and Kaltenthaler point out, to become a full member, every 'student' has to undergo a long and selective process, requiring deep financial and personal engagement in the organization. This could explain the relatively low number of activists compared to the large number of sympathizers. According to Simcox, Stuart, and Ahmed (2010), 18% of UK terror-related convictions between 1999 and 2009 were linked to AM, a figure that also underlines the group's human capital over the past decade.
21. Only Hassan Butt declared as early as 2002 that 'the Mujahideen that are coming in from Britain [to AM's offices in Lahore, Pakistan, to fight alongside the Taliban] should strike at the heart of the enemy which is their own country, within Britain [sic]'. It was not until spring 2004 that AM's leaders started more openly encouraging their British followers to target their own country (Clément 2013).

**References**

Alt, J. E., R. L. Calvert, and B. D. Humes. 1988. "Reputation and Hegemonic Stability: A Game-Theoretic Analysis." *The American Political Science Review* 82: 445–466. doi:10.2307/1957395.

Buzan, B., O. Wæver, and J. de Wilde. 1997. *Security: A New Framework for Analysis*. Boulder, CO: Lynne Rienner Publishers.

Clément, M. 2013. "Radicalisation violente islamique: le rôle des emotions dans le nexus non-respect – propension à la mobilisation violente." Paper presented at the Congress of the French Political Science Association, Paris, July 9–11. Accessed April 21, 2014. http://www.congres-afsp.fr/ateliersdoctoraux/ad4clement.pdf

Commins, D. D. 2007. "The Jihadi Factor in Wahhabi Islam." Lecture delivered at the Conference on Jihadi Islam held at the UCLA Faculty Center, Los Angeles, CA, November 13.

Doty, R. L. 1993. "Foreign Policy as Social Construction: A Post-Positivist Analysis of U.S. Counterinsurgency Policy in the Philippines." *International Studies Quarterly* 37 (3): 297–320. doi:10.2307/2600810.

El Fadl, K. A. 2001. "Islam and the Theology of Power." *Middle East Report* 31 (221): 28–33. doi:10.2307/1559337. Accessed April 21, 2014. http://www.merip.org/mer/mer221/islam-theology-power

El Fadl, K. A. 2003. "Between Functionalism and Morality: The Juristic Debates on the Conduct of War." In *Islamic Ethics of Life: Abortion, War, and Euthanasia*, edited by J. E. Brockopp, 103–128. Columbia: University of South Carolina Press.

Fattah, K., and K. M. Fierke. 2009. "A Clash of Emotions: The Politics of Humiliation and Political Violence in the Middle East." *European Journal of International Relations* 15 (1): 67–93. doi:10.1177/1354066108100053.

Fierke, K. M. 2014. *Political Self-Sacrifice: Agency, Body and Emotion in International Relations*. Cambridge: Cambridge University Press.

Hansen, L. 2006. *Security as Practice: Discourse Analysis and the Bosnian War*. London: Routledge.

Hashmi, S. H. 1996. "Interpreting the Islamic Ethics of War and Peace." In *The Ethics of War and Peace: Religious and Secular Perspectives*, edited by T. Nardin, 146–166. Princeton, NJ: Princeton University Press.

Hegel, G. W. F. 2010 [1807]. *Phänomenologie Des Geistes*. Berlin: Suhrkamp Verlag.

Heins, V. 2012. "The Global Politics of Recognition." In *Recognition Theory as Social Research*, edited by S. O'Neill and N. H. Smith. London: Palgrave Macmillan.

Hirschman, A. O. 1982. *Shifting Involvements: Private Interest and Public Action*. Princeton, NJ: Princeton University Press.

Honneth, A. 1995. *The Struggle for Recognition: The Moral Grammar of Social Conflicts*. Cambridge: Polity Press.

Honneth, A. 2007. *La Réification. Petit Traité De Théorie Critique*. Paris: Gallimard.

Honneth, A. 2010. *Das Ich Im Wir. Studien Zur Anerkennungstheorie*. Berlin: SuhrkampVerlag.

Keller, R. 2005. "Analysing Discourse: An Approach from the Sociology of Knowledge." *Forum Qualitative Sozialforschung* 6 (3). Accessed April 21, 2014. http://www.qualitative-research.net/index.php/fqs/article/view/19/41

Keller, R. 2011. *Diskursforschung. Eine Einführung Für Sozialwissenschaftlerinnen*. 4th ed. Wiesbaden: VS Verlag für Sozialwissenschaften.
Kelsay, J. 2007. *Arguing the Just War in Islam*. Cambridge, MA: Harvard University Press.
Laclau, E., and C. Mouffe. 1985. *Hegemony and Socialist Strategy: Towards a Radical Democratic Politics*. New York: Verso.
Lindemann, T. 2010. *Causes of War: The Struggle for Recognition*. Wivenhoe Park: ECPR Press.
Lindemann, T. 2013. "A Rundown on (Non) Recognition in Hollywood Action Movies and War Narratives: Understanding the Framing of Emotions in Al Qaeda's and Bush's Discourse." Paper presented at the ECPR Joint Session 28, Mainz, March 13.
Lindemann, T., and E. Ringmar, eds. 2012. *The International Struggle for Recognition*. Boulder, CO: Paradigm Publisher.
Lindemann, T., and J. Saada 2012. "Théories de la reconnaissance dans les relations internationals: Enjeux symboliques et limites du paradigme de l'intérêt." *Cultures & Conflits* 87: 8–25. Accessed April 21, 2014. http://conflits.revues.org/18461
Maslow, A. H. 1954. *Motivation and Personality*. New York: Harper and Row.
Mazid, B.-E. M. 2008. "Cowboy and Misanthrope: A Critical (Discourse) Analysis of Bush and Bin Laden Cartoons." *Discourse & Communication* 2 (4): 433–457. doi:10.1177/1750481308095939.
Mead, G. H. 1934. *Mind, Self and Society*. Chicago, IL: University of Chicago Press.
Mercer, J. 1996. *Reputation and International Politics*. Ithaca, NY: Cornell University Press.
Mitzen, J. 2006. "Ontological Security in World Politics: State Identity and the Security Dilemma." *European Journal of International Relations* 12 (3): 341–370. doi:10.1177/1354066106067346.
Neumann, I. B. 2009. "Discourse Analysis." In *Qualitative Methods in International Relations: A Pluralist Guide*, edited by A. Klotz and D. Prakash. London: Palgrave Macmillan.
Neumann, P. R. 2008. *Joining Al-Qaeda: Jihadist Recruitment in Europe*. London: Routledge.
O'Neill, S., and N. H. Smith. 2012. *Recognition Theory as Social Research*. London: Palgrave Macmillan.
Paveau, M.-A., and L. Rosier. 2005. "Éléments pour une histoire de l'analyse du discours." Paper presented at the Franco-German Conference on Discourse Analysis held at the University of Paris, Paris, July 2, 2012.
Pew Forum on Religion and Public Life. 2010. *Muslim Networks and Movements in Western Europe*. Washington, DC: Pew Research Center.
Saurette, P. 2006. "You Dissin Me? Humiliation and Post 9/11 Global Politics." *Review of International Studies* 32: 495–522. doi:10.1017/S0260210506007133.
Shannon, M., C. Thyne, S. Hayden, and A. Dugan. 2014. "The International Community's Reaction to Coups." *Foreign Policy Analysis*. doi:10.1111/fpa.12043.
Simcox, R., H. Stuart, and H. Ahmed. 2010. *Islamist Terrorism: The British Connections*. London: The Centre for Social Cohesion.
Taylor, C. M. 1994. *Multiculturalism: Examining the Politics of Recognition*. Princeton, NJ: Princeton University Press.
Vidino, L. 2007. "Current Trends in Jihadi Networks in Europe." *Terrorism Monitor* 5 (20). http://www.jamestown.org/programs/tm/single/?tx_ttnews%5Btt_news%5D=4499&tx_ttnews%5BbackPid%5D=182&no_cache=1#.U39LBfldVjR
Wæver, O. 1989. "Security, the Speech Act – Analysing the Politics of a Word." 2nd draft. Paper presented at the Research Training Seminar, Sostrup Manor, June 1989. Revised, Jerusalem/Tel Aviv, June 25–26.
Wendt, A. 1999. *Social Theory of International Politics*. Cambridge: Cambridge University Press.
Wiktorowicz, Q., and K. Kaltenthaler. 2006. "The Rationality of Radical Islam." *Political Science Quarterly* 121 (2): 295–319. doi:10.1002/j.1538-165X.2006.tb00573.x. Accessed April 21, 2014. http://www.psqonline.org/article.cfm?IDArticle=17983
Wolf, R. 2008. "Respekt. Ein Unterschätzter Faktor in Den Internationalen Beziehungen." *Zeitschrift Für Internationale Beziehungen* 1: 5–42. doi:10.5771/0946-7165-2008-1-5
Wolf, R. 2011a. "Respect and Disrespect in International Politics: The Significance of Status recognition." *International Theory* 3 (01): 105–142. doi:10.1017/S1752971910000308.
Wolf, R. 2011b. "Respecting Foreign Peoples: The Limits of Moral Obligations." Unpublished manuscript, Goethe University, Frankfurt am Main.
Zara Raymond, C. 2010. "Al Muhajiroun and Islam4UK: The Group behind the Ban." In *Developments in Radicalisation and Political Violence Papers*. London: International Centre for the Study of Radicalisation, King's College London.

# REPLY

## Terrorism, discourse and analysis thereof: a reply to Clément

Lee Jarvis

*School of Political, Social and International Studies, Faculty of Arts and Humanities, Norwich Research Park, University of East Anglia, Norwich, UK*

This is a reply to:

Clément, Maéva. 2014. "Al-Muhajiroun in the United Kingdom: the role of international non-recognition in heightened radicalization dynamics." *Global Discourse*. 4 (4): 428–443. http://dx.doi.org/10.1080/23269995.2014.918306

Clément's discussion of Al-Muhajiroun (AM) presents, in my view, an important contribution to discursive studies of 'terrorism' and 'counterterrorism' on two principal grounds. In the first instance, it focuses on the written and spoken language of a relatively under-explored group, which had been extremely visible within UK politics until its proscription in 2010. Most significant here – as Clément demonstrates – is that AM's language departed quite markedly from that of more intensively analysed organisations, not least in its initial ambiguity towards the meaning of the 9/11 attacks and the lessons thereof. In this sense, Clément usefully broadens our understanding of the different ways in which groups that might be deemed 'terrorist' legitimise their campaigns and of the significance of changes therein. The second reason that this article merits wide reading is the use to which recognition theory is put in its attempt to explore transformations in AM's articulation of its own struggle. Of particular interest here is the turn towards self-recognition and divine recognition as sources for self-validation, a turn that was made necessary, for Clément, following the denial of the 'West's' status as a significant other with whom recognition might be negotiated.

In making these contributions, Clément's analysis speaks to (yet does not directly address) contemporary developments within what some have termed 'critical terrorism studies' (e.g., Jackson, Breen Smyth, and Gunning 2009; Jackson et al. 2011). Although heterogeneous, contributions to this 'project' – if it may be described thus – share Clément's desire to engage with, destabilise and deconstruct representations of (counter-)terrorist violence. In the process, they pull attention to the constitutive and performative functions of such representations and to their role in the continuous (re)making of social worlds. Where recent work in this area goes beyond Clément's, however, is by demonstrating that categories such as 'radicalisation' must also be approached as discursive productions rather than given the taken-for-granted status they are afforded in this discussion (e.g., Baker-Beall, Heath-Kelly, and Jarvis forthcoming). Thus, whilst Clément takes the growing radicalisation of AM as her object of analysis – as something to be explained (here, through recognition theory and discourse analysis) – it might be more useful, I think, to begin our analysis with the ways in which AM is itself discursively constructed as a radicalising entity by legislators, academics and other interested parties. As Heath-Kelly (2013) argues (focusing – as does Clément – on the UK context), 'radicalisation' has a particular history and an important role in contemporary security politics, each of which should be acknowledged in the discussion and analysis of groups such as AM before they are described thus.

This brings me to my second point, which is Clément's treatment of discourse more generally. Although not fully elaborated, Clément makes a distinction, following Neumann, between two types of discourse analysis. These might be thought of as forward and backward looking variants that seek either to explore the range of possible outcomes from discursive acts or, alternatively, to begin with such outcomes and investigate their (prior) conditions of possibility within the realm of representation. While potentially useful, discourse here is treated with a thinness that implies that there exists something beyond or beneath it. This comes through in the article's empirical analysis in which AM's struggle for recognition is connected to, but seemingly distinct from, the articulation of events and identities. In other words, a desire for recognition is depicted here that exceeds the relational construction of identity to which Clément points: a desire that may be satisfied or frustrated given how discursive developments play out.

Whether we agree with Clément's ontology or not, her approach to discourse is one in which it is possible to say something about the 'truth' of particular social meanings away from their content. It is possible, put otherwise, to engage in explanatory analysis of this group's discursive practices and the consequences thereof *because* of the importance of recognition within social interaction. This example of what we might call 'discursive discovery' may be contrasted with two alternative approaches to discourse analysis (see Howarth 2000, 128–130; Jarvis 2009). The first, 'discursive recovery', involves reconstructing the purposes or intentions behind discursive acts. This would involve, in this example, asking *why* AM sought to construct its struggle as it did and searching for intentionality within this construction. The second, termed here 'discursive invention' (see Caputo 1997), approaches the meaning of discourse instead as something that is invented in the context-bound, active negotiation that takes place between discourse and analyst. This type of study would likely focus on destabilising and deconstructing AM's struggle – in its own terms – rather than seeking to explain this via the extra-discursive role of affective factors such as recognition. And, in so doing, it would recognise that any destabilisation was a product of the inventive reading of the analyst herself. In this sense, it might be more useful, I suggest, to substitute Clément's two approaches to discourse analysis with three that are organised around an epistemological rather than temporal division.

## References

Baker-Beall, C., C. Heath-Kelly, and L. Jarvis, eds. Forthcoming. *Counter-Radicalisation: Critical Perspectives*. Abingdon: Routledge. ISBN: 978-1-13-877663-0.

Caputo, J. 1997. *Deconstruction in a Nutshell: A Conversation with Jacques Derrida*. New York: Fordham University Press.

Heath-Kelly, C. 2013. "Counter-Terrorism and the Counterfactual: Producing the 'Radicalisation' Discourse and the UK PREVENT Strategy." *British Journal of Politics and International Relations* 15 (3): 394–415. doi:10.1111/j.1467-856X.2011.00489.x.

Howarth, D. 2000. *Discourse*. Buckingham: Open University Press.

Jackson, R., M. Breen Smyth, and J. Gunning, eds. 2009. *Critical Terrorism Studies: A New Research Agenda*. Abingdon: Routledge.

Jackson, R., L. Jarvis, J. Gunning, and M. Breen Smyth. 2011. *Terrorism: A Critical Introduction*. Basingstoke: Palgrave.

Jarvis, L. 2009. *Times of Terror: Discourse, Temporality and the War on Terror*. Basingstoke: Palgrave.

# Recognition and the origins of international society

Erik Ringmar

*Department of Political Science, Lund University, Lund, Sweden*

> The international system of civilized states that came to develop in Europe in the course of the nineteenth century was formed through practices of recognition, which created and affirmed similarities between all European states, but also through practices of non-recognition, which created and affirmed differences between Europeans and non-Europeans. Practices of non-recognition are generally ignored in liberal accounts of the origins of international society. A theory of recognition allows us to retrieve this alternative history and make it explicit.

In his account of the logic of world history in the *Phenomenology of Spirit*, G.W.F. Hegel envisioned two parties locked into a deadly struggle for recognition.[1] 'They must engage in this struggle,' Hegel explained, 'for they must raise their certainty of being *for themselves* to truth, both in the case of the other and in their own case' (Hegel 1979, sec. 187:113–114). There was at the time of Hegel's writing a real-life example of such a deadly struggle – the slave rebellion on the Caribbean island of Saint-Domingue, and there are good reasons to believe that this event directly inspired Hegel's philosophical account. 'The actual and successful revolution of Caribbean slaves against their masters is the moment when the dialectical logic of recognition becomes visible as the thematics of world history, the story of the universal realization of freedom' (Buck-Morss 2009, 59–60). In fact, there were two separate struggles of recognition going on in Saint-Domingue. First, the slaves struggled to be recognized by their former masters, but secondly, the new nation of Haiti struggled to gain international recognition as an independent state. Recognition, we could argue, was always a matter of international politics, and it was always a matter of non-European nations gaining recognition from European.[2]

As Hegel explained, a failure to be recognized on one's own preferred terms was not the end of the story. Instead, it was only the beginning. A failure of recognition initiated a process of progressive change whereby the inferior party – the slave, the non-European – was forced to work on himself, to improve himself, to the point where the superior party – the master, the European – finally would be able to recognize him as one of his own (Kojève 1980, 31–70; Horkheimer and Adorno 2007, 3–42). This dialectical process of acculturation describes the very logic of world history, and its final end is a steady state in which full recognition is universally extended, on equal terms, by everyone to everyone else.

Or, to translate the same logic into terms valid within the international politics of the nineteenth century: there was an international society made up of civilized European states, considered as sovereign actors who all granted each other formal recognition as equals. International society was kept together through what we could call 'practices of recognition' – everyday forms of behavior into which the recognition which states granted each other was embedded. Non-European states, on the other hand, were not members of international society; they had at best a partial standing in international politics, and they did not enjoy full rights to sovereignty. But just as Hegel had explained, this was not the end of the story. The non-Europeans could be recognized as full members if they only worked on themselves, improved themselves, that is, became sufficiently Europe-like. Having busied themselves at this task through internal reforms and diplomatic measures, Turkey was formally invited to become a member of Europe-led international society in 1856 and Japan in 1899.

The logic which Hegel elucidates is not, however, the only one possible. The process of acculturation does not necessarily work. There is no reason, for example, why the already established members of international society cannot refuse to admit non-members, no matter what they do to improve themselves. It is through exclusion, after all, that the exclusivity of a membership club is best maintained. As Groucho Marx famously noted, once everyone is admitted on equal terms, membership loses its social prestige (Marx 1995, 321). In this alternative scenario, recognition takes place not between a master and a slave, but between a group of masters who provide an identity for themselves by exaggerating the features that separate, and thereby distinguish, them from others.[3] They recognize each other as superior because of their differences from everyone else.

This, we will argue, is how international society came to be constituted. International society was *not* formed once a core of like-minded European states realized how much they had in common and as they generously extended the benefits of their solutions to everyone else. This is how members of the English School have explained the origins of international society, and this explanation is incorrect (Bull and Watson 1985; Watson 2009, 288–298). Rather, international society was formed as the Europeans drew as sharp a distinction as ever possible between themselves and others, accentuating and exaggerating the differences and forgetting nuances and variations. This demarcation, moreover, constituted the rationale for two entirely different sets of behaviors: practices of mutual recognition among the Europeans themselves, but practices of non-recognition in relation to non-Europeans. It was through practices of recognition, affirming sameness, and through practices of non-recognition, affirming difference, that international society came to constitute itself as such. And the story is, arguably, on-going. Practices of non-recognition are constitutive of international society also as it currently exists.

The aim of this article is to briefly review these two sets of practices – practices of recognition and of non-recognition – as they developed within three separate fields – diplomacy, trade, and warfare – and to study how the respective practices gave rise to the distinction between the European and the non-European through which international society was constituted. As an illustration of this process of identity-creation, we briefly look at the legal stipulations that emerged among international lawyers in the course of the nineteenth century regarding the protection of cultural artifacts in times of war.

## Practices of recognition

International relations in Europe are often thought of as simultaneously both anarchical and societal in nature (Bull 1977, 23–52). That is, despite persistent wars and threats of war, relations between states are not best described in terms of a Hobbesian state of nature. In their everyday practices, states follow norms and customs which help determine the way they participate in balance of power politics, alliances and international organizations, as well as the way they conduct their trade, diplomacy, and wars. Although atrocious counter-examples are easy to cite, international society does contribute a measure of order, a degree of civilized behavior, and it assures a modicum of predictability and peace to relations between states. Since these everyday practices presuppose that we recognize the other participants as formally equal to ourselves, we could call them 'practices of recognition.'

Practices of recognition presuppose reciprocity. By engaging in a certain practice, we expect our counterparts to respond in kind: to mirror our behavior and to return favors, if not in every interaction, at least over the longer haul (Keohane 1986, 19–24). Although the rules of the game may be largely tacit, states know how to go on behaving towards each other, and they all go on behaving much in the same way. This knowing-how-to-go-on is founded not only on formal similarities between us but on the fact that we share in a certain way of life. As a party to these practices, we can expect all other parties to automatically recognize us as one of their own; non-parties, however, can make no such assumptions. 'It is scarcely necessary to point out,' the British lawyer William E. Hall pointed out in 1884,

> that as international law is a product of the special civilisation of modern Europe, and forms a highly artificial system of which the principles cannot be supposed to be understood or recognised by countries differently civilised, such states only can be presumed to be subject to it as are inheritors of that civilisation. (Hall 1884, 40)

This does not preclude disagreements between members of the same international society and it does not rule out that violence will be used, but it does make wars between members of the same international society into fratricides or into peculiarly international species of civil wars.

Compare the new science of international, positive, law as it came to develop in the course of the nineteenth century (Koskenniemi 2004, 11–97). According to its enthusiastic proponents, international law is not declared into existence by political fiat but emerges instead from the everyday practices in which states engage (Bull 1977, 59–71). International law is customary law, case-law, which resembles the law of stateless societies, in that it is constructed from the bottom up rather than the top down. *Ubi societas ibi ius est*, as John Westlake, the British international lawyer, put it in 1894, 'where there is a society there is law' (Westlake 1894, 3). 'When we assert that there is such a thing as international law, we assert that there is a society of states: when we recognise that there is a society of states, we recognise that there is international law.' Yet since customary law can only be as strong as the customs on which it rests, international law will inevitably fall apart if international society is too diverse and the practices in which states engage too divergent. To make international society more coherent and more unified, according to the new generation of international lawyers, was consequently the best way to strengthen the force and increase the reach of the law. The more unified and homogeneous international society became, the more viable the law, and the more viable the law, the more unified and homogeneous international society (Lorimer 1884, 2:112–113).

The practices of diplomacy provide an example. In Europe, the first permanent ambassadors were dispatched from the court one of ruler to the court of another in the course of the Renaissance (Mattingly 1937, 423–439, 1988, 61–77). Despite mutual suspicions and recurring hostilities, this expanding diplomatic network provided a means of gathering information, of spying, but also a way of keeping in touch with one another, of carrying out negotiations and concluding deals. A number of practices developed, which facilitated the work of the new diplomats: extraterritoriality for their embassies, immunity for the diplomats themselves, inviolability of diplomatic dispatches, the right to worship the god of their choice, and so on. Or consider the many rituals in which the diplomats engaged. There were rules for how they should carry themselves, for how they should dress, walk, and talk; there were prescriptions for how to arrange audiences, dinners; for which presents to bring on what occasions; and for how letters of accreditation should be written, presented, and acknowledged (Satow 1917). A large number of rules concerned how to determine matters of rank and standing: the way diplomats should be seated during negotiations, in conferences and at dinner tables; who had the right to enter a gate before whom; and the order in which treaties should be signed and ratified.

An analogous argument can be made regarding international trade. In early modern Europe, with Holland and then Britain taking the lead, new markets were discovered and new products – Atlantic herring, Baltic wheat, West-Indian sugar – developed and promoted (see, inter alia, Braudel 2002a, 81–114, 138–204; De Vries and van der Woude 1997, 350–408). The vast profits made in these markets were fed back into expanding commercial enterprises and a large number of practices developed, which organized, facilitated, and policed the new trade. Commerce required ships and the ships required harbors, shipwrights, sea-captains, and crews, but also pilots, better maps, and more reliable commercial intelligence. The goods needed to be safely transported, insured against storms and pirates, stored in granaries and warehouses, then distributed. Financial instruments, such as bills of exchange, were required to pay for the purchases, and the financial instruments needed banks that were connected to each other in an all-European network. In addition, once each respective state got involved in the commercial transactions, an entirely new set of political practices developed concerned with ways of organizing tolls and duties, ways of avoiding tolls and duties, ways of smuggling and preventing smuggling, with patents and monopolies, with the collection of taxes, and with ways of giving and receiving bribes. Or consider a practice such as the granting of 'most favored nation' status, whereby countries promised each other not to treat each other less advantageously than their best-treated trading partner.

The practices of diplomacy and trade embodied a shared set of values which governed relations within the European international system. The principal such value was sovereignty (Bull 1977, 8–9, 36–37; Koskenniemi 2004, 143–152). In Europe, each state was regarded as a sovereign subject that followed its own preferred course of action. The goal of diplomacy was to further each state's national interest, and the purpose of trade was to enrich the nation. European states had, for example, an obvious right to control which goods that moved across their borders, or, indeed, if any goods moved across their borders at all (Heffter 1857, 67–68; Hont 2010, 185–266). Sovereignty and formal equality led to the problem of anarchy – to the problem of how to assure peace in the absence of a world state. However, at least as strong as these centrifugal tendencies was the centripetal pressure for social conformity. Consider the practices of diplomacy. European diplomats showed up in the same place at the same time, following the same elaborate protocol, wearing the same kinds of clothes and powdered wigs. Through practices such as these, the European states recognized each other as sovereign, as formally equal, and also and at the same time, as rivals and enemies.

## Practices of non-recognition

International society thus described was sharply distinguished from the assorted political entities which the Europeans encountered once they left their own continent. In the nineteenth century, it was common to make a distinction between two kinds of non-Europeans: 'savages' and 'barbarians.' 'Savages' were peoples, predominantly in Africa and the Americas, who lived in societies that had no state. Roaming around in vast forests, they could not properly defend themselves from outsiders and they had no means of controlling and administering their own territories (Lorimer 1884, 2:2:157; Westlake 1894, 136). 'Barbarians,' on the other hand, were predominantly to be found in the ancient monarchies of Asia. Here there were states – states which more than perfectly fulfilled the European requirements for statehood – yet since they were states of a distinctly non-European kind, it was impossible to include them in Europe's international society. The problem was their unwillingness, or perhaps inability, to reciprocate. Asian states were 'despotic,' the Europeans decided, meaning that they were arbitrarily ruled by omnipotent rulers who cared little for the welfare of the people (Rubiés 2005, 109–180). Taking themselves as the centers of their respective worlds, they refused to regard other states as equals. With states such as these, there could be no mirroring and no trust.

As a result of the drawing of these distinctions, savages and barbarians were given an entirely different standing in international law than European states (Lorimer 1884, 2:101; Wheaton 1855, 27–82; Bluntschli 1874, 61–109). European states enjoyed the full rights and obligations of sovereignty – the inviolability of borders and the right to self-determination. A civilized state could conduct both domestic and foreign policy without interference from others, and if it was attacked, it had an unquestionable right to self-defense. Savages, by contrast, had no standing in international law; they enjoyed no sovereign rights and could rely only on the kind of benevolence which all human beings owe each other by virtue of their shared humanity. 'The right of undeveloped races, like the right of undeveloped individuals,' said James Lorimer, professor of public law at the University of Edinburgh, 1884, 'is a right not to recognition as what they are not, but to guardianship that is, to guidance in becoming that of which they are capable, in realising their special ideals' (Lorimer 1884, 2:157). As a consequence, there was nothing stopping the Europeans from appropriating their land for themselves. As for barbarians, they occupied an intermediary position between the civilized and the barbarians (Lorimer 1884, 2:216–218; Westlake 1894, 142; Oppenheim 1912, vol. I:155). They had an international status and standing, but they were international subjects only in certain respects. Barbarian states were formally independent but not fully sovereign, and they periodically saw their territories invaded and parts of their political systems taken over by foreigners. Their actions were often constrained by unequal treaties and by military intimidation.

The practices of diplomacy were altered in line with these distinctions. As for the savages, it was obviously quite impossible to establish proper diplomatic relations with people who did not have a state of their own, and besides, Europeans were convinced, savages were far too uncouth to master the elaborate protocol required (Westlake 1894, 129–189; Anghie 1999, 1–80). The diplomatic engagements that did take place with such peoples were farcical exchanges where the natives dressed up in what they took to be the required outfits, while the European visitors struggled to repress their laughter. Diplomatic relations with the monarchies of Asia was quite a different matter. These states had long traditions of receiving foreign diplomats, not least from Europe, and medieval European visitors had often been amazed at the sumptuousness of the courts and the dignity of the rituals involved. Yet once the Euro-centric international society came to constitute itself as such, these traditional practices were found wanting. A particular problem was the headlong prostration, the *proskynesis* or *koutou*, which Asian rulers insisted that visitors perform (Rockhill 1897, 627–643; Ringmar 2012, 68–80). The prostration, the Europeans decided, constituted proof of Asian despotism since only Asian monarchs required such ceremonies and only Asian subjects were servile enough to perform them. The insistence that European visitors participate in the same ritual demonstrated how difficult it was to do business with Asiatic rulers. A European diplomat who prostrated himself before an Asian king would not only degrade himself but also his country. While European visitors in previous ages had followed the local customs when visiting Asia, by the nineteenth century they stubbornly refused to humiliate themselves in this manner.

Trade provides another example of practices of non-recognition. Trade with savages was easy to conduct. Since savages had no state they had no way of policing their own borders and no way of stopping the Europeans from engaging in whichever exchanges for which they could find a business partner. In Africa, for example, the Europeans bought ivory, hardwoods, and slaves in exchange for shotguns, mirrors, and alcohol (Braudel 2002b, 430–441). As for the barbarian states of Asia, they did indeed have the power to stop European attempts to trade, and in the case of China and Japan, they famously did. In China, before 1842, foreign trade was only allowed at the southern port of Guangzhou, and in Japan, before 1869, trade was only possible at Deshima in Kyushu. Yet since these barbarian kingdoms were not full members of international society, the Europeans saw no reason to respect these constraining arrangements. In 1853, Japan was threatened by the Black Ships of Commodore Perry, and between 1839–42 and 1856–60, the Europeans made war on the Chinese in order to gain trading rights, in particular the right to sell opium. In Europe, needless to say, similar practices would have been perfectly unthinkable.

The arguments used to justify Europe's military aggression throw further light on the distinction which international lawyers made between the civilized and the uncivilized. According to the medieval understanding, based on the stipulations of natural law, the right to trade was given equally to all men by Providence itself (Viner 1976, 32–33, 37). Providence has so wisely organized matters, went the argument, that the objects which human beings require are scattered around the globe. We must consequently exchange with one another if we are to provision for ourselves, and in the process, friendly relations between individuals and societies will quite naturally come to develop. It is consequently against the stipulations of natural law to restrict trade, in particular in the kinds of goods that are necessary for our survival. This, indeed, was the premise of Hugo Grotius' celebrated argument in favor of freedom of the seas (Grotius 1916). Yet in the nineteenth century, this argument was discarded together will all other parts of the natural law heritage, and the cunning of Providence was replaced by appeals to economic advantage. Free trade, Adam Smith explained, is beneficial to all parties, yet among civilized states, trade was never freer than the national imperatives permitted. Sovereign states could, and did, restrict trade in order to benefit themselves. It was only in relation to people outside of Europe that the old natural law arguments remained in force. As the *Dictionary of Commerce*, 1842, explained: if a country abundant in resources 'insulates itself by its institutions, and adopts a system of policy that is plainly inconsistent with the interests of every other nation,' then 'such nation may be justly compelled to adopt a course of policy more consistent with the general well-being of mankind' (McCulloch 1842, 72). Since arguments regarding economic advantage carried no force with barbarians, and since the laws of Euro-centric international society did not apply to them, natural law was used to 'justly compel' them.

In the Euro-centric international system, we said, practices of recognition create similarities between the states that participate in them by embedding presumptions regarding formal equality into the very structure of interaction. In relation to non-Europeans, on the other hand, practices of non-recognition create differences between states by embedding presumptions regarding inequality into the structure of interaction (Anghie 1999, 1–80). First, the Europeans drew as sharp a distinction as ever possible between themselves and everyone else, accentuating and exaggerating the differences and forgetting nuances and variations, and then, when acting in terms of the distinction thus drawn, the differences which the Europeans had invented were made manifest and obvious for everyone to see. As a result, all Europeans really were alike, and they were distinctly different from non-Europeans. It was the invention of the categories of 'barbarians' and 'savages' which made civilization possible.

## A short case-study: the protection of cultural artifacts

As a way to study the practices through which recognition was granted and withheld, consider a short case study regarding the protection of cultural artifacts during times of war. Cultural artifacts are not resources that can be used for the purposes of warfare, instead they are prizes which a victor brings home in triumph, demonstrating that he is strong enough to take what the vanquished opponent cannot protect. Alternatively, they are things which the victor deliberately choses to respect, thus displaying his respect not only for the objects concerned but also for the opponent . As such, the cultural artifact, and its degree of protection in times of war, provides a way to understand the nature of the relations that obtain between the participants in a war.

Before the nineteenth century, international law had little to say about the protection of museums, libraries, and art collections (Auzillion 1897; Ringmar 2013b, 265–267). Occupying armies would deal with such artifacts in whatever way they saw fit, and there were no legal prohibitions against looting and pillaging. However, once the science of positive international law came to be established in the course of the nineteenth century, destruction and appropriation of cultural artifacts came to be explicitly banned by international treaties and surprisingly often also honored in the practices in which European states engaged.

A first requirement of the new laws was that wars can only be fought between soldiers, not against civilians and that only military targets legitimately can be attacked. This stipulation had implications for cultural artifacts, since all privately held property was regarded as off limits to an occupying army. The occupiers could certainly provision for themselves in enemy territory, set up camp, and requisition horses and vehicles, but when they did so they had to pay a fair price for what they took (Bluntschli 1874, §§653–657, 366–69). A different set of provisions governed the property of the enemy state. Although all public property automatically fell into the hands of an occupying army, there were limitations here too. Cultural artifacts which rightly belonged to the people, but of which the state was the custodian, could not be appropriated. The destruction of archives and libraries was not permitted since that disproportionately would disadvantage civilians. The only exceptions both in the case of private and public property concerned 'military necessity' – but any military benefit must be immediate, overwhelming, and easily demonstrable (Lieber 1863, §14, 4; Bluntschli 1874, §549, 309; Wheaton 1855, §6, 421; Moore 1906, 178). Cultural artifacts were unlikely to fall into this category.

Unrealistic though these requirements may appear, they reflected the way armies already for some time had conducted themselves on the battlefields of Europe (Ringmar 2013b, 265–267). During the Napoleonic Wars, the British had paid for the provisions they requisitioned, and they did the same during the Crimean War. Pillaging and looting were punished in all armies, and the cultural and architectural treasures of enemies were generally respected. The near universal cries of 'barbarism' which the exceptions to these rules evoked demonstrate the relevance of the new practices. Napoleon, for example, looted art collections in Italy, but after Waterloo, most of the objects were returned and even the French admitted that the actions had constituted war crimes. Similarly, public opinion was outraged when British troops in 1814 burned down government buildings in Washington, DC, including the White House (Moore 1906, 200). Later in the century, these new practices of warfare were increasingly codified. The 'Lieber Code' of 1863, which provided rules of engagement for the soldiers of the Northern states in the American Civil War, is an early celebrated example, but the British, German, and French armies soon adopted similar legally inspired regulations (Lieber 1863; Ringmar 2009, 52–60).

However, when it comes to wars conducted in non-European settings, an entirely different set of rules applied (Colby 1927, 279–288; Ringmar 2013b, 267–270). The practices developed here recognized the differences between Europeans and non-Europeans, not their similarities. In these colonial wars, works of art and buildings of religious and architectural importance were not only not protected but often explicitly singled out as targets. The destruction of cultural artifacts came to be identified as an integral part of colonial warfare and as a particularly efficient way of striking at intractable natives. The wars fought by France in Algeria in the 1830s and 40s, by Britain in Afghanistan, 1841–42, and in India after the Uprising in 1857 provide numerous examples. In all three locations, the Europeans met with fierce resistance from the locals, and in each case they came close to being defeated. Changing from European-style, civilized, practices of warfare to uncivilized practices, their fortunes eventually turned. In Algeria, civilians were explicitly targeted and the bases of their livelihoods – herds, fields, orchards – were destroyed (Porch 1986, 376–407). After the British had lost an entire army in Afghanistan in the winter of 1842 and been forced into a humiliating retreat, they returned in the fall of the same year to get revenge. Here too civilians were targeted and the Grand Bazaar of Kabul was reduced to pebbles (Kaye 1851, 638–639). In India, after the British had retaken Delhi, the city was subject to a spectacular loot in which private and public property alike was stolen and wantonly destroyed. Particularly notorious was the practice of strapping rebels to the mouths of cannons and firing them off to eternity (Davis 1994, 293–317; Craig 1858, 348–350).

Another spectacular case of destruction took place northwest of Beijing in October 1860 (Ringmar 2013a, esp. 69–85; Ringmar 2011, 273–297). It was here, at Yuanmingyuan, that the emperor of China had his residence, an enormous park filled with palaces, pagodas, temples, galleries, and archives. The buildings represented architecture drawn from various parts of China and beyond, and the collections included jewelry, clocks, mechanical dolls, furniture, silks, paintings, calligraphy, and a library with a copy of every book printed in the Chinese language. It was one of the most remarkable collections of cultural artifacts ever assembled. Yet between October 6 and 9, 1860, Yuanmingyuan was thoroughly looted by a French army, and on October 18 and 19, the whole compound was burned to the ground by the British. As even some of the participants themselves admitted, this was a 'Vandal-like' and a 'barbaric' act (Hake 1884, 33).

The question is what the relationship might be between the way the Europeans behaved in these two geographical settings. Why did the Europeans agree to protect cultural artifacts in Europe itself while they at the very same time targeted them, in non-European settings, as a matter of explicit and officially sanctioned policy? The most charitable interpretation is to say that the discrepancy was nothing but a coincidence, but we may be more inclined to see it as a particularly blatant case of double-standards. In fact it was neither. Instead the two sets of behaviors causally entailed one another. The two distinct sets of practices first created and then affirmed the differences between the European and the non-European, constituting the identity of a European self as well as a non-European other. It was *because* the Europeans committed acts of barbarism outside of Europe that they became increasingly civilized in Europe itself, and *because* they became increasingly civilized in Europe itself, that they committed acts of barbarism outside of Europe. Through the practices of recognition embedded in war-making, Europeans were made alike, and through the practices of non-recognition, non-Europeans were made different. It was on the bases of these similarities, and these differences, that international society rested.

This categorization explains why the Europeans fought the non-Europeans in such ferocious fashion. Although the destruction of a cultural artifact had no military value, it was an efficient way of demonstrating one's might and of intimidating one's enemies. Such demonstrative effects were particularly important when it came to colonial warfare (Ringmar 2013a, 147–149). Despite their obvious military superiority, the Europeans were not generally able to impose their will on the kingdoms of Asia by regular military means alone. Wars were logistical nightmares at a time when a single journey to East Asia took three months to complete and instructions took just as long to reach a commander in the field. A country such as China was impossible to occupy and administer, and although India was colonized, the British military presence here was exceedingly thin on the ground, a weakness exposed during the uprising of 1857. Under such circumstances, the most successful military actions were those that terrified the locals. Colonial wars were pieces of theater designed to showcase a military superiority which did not necessarily exist (Ringmar 2013a, 147–149). This is why cultural artifacts were targeted. It was because the palaces, temples, and bazaars contained such irreplaceable treasures that they were destroyed. This, the Europeans decided, was the quickest way to intimidate their uncivilized enemies (Porch 1986, 378–382). In addition, the radical distinction between practices of recognition and of non-recognition served to remind the Europeans of who they took themselves to be. Spectacular acts of destruction undertaken in extra-European settings were a way of policing the boundary they had drawn between the civilized self and the uncivilized other. Treating non-Europeans differently, and making war on them in explicitly uncivilized ways, strengthened and affirmed this distinction. In this way, the coherence of European international society was enhanced.

## On the origins of international society

According to a reformist narrative common to American liberals and to members of the English School, international society has its origin in the shared practices, which developed among European states in fields such as diplomacy, trade, and warfare. We called these 'practices of recognition' since they embedded norms of formal equality and reciprocity in everyday, routinized, behavior. International society became global in scope as the Europeans, in the nineteenth century, colonized the rest of the world and as the former colonies, in the twentieth century, achieved their independence on European terms. As a result, in 1945, all states were recognized as sovereign and as formally equal, as subjects of international law, and as members of the United Nations. In the twenty-first century, on the received account, this international society still helps bring a measure of predictability and order to relations between states (Bull and Watson 1985; Watson 2009, 288–298).

Common though this narrative may be, it rests on a fatal omission. International society, we argued, was not formed once a core of like-minded European states realized how much they had in common and as they generously extended the benefits of their solutions to everyone else. Rather, international society was formed as the Europeans drew as sharp a distinction as ever possible between themselves and everyone else. The Europeans were 'civilized,' they agreed, and the non-Europeans were either 'savages' or 'barbarians.' This distinction did not name a preexisting difference as much as it constituted a difference which previously did not exist. This difference, moreover, constituted a rationale for practices of non-recognition – forms of behavior through which presumptions regarding inequality came to be routinized in everyday interactions – which excluded the non-Europeans and made them legitimate targets for European interventions and wars. The practices of non-recognition were not an aberration, not a mistake, and not even a regrettable by-product of imperialism. Instead they were constitutive of international society as it currently exists.

Much as Hegel suggested in the *Phenomenology*, the only way for the non-Europeans to avoid this predicament was to emulate the European understanding of international politics and to quickly become Europe-like countries. They had to work on themselves, improve themselves, before they could gain membership in international society. On 30 March 1856, in the wake of the Crimean War, Turkey was expressly 'admitted to participate in the advantages of the public law and system of concert of Europe,' but critics soon complained that the admission had been premature since Turkey's laws still were distinctly uncivilized (Moore 1906, vol. I:9; Krauel 1877, 388). 'The Turks, as a race,' James Lorimer decided, 'are probably incapable of the political development, which would render their adoption of constitutional government possible.' Islam is an 'exclusive religion' which stands between Turkey and the world and contradicts 'its constitutional professions of reciprocating will' (Lorimer 1884, vol. 2:123). Compare the discussions which today are pursued regarding a Turkish application for membership in the European Union (Nas and Özer 2012). After decades of attempts to approach the Europeans, Turkey was finally admitted as an official candidate country in December 1999, but negotiations have since stalled and leading European politicians have insisted that the country cannot be admitted since 'Turkey is not a proper European country' (Bilefsky 2007; Finkel 2012).

Or take the case of Japan. After very extensive domestic reforms in the 1870s and 80s and full acceptance of the Euro-centric rules on diplomacy and international law, the country was finally admitted into the 'circle of law-governed countries' 'as a fully independent sovereign power' in the summer of 1899 (Moore 1906, vol. I:9; von Siebold 1901). And although the Japanese leaders played along with the Europe-directed balance of power politics during the First World War, they began to break the rules in the 1930s. Japan, it turned out, was a revisionist power and not a very civilized country at all. As far as China was concerned, the imperial authorities undertook sweeping reforms of its foreign policy in the 1860s, including the establishment of a European-style ministry of foreign affairs – the Chinese began sending diplomats abroad in the 1870s, and participated in international conferences in the 1890s – and yet the Europeans remained profoundly skeptical regarding the country's progress. China's reforms never seemed to be radical enough. In 1912, according to Lassa Oppenheim, China still belonged to a small group of countries where 'neither their governments nor their populations are at present able to fully understand the Law of Nations and to take up an attitude which is in conformity with all the rules of this law' (Oppenheim 1912, vol. I:155).

Lets note the paradoxical nature of this game of recognition and non-recognition (Ringmar 2002, 115–136). To the extent that countries such as Turkey, Japan, and China ignored the rules of the Euro-centric international system, they were denied the rights of sovereignty and they could be bullied by the Europeans with impunity. It was consequently only by following Europeans practices that they could gain the right to act freely; only by modeling themselves on foreigners would they be allowed to be themselves. Sovereignty, once gained, would give them the right to do whatever they wanted, but sovereignty could only be granted to states that lived up to the European norm. Self-determination, much as in Hegel's formulation of the struggle for recognition in the *Phenomenology*, required determination by others.

The paradox of sovereignty placed, and continues to place, European and non-European states on an unequal footing despite all the rhetoric regarding equality and universal rights. Today, at the beginning of the twenty-first century, all states are considered sovereign, they have their respective seats in the United Nations, and they are all formally equal subjects of international law, trade, warfare, and diplomacy. Yet the civilized states of the world still need savages and barbarians who can help confirm them in their perceptions of themselves. Although there are few remaining formal criteria by which such distinctions can be drawn, there are a number of informal practices – informal practices of non-recognition – that serve the same purposes. Countries are still called uncivilized by European and North American TV viewers watching reports of bloody wars in faraway places, by investment bankers drawing up plans in their air-conditioned offices, by development experts frustrated by the inefficiencies of the local government, and by expats as they look out on shantytowns from their chauffeur-driven sedans. Or consider the discourse on human rights (Mutua 2001, 201–245). Despite the norm regarding sovereignty, to which all independent countries are subject, sovereignty, the Europeans insist, should not give rulers a pretext for treating their own people in degrading, dehumanizing, and savage ways. And while there is no doubt that human rights continue to be broken in various non-European locations around the world, and that such abuses should be condemned and stopped, it is equally obvious that the human rights discourse serves Europeans well in drawing the same line they have drawn since the nineteenth century – the line between themselves as civilized and the non-Europeans as savages and barbarians.

## Notes

1. I am grateful to Jens Bartelson, Shannon Brincat, and John Hobson for comments on a previous version of this article.
2. 'Europeans' here, and throughout this article, includes the inhabitants of the former European colonies in North America.
3. This possibility was always occluded by Hegel's own account where there were only two parties to the interaction.

## References

Anghie, A. 1999. "Finding the Peripheries: Sovereignty and Colonialism in Nineteenth-Century International Law." *Harvard International Law Journal* 40 (1): 1–80.
Auzillion, C. 1897. *La Propriété privée et la guerre continentale*. Paris: Troublé.

Bilefsky, D. 2007. "Sarkozy Blocks Key Part of Eu Entry Talks on Turkey." *New York Times*. June 25. http://www.nytimes.com/2007/06/25/world/europe/25iht-union.5.6325879.html

Bluntschli, J. C. 1874. *Le droit international codifié*. Originally published in 1869. Paris: Guillaumin et cie.

Braudel, F. 2002a. *The Wheels of Commerce*. New York: Weidenfeld & Nicolson.

Braudel, F. 2002b. *The Perspective of the World*. Originally published in 1979. London: Phoenix Press.

Buck-Morss, S. 2009. *Hegel, Haiti, and Universal History*. Pittsburgh, PA: University of Pittsburgh Press.

Bull, H. 1977. *The Anarchical Society: A Study of Order in World Politics*. New York: Columbia University Press.

Bull, H., and A. Watson, eds. 1985. *The Expansion of International Society*. Oxford: Oxford University Press.

Colby, E. 1927. "How to Fight Savage Tribes." *The American Journal of International Law* 21 (2): 279–288. doi:10.2307/2189127.

Craig, G. 1858. "Blown Away." *Household Words*. March 27. https://archive.org/details/householdwords17dick

Davis, R. H. 1994. "Three Styles in Looting India." *History and Anthropology* 6 (4): 293–317. doi:10.1080/02757206.1994.9960832.

De Vries, J., and A. M. van der Woude. 1997. *The First Modern Economy: Success, Failure, and Perseverance of the Dutch Economy, 1500–1815*. Cambridge: Cambridge University Press.

Finkel, A. 2012. "It's Turkey's Time." *New York Times*. March 23. http://latitude.blogs.nytimes.com/2012/05/23/turkey-has-shot-at-the-european-union-thanks-to-europes-troubled-times/

Grotius, H. 1916. *The Freedom of the Seas: Or, the Right Which Belongs to the Dutch to Take Part in the East Indian Trade*. New York: Oxford University Press.

Hake, A. E. 1884. *The Story of Chinese Gordon*. London: Remington.

Hall, W. E. 1884. *Treaties on International Law*. Oxford: Clarendon Press.

Heffter, A. W. 1857. *Le droit international public de l'Europe*. Paris: Cotillon.

Hegel, G. W. F. 1979. *Phenomenology of Spirit*. Originally published in 1807. New York: Oxford University Press.

Hont, I. 2010. *Jealousy of Trade: International Competition and the Nation-State in Historical Perspective*. Cambridge: Belknap Press.

Horkheimer, M., and T. W. Adorno. 2007. *Dialectic of Enlightenment*. Stanford, CA: Stanford University Press.

Kaye, J. W. 1851. *History of the War in Afghanistan*. 2 vols. London: Richard Bentley.

Keohane, R. O. 1986. "Reciprocity in International Relations." *International Organization* 40 (1): 1–27. doi:10.1017/S0020818300004458.

Kojève, A. 1980. *Introduction to the Reading of Hegel: Lectures on the Phenomenology of Spirit, [1947]*. Ithaca, NY: Cornell University Press.

Koskenniemi, M. 2004. *The Gentle Civilizer of Nations: The Rise and Fall of International Law 1870–1960*. Cambridge: Cambridge University Press.

Krauel, A. 1877. "Applicabilité du droit des gens européen à la Chine." *Revue de droit international et de législation compare* 9: 387–401.

Lieber, F. 1863. *Instructions for the Government of Armies of the United States, in the Field*. New York: D. van Nostrand.

Lorimer, J. 1884. *The Institutes of the Law of Nations: A Treatise of the Jural Relations of Separate Political Communities*. 2 vols. Edinburgh: Blackwood.

Marx, G. 1995. *Groucho and Me*. New York: Da Capo Press.

Mattingly, G. 1937. "The First Resident Embassies: Mediaeval Italian Origins of Modern Diplomacy." *Speculum* 12 (4): 423–439. doi:10.2307/2849298.

Mattingly, G. 1988. *Renaissance Diplomacy*. Mineola, NY: Dover Publications.

McCulloch, J. R., ed. 1842. "Tea, the Trade In." *A Dictionary, Practical, Theoretical, and Historical, of Commerce and Commercial Navigation*. London: Longman, Brown, Green and Longmans.

Moore, J. B. 1906. *A Digest of International Law*. 8 vols. Washington, DC: Government Printing Office.

Mutua, M. 2001. "Savages, Victims, and Saviors: The Metaphor of Human Rights." *Harvard International Law Journal* 42 (1): 201–245.

Nas, C., and Y. Özer, eds. 2012. *Turkey and the European Union: Processes of Europeanisation.* Farnham: Ashgate.
Oppenheim, L. 1912. *International Law: A Treatise.* London: Longmans.
Porch, D. 1986. "Bugeaud, Gallieni, Lyautey: the Development of French Colonial Warfare." In *Makers of Modern Strategy from Machiavelli to the Nuclear Age*, edited by P. Paret, G. A. Craig, and F. Gilbert, 376–407. Oxford: Oxford University Press.
Ringmar, E. 2002. "The Recognition Game: Soviet Russia against the West." *Cooperation & Conflict* 37 (2): 115–136. doi:10.1177/0010836702037002973.
Ringmar, E. 2009. "Francis Lieber, Terrorism, and the American Way of War." *Perspectives on Terrorism* 3 (4): 52–60.
Ringmar, E. 2011. "Malice in Wonderland: Dreams of the Orient and the Destruction of the Palace of the Emperor of China." *Journal of World History* 22 (2): 273–298. doi:10.1353/jwh.2011.0031.
Ringmar, E. 2012. "The Ritual-Performance Problem in Foreign Policy Analysis: European Diplomats at the Chinese Court." In *The Agency-Structure Problem and the Study of Foreign Policy: Essays in Honor of Walter Carlsnaes*, edited by F. Bynander and S. Guzzini, 68–80. London: Routledge.
Ringmar, E. 2013a. *Liberal Barbarism: The European Destruction of the Palace of the Emperor of China.* New York: Palgrave.
Ringmar, E. 2013b. "'How to Fight Savage Tribes': The Global War on Terror in Historical Perspective." *Terrorism and Political Violence* 25 (2): 264–283. doi:10.1080/09546553.2012.661321.
Rockhill, W. W. 1897. "Diplomatic Missions to the Court of China: The Kotow Question II." *The American Historical Review* 2 (4): 627–643. doi:10.2307/1833980.
Rubiés, J.-P. 2005. "Oriental Despotism and European Orientalism: Botero to Montesquieu." *Journal of Early Modern History* 9 (1): 109–180. doi:10.1163/1570065054300275.
Satow, E. M. 1917. *A Guide to Diplomatic Practice.* 2 vols. London: Longmans, Green.
Viner, J. 1976. *The Role of Providence in the Social Order: An Essay in Intellectual History.* Princeton, NJ: Princeton University Press.
von Siebold, A. 1901. *Japan's Accession to the Comity of Nations.* Translated by Charles Lowe. London: Kegan Paul, Trench, Trübner.
Watson, A. 2009. *The Evolution of International Society: A Comparative Historical Analysis.* Originally published in 1992. London: Routledge.
Westlake, J. 1894. *Chapters on the Principles of International Law.* Cambridge: Cambridge University Press.
Wheaton, H. 1855. *Elements of International Law.* Originally published in 1836. Boston, MA: Little, Brown.

# REPLY

## Recognition and the origins of international society: a reply to Erik Ringmar

John M. Hobson

*Department of Politics, University of Sheffield, Sheffield, UK*

This is a reply to:

Ringmar, Erik. 2014. "Recognition and the origins of international society." *Global Discourse*. 4 (4): 446–458. http://dx.doi.org/10.1080/23269995.2014.917031.

This special issue is concerned with the issue of the potential for the process of 'recognition' to pacify relations between states, groups and individuals and to develop recognition processes in the global community. In his insightful and stimulating article, Ringmar (2014) argues that European international society has from the outset been constructed as a means of *preventing* the West's recognition of Eastern polities and societies. The author, in effect, relays the story of how the Europeans constructed the 'standard of civilisation' which divides the world into three tiers. In this civilisational league table, we find the civilised Europeans perched at its apex enjoying full sovereignty; down one notch are the Eastern 'barbaric' states (oriental despotisms) with the 'savage' East languishing at the bottom. Critically, this construct prescribed that Eastern polities and societies should be denied full sovereign recognition on account of their uncivilised natures that in turn meant that they would be unable to fully reciprocate were they given a seat within the Western club known as European international society. Not surprisingly, then, this Eurocentric construction became embedded within positive international law in the nineteenth century, which prescribed the civilised European states as having a right to remake or culturally convert non-Western societies along Western lines so that they could be brought successfully into international society. For only becoming Western – i.e. civilised – could such societies, or so it was assumed, come to fully reciprocate.

The article does an excellent job of narrating this story, and it is one with which I am in complete agreement. Indeed, it does a marvellous job of showing how the fraught process of European identity construction has created an antagonist world of a superior European Self and an inferior non-Western Other in which the former refuses to recognise the latter. As a result, global international society today remains bifurcated, and the refusal of mutual recognition between East and West means that the present Eurocentric conceptions of recognition will necessarily prevent the pacification of inter-civilisational struggle and conflict that have marked the last couple of hundred years of world politics. But this, in turn, begs the question as to how we can move beyond the sterility of what is in effect a hierarchical Eurocentric conception of recognition and indeed whether this is even possible. Given that this excellent article does not consider such a concern, I want to think through some generic ways in which global reconciliation might be effected, given that a lack of space precludes a fuller treatment.

The basic problem is that which Ashis Nandy first discussed in his seminal book, *The Intimate Enemy* (Nandy 1983). The centrepiece of Eurocentrism is that it in effect constructs a line of civilisational apartheid that separates a pure and exceptional self-generating and superior West from the failed and inferior Eastern world of barbarism (autocratic/Oriental Despotisms/rogue states/axis of evil) and savage societies (failed/collapsed states). Eurocentrism has constructed the great illusion of an autonomous and exceptional West in which all of its irrational 'impurities' have been purged and projected onto the irrational East. So, a first move that needs to be undertaken is to recognise that this is a false construct because if we examine the rise of the West in the last 1000 years we can find strong Eastern influences in its formation; all of which means that there is no such thing as a 'pristine West' but rather an 'Oriental West' (Hobson 2004). Recognising the Eastern origins of, and influences in, Western civilisation means that the binary construction of the world cannot hold because what it obscures are the mutual co-constitutive influences that have driven development, Western and non-Western as well as world politics, forward all of which ricochet backwards and forwards across the constructed 'civilisational frontier'. This vital process of recognition is the first move that needs to be executed if we are to call to account the West's hubris that underpins its extant refusal to properly recognise the so-called Eastern Other. And, at the same time, it urges a sense of humility on the part of the West in order to counter its puffed-up sense of hubris. But, there is a second process of recognition that must follow if we are to have any chance of effecting a genuine process of global reconciliation.

The second step requires a process of mutual dialogue; one which I believe needs to speak in the language of Western civilisation. If this sounds contradictory I would point out that just such a process underpinned the successful project of decolonisation, wherein the Eastern nationalist movements rhetorically prosecuted the Western colonial powers in an imaginary court of social justice by revealing how they failed to live up to their own civilisational norms when dealing with the non-Western world. This was crucial in undermining the legitimacy of empire. Likewise, I suggest that today's Eastern spokes-people need to emphasise the contradictions and double standards that underpin past and present Western treatment of the East by prosecuting the West for its unfair and hypocritical practices within the 'global court of social justice'.

Still, this dialogical project is one that can simultaneously benefit the West (see Nandy 1983; Todorov 1984; Inayatullah and Blaney 2004). For as noted, Eurocentrism leads to the repression and sublimation of the Other in the Self. Thus, doing away with Eurocentrism can end the socio-psychological angst and alienation that necessarily occurs through such sublimation. Indeed, the ultimate irony is that the consistent Eurocentric practice of non-recognition of the East has, most paradoxically, *underdeveloped* the Western Self. And so, hopes for Western emancipation must to an important extent lie with the 'Eastern rhetorical civilising mission', which can launch the Western peoples on an ethnographic maiden Voyage of Self-Discovery that, with humility, empathy, love and above all sincerity, steers around the icebergs of tragic Eurocentric self-deception to return fully humanised (see also Ling 2013). In the process, we take one giant leap towards a global dream that exorcises the global nightmare of cycles of war and Western civilising missions – a dream in which the dusk of Eurocentric non-recognition brings in its wake the dawn of a new era wherein the line of civilisational apartheid that divides the peoples of the world is erased so that all peoples can finally sit down at the table of global humanity and mutually recognise each other as equal partners as they go about forging a new project of progressive global politics.

## References

Hobson, J. M. 2004. *The Eastern Origins of Western Civilisation*. Cambridge: Cambridge University Press.
Inayatullah, N., and D. L. Blaney. 2004. *International Relation and the Problem of Difference*. London: Routledge.
Ling, L. H. M. 2013. *The Dao of World Politics*. London: Routledge.
Nandy, A. 1983. *The Intimate Enemy*. Delhi: Oxford University Press.
Ringmar, E. 2014. "Recognition and the Origins of International Society." *Global Discourse* 4 (4): 446–458. http://dx.doi.org/10.1080/23269995.2014.917031.
Todorov, T. 1984. *The Conquest of America*. New York: Harper and Row.

# Treating Asian nations with respect: promises and pitfalls of status recognition

Reinhard Wolf

*Department of Political Science, Goethe University, Frankfurt, Germany*

> Both nations and their political representatives demand respectful treatment from their international peers. In particular, Asian publics and leaders increasingly insist on their improved status being properly recognized by Western state representatives. Research in both social psychological and political science strongly indicates that meeting such claims can foster international understanding while status misrecognition fuels conflicts. Yet what do such findings imply for political practitioners? How can they make use of the positive effects of respectful gestures without compromising their own status or other foreign policy objectives? After defining respectful behavior as status recognition, the article first summarizes empirical research on the impact of (dis)respect, before it addresses potential drawbacks of satisfying other states' status claims. This discussion will be used as a basis for formulating policy recommendations aimed at facilitating international cooperation without lowering the perceived status of the acting state. In this context, particular emphasis will be given to efforts to meet Chinese and Indian demands for respectful treatment by 'the West.'

Actors seek social recognition for many aspects or dimensions of their particular identities: for meaningful events in their biographies, for certain roles they play in society, or for the sufferings they had to endure at the hand of perpetrators. In particular, however, actors care for the proper recognition of their social status, that is, they care for respect. In fact, humans all over the world deem themselves entitled to receiving respectful treatment. A sense for respectful behavior toward authority appears to be one of the few universal moral intuitions shared by all humans and probably even by some of their closest biological relatives. Conversely, humans deem others morally obliged to respect their own social position (Frank 1986; Haidt and Joseph 2004; Rosen 2007; Wright 1994). Insufficient status recognition thus provokes anger and indignation as well as an instant desire to put the disrespectful offender back in his/her place (Frank 2010, chap. 9; Miller 2001). The same gut reactions occur at the group level to the extent individuals identify with a given group. Accordingly, even disrespect for one's nation can deeply offend such an *Imagined Communities* (Anderson 1983) and can put pressure on its representatives to restore 'national dignity' by teaching arrogant foreigners an 'appropriate lesson.' Disrespecting other nations can thus be costly. While it will rarely instigate violent reactions, it will often impede cooperation.

This issue deserves particular attention in Western relationships with Asian nations, and above all in the interaction with China, Iran, and India. All three countries embody ancient civilizations which, for centuries, had to endure colonial subjugation and arrogant infringements by Western states which they considered uncivilized upstarts. Naturally then, these nations increasingly experienced 'status mismatchs' which, to this day, made them highly susceptible to narratives of victimization and status infringement (Miller 2013, 130–135). These historical status sensibilities are further aggravated by cultures with a stronger sense for status differences. Status values are particularly prevalent in Confucian countries with their great emphasis on authority rankings and public face (Gries 2004; Shambaugh 2013, 53–59). Psychological research has confirmed that East Asians indeed are less prone to think of themselves as autonomous individuals. When asked about themselves, they are far more likely than typical Westerners to mention their roles and relationships, rather than their internal psychological characteristics. Accordingly, such societies tend to develop cultures of morality which emphasize the concerns of groups and social communities, rather than individual needs (Ames 1997; Haidt 2013, 113–114; Wang 2012, 155). This again should make East Asians more sensitive to perceived offenses against what they see as the 'proper status' of their nation. Given the ever growing economic and military clout of Asian nations, Western nations seem well advised to take these enhanced sensibilities into account by looking for policies and gestures which convey greater respect for the erstwhile 'underlings.'

In fact, the discourses and foreign policies of many Asian nations provide ample evidence that they attach great importance to adequate status recognition. China perhaps is the most conspicuous example. One prominent expert has even suggested that 'the PRC may very well be the most status-conscious country in the world' (Deng 2008, 8). Many other observers similarly stress the paramount importance China's leaders and citizens attach to restoring the preeminent status lost during the 'century of humiliation' and to gaining foreign respect (Gries 2004; Liao 2013; Shambaugh 2013, chaps. 2 and 3; Shirk 2008, 77, 266; Tan 2011, 230; Wang 2012; Yan 2001).[1] Similar narratives of past glory, more recent victimization, and regained international status pervade the Iranian discourse. Along with 'an elevated sense of the country's strategic importance and significance as an "indispensable actor"' (Farhi and Lotfian 2012, 122), these perceptions fuel the Iranian nation's desire to undo the current global hierarchy and the Western 'arrogance' which it is supposedly built upon. India's colonial past is likewise seen as a cause of its recurrent displays of 'extreme ... touchiness' (Malone 2011, 271). Past and present India is said 'to place an inordinate amount of importance on attaining international status' (Ollapally and Rajagopalan 2012, 79) which repeatedly has prevented its diplomats to consent to cooperative projects because they allegedly failed to reflect India's status as a great civilization (Narlikar 2006, 72).

Over the past couple of years, the Western hegemon has indeed tried to take such sensitivities into account. The Obama Administration vowed to put an end to the problematical habits attributed to the previous administration, such as lecturing foreign governments or confronting them with faits accomplis. Instead, the administration announced its intention to listen and consult – particularly to the concerns of East Asian nations which had felt neglected by the preceding administration (Clinton 2011; Congressional Research Service 2012, 2, 16). Already during his campaign, candidate Obama had envisioned rebuilding transatlantic relations by treating European 'allies with respect,' while in his inaugural address, the President offered the Muslim world a new relationship 'based on mutual interest and mutual respect' (Obama 2009a, 2; Obama and Biden 2008a). Only weeks later, Obama publicly declared his nation's esteem for the accomplishments of Iran's 'great civilization' and offered 'engagement that is honest and grounded in mutual respect' (2009b, 10). This was to be followed by a historic speech in Cairo in which the President expressed his admiration for Muslim achievements and outlined his vision for a new kind of relationship. The administration also vowed to 'treat

[America's] hemispheric partners and neighbors with dignity and respect' (Obama and Biden 2008b). Finally and perhaps most importantly, the President repeatedly expressed his commitment to American–Chinese relations 'based on mutual interests and mutual respect,' a pledge which apparently was highly appreciated by his Chinese counterparts (Bader 2012, 126–127; Indyk, Lieberthal, and O'Hanlon 2012, 12 and chap. 2).

So far, however, this charm offensive has brought about few tangible results. While America's global image has recovered from its nadir during the Bush presidency, the new policy style has hardly affected the substance of official relations. Foreign governments may appreciate the changed tone, yet they have not become more accommodating to Washington's wishes or ideas. Former Iranian President Ahmadinejad responded to Obama's 'open hand' with demands for American apologies and real concessions, while his country's nuclear program proceeded unabated (Fathi 2009). In the Middle East, prospects for American peace initiatives seem as bleak as ever. Chinese–American relations have become more strained in the wake of Beijing's supposed turn to 'assertiveness' and the US 'pivot' to Asia (Bader 2012, chap. 7; Indyk, Lieberthal, and O'Hanlon 2012, chap. 2; Xiang 2012). More than five years after its launch, the new diplomacy seems to have achieved little more than opening the President to Republican charges that he is too soft with America's opponents in the Muslim world.

Yet, it would be premature to abandon this approach once and for all. The policy of respect is neither a panacea for healing strained relationships, nor is it a naive project which holds little promise of promoting international progress. Just as disrespect can fuel conflicts, respect shown for foreign nations and their leaders can often facilitate dialog and cooperation. In this regard, evidence from social psychology clearly matches diplomatic experience. To be successful, however, the display of respect must be tailored to the situation at hand. Potential benefits of such gestures must be carefully balanced against their costs and risks. Often, this will require meticulous analysis of foreign cultures and idiosyncratic perceptions. Yet, there is no alternative, as both respect and disrespect will become more consequential in a globalizing world undergoing profound shifts in power and status relations.

## Respect and disrespect

Over the years, 'respect' has become a buzzword used in all kinds of social contexts. In western democracies, ethnic or social groups increasingly demand respect from the government or mainstream society. When doing so, they express their dissatisfaction with their current treatment because it allegedly fails to reflect their actual rank or the social place they feel entitled to claim. Thus, by calling for more respect, people do not just utter their desire for a better treatment. Rather, they make a moral statement: they contend that they do not get what they truly deserve (Dillon 2007; Hudson 1980). Social respect can thus be seen as an attitude we expect others to show by the way they treat us. When striving for respect, actors seek *adequate consideration of their social importance and worth*. Specifically, they watch out for the due recognition of their ideas and values, physical needs and interests, achievements, efforts, qualities and virtues, and rights (Wolf 2011).

Of course, those who seek respect and those who are supposed to show it may profoundly disagree as to what should be regarded as *adequate* consideration. In the international sphere, there are especially wide disagreements concerning the appropriate standards for evaluating national importance, achievements or virtues (Wolf forthcoming). Though such differences may seem only natural (and thus unobjectionable) among people with diverse cultural backgrounds, the mere awareness of value pluralism will scarcely alleviate the social pain experienced by disrespected actors. Even when such behavior violates only the victims' idiosyncratic norms, they will often experience it as an undeserved infringement upon their sense of self-worth or social importance. Inadequate consideration thus easily incites indignation, anger, and sometimes even violent reactions.

Conceptualizing 'respect' as an attitude expressing adequate recognition for another actor's status draws attention to interlinkages with various strands of social research, especially with philosophical discussions of recognition, psychological research on respect, and a renewed focus on status among international relations (IR) scholars. Interest in the 'politics of recognition' (Taylor) has been stimulated by the seminal contributions of Axel Honneth (1996) and Charles Taylor (1995). Their ideas have been taken up by numerous scholars with an interest in domestic struggles against the symbolic discrimination of disadvantaged groups (Fraser and Honneth 2003; Kymlicka 2001; Laden and Owen 2007; Tully 2004; Van Den Brink and Owen 2007). More recently, they have also inspired research on international interactions among collective actors with conflicting symbolic desires (Heins 2008; Lindemann 2010; Lindemann and Ringmar 2012; Ringmar 1996; Wendt 2003). However, most of these contributions assume that actors engage in these struggles to achieve social recognition of their specific identities (see particularly Taylor 1995). Hence, they tend to gloss over the fact that actors may not want to draw attention to particular aspects of their identities, for instance, aspects which they deem trivial or embarrassing. Moreover, most of these publications have little to say about actors' desire to be treated as consequential members of society which deserve to be taken seriously irrespective of any specific identity claims based on individual traits or biographies. By focusing on the desire to see one's status recognized, the concept of 'respect' thus draws attention precisely to those recognition needs which actors care most about.

This focus on status recognition also provides a useful opening for integrating related insights into social psychology. This research has resulted in various findings on personal reactions to treatment experienced in small groups or institutional settings. Psychologists have been particularly interested in the effects such experiences have on prosocial and antisocial behavior (see the following section). In these studies, 'respect' is also understood as affirmation of a person's status within a group (Tyler and Blader 2001, 211), rather than as indiscriminate recognition of an actor's overall identity. Finally, an emphasis on status aspects is also helpful in the context of a renewed interest in the empirical investigation of international status conflicts (Deng 2008; Larson and Shevchenko 2010; Lebow 2008; Onea 2014; Suzuki 2008; Wohlforth 2009). To some extent, the policy recommendations presented in the following discussion thus are meant to provide a practical answer to those who want to avoid such disputes or at least hope to minimize their damaging effects on other international issues.

## How respect affects social relationships

Previous experience of respect increases the chances of cooperative behavior. This has repeatedly been established by social psychologists (Cremer 2002; Tyler and Blader 2000). Recognizing another actor's status, importance, faculties, or merits indicates that one basically shares his positive self-concept. Such signals will enhance confidence in one's partner's commitment to prosocial behavior, especially if this respectful attitude has been shown over an extended period of time. This greater trust tends to alleviate two widely discussed impediments to international collaboration: it diminishes concerns over asymmetric power shifts and it dampens the desire for autarchy, as the latter is often due to fears that commercial partners might suddenly exploit one's dependence on some good or commodity. Mutual respect should also make partners less concerned about the status effects which might result from a particular distribution of benefits, for well-recognized partners no longer need to take this allocation as a 'test' of their relative social standing.

Respecting the partner's views, values, and rights is also crucial for an open and thorough exchange of ideas. It facilitates mutual learning and persuasion which tend to make cooperative agreements both more attractive and more legitimate. Moreover, mutual respect for importance, standpoints, values, and achievements is crucial for avoiding status conflicts in deliberative exchanges as controversies about preferred options will no longer assume a prestige dimension. Thus, mutual respect is a sine qua non for jointly identifying the most efficient solution for a common problem.

Perhaps, even more important is the careful avoidance of disrespectful behavior, for it causes resistance and tends to aggravate ongoing conflicts. Indeed, forceful reactions to contempt or outright humiliation are the most powerful indicators of the social importance of respect (Lebow 2008; Lindemann 2010; Miller 2001). Just as with oxygen, being denied respect suddenly brings to the fore how vital the stuff actually is. The majority of disrespected people and collective actors almost immediately try to redress the situation.

Furthermore, open denial of respect may severely harm an actor's reputation as a resolute defender of its interests, thereby compromising an actor's capability to prevail in some future crisis (Frank 2010, chap. 9; Gould 2003). Disrespect for achievements, standpoints, and faculties can weaken an actor's prestige or lower its rank to 'a second-class actor.' This, in turn, reduces its 'soft power' and thus can diminish its chances for influencing all kinds of negotiations and debates.

Additional motives for defection and resistance to disrespect result from actors' *needs to maintain their self-esteem and self-respect* (Horowitz 1985, chaps. 4 and 5; Lebow 2008; Ringmar 1996). Belittling the victim's historic achievements or denigrating its essential cultural values can put the very foundation of its self-esteem into question. By openly resisting such an affront, an actor in effect makes a public statement about the importance of these values or achievements (Honneth 1996). To some extent, the mere act of fighting already establishes equality, as it tends to force the transgressor to take its victim seriously as an equal opponent. By failing to respond, however, the victim would effectively consent to its classification as a member of a lower status group. Even in situations without any significant audience, not responding to such acts would entail considerable psychic discomfort, especially in humiliating encounters.

The typical *emotional reaction to disrespect* is likely to further intensify the urge for open resistance. Disrespect almost automatically arouses anger which is well known to constrain information processing and to promote strong reactions against the disrespectful actor. Psychological experiments have demonstrated that the experience of anger leads to negatively biased perceptions, reduces the demand for information, shortens decision times, and consequently leads to more risk prone and more aggressive behavior (Van Kleef et al. 2008; Lerner and Keltner 2001; Miller 2001).[2]

Finally, in addition to immediate reactions, experiences of disrespect can also incite long-term feelings of resentment which become manifest and stabilized in public discourses. Typically, resentment results from a perception of an undeserved status difference which cannot be immediately corrected by the weaker party (Feather and Nairn 2005; Oldmeadow and Fiske 2012; Petersen 2002, 40–41). Due to their 'undeserved' status, targets of resentment are described as morally inferior and thus as less friendly and trustworthy (Oldmeadow and Fiske 2012).[3] This, in turn, makes cooperation less attractive and more difficult to justify in front of suspicious national publics. Moreover, resentment often fuels a desire to 'cut down' the higher ranking actor (Feather and

Nairn 2005; Feather and Sherman 2002, 958). Through inciting stable discourses of resentment, repeated acts of disrespect may thus seriously wreck prospects for cooperation in the longer run.

## Dis(respect) between nation-states

But can such findings be directly applied to exchanges between governments and nations, that is, to interactions between institutionalized collective actors or among rather amorphous groups? States after all lack feelings and their political representatives are expected to make rational decisions by choosing the option with the best prospects for promoting the country's interests.[4] Moreover, greater social distance between nations should also mitigate the effects of (dis)respect. After all, individuals care more strongly for the judgments of their peers than for the opinions of complete strangers with whom they may have little in common (Abrams et al. 1990; Haslam, McGary, and Turner 1996; Turner et al. 1987, chap. 4). Disrespectful or humiliating treatment on the part of outsiders tends to hurt less than abuse by familiar group members because it often can be 'explained away' with the outsiders' 'bad character' or their lack of better knowledge.

Yet while respect expressed by fellow members of one's peer group often is more cherished than respect shown by another group, respect (or disrespect) expressed by outgroups can still be very important – both for the collective self-esteem of the in-group and for the self-esteem of its individual members. Depending on the circumstances, being a member of a given group may figure prominently in an individual's social identity (Bloom 1993; Druckman 1994, 49–54). Respect for their group, its representatives, and its symbols can thus profoundly affect individuals' self-esteem and consequently also their behavior in various political contexts (Mackie, Devos, and Smith 2000; Mackie, Smith, and Ray 2008).

Rather than countervailing such emotional experiences, national decision-makers often tend to aggravate these feelings. Political leaders actually may share strong national sentiments, or they might seek international status for themselves. Status conscious as they typically are, political leaders themselves may be even more strongly aroused by foreign (dis)respect than ordinary citizens (Lindemann 2012).[5] In this case, they will be motivated to bring the nation along by promoting a public discourse which accords well with their own convictions or prestige ideas. At other times, policy-makers might stir up national sentiments for strictly instrumental reasons by using society's nationalist inclinations to boost the regime's domestic legitimacy. Often, governments will use the leeway for interpreting ambivalent foreign acts in ways that will aggravate rather than moderate their citizens' sensitivity to alleged instances of foreign disrespect. On the other hand, a weak domestic leader faced by a patriotic public would also benefit from exaggerating the symbolic salience of friendly foreign gestures by construing them as evidence of successful efforts to gain international recognition.

Domestic institutions can likewise enhance the touchiness of nations. The institutionalized propagation of national narratives and an organizational bias in favor of conflict norms might make nations even more sensitive than individuals who have been subjected to alleged disrespect. State institutions, after all, play an important role in the construction, promotion, and stabilization of national narratives (Ringmar 2012). Nation-states have founded university departments to study the nation's (alleged) roots and past achievements and have set up public schools to disseminate official historical interpretations. They have established national symbols (such as monuments, flags, and anthems) for public worship and have come up with all kinds of public rituals, which help citizens enacting their identification with the nation (Assmann 2006; Gellner 1983; Giesen 1999).

In addition, states have set up peace-time military institutions for national protection, which also promote national sentiments by routinely warning against dubious foreign designs and by continuously training large numbers of men and women for the defense of their country. Conflict norms that these institutions, the military in particular, tend to propagate can severely compromise the political leeway for leaders interested in pragmatic international cooperation.

Compared to its relevance for strictly personal interactions, the significance of international recognition problems thus is not only more nuanced but also more variable. Due to the great complexity of nation-states (and of their foreign policy apparatus), it is much more difficult to anticipate the former's reactions to external stimuli. Apparently, a great number of factors need to be considered. Particular attention must be given to the *behavior of policy-makers and prominent intellectuals*, for these leaders can exert critical influence on how the broader community comes to see both the status of its own nation and the symbolic implications of foreign acts. In shaping these perceptions, however, leaders themselves will pay close attention to salient *domestic cleavages*. Playing up alleged foreign slights may work wonders for authoritarian leaders embattled by democratic oppositions or by social movements insisting on economic redistribution. On the other hand, it may utterly fail when domestic society is divided between groups holding on to rather different national narratives.

Another major factor influencing the likelihood or intensity of recognition politics concerns the nature of the *norms that shape domestic political cultures*. Apparently, a nation-state in which individualistic and materialist-hedonistic views predominate will be less sensitive to foreign (dis)respect than a nation-state whose society stresses collectivist norms and the honor of family clans or other status groups. If protecting one's honor is an essential purpose for individuals and domestic groups, it seems quite likely that they will externalize such an outlook to IR (Lebow 2008, chap. 2). In this case, norms mandating the resolute defense of group standings within society may also be applied to foreign policy. Strong collectivist norms make it easier for nationalists to equate dissent with disloyalty and thus discourage both political leaders and intellectuals from advancing more nuanced arguments on the relative merits of insiders and outsiders. Consequently, such norms create a political climate that promotes negative stereotyping and self-righteous positions in international conflicts. Thus, when confronted with such a national culture, foreign political leaders should take even greater care to avoid disrespectful actions and to search for unambiguous ways for conveying their country's respectful attitude. Otherwise, they risk alienating foreign nations and missing opportunities for enhancing the prospects for international cooperation.

International history provides ample evidence for this claim. There are numerous well-known examples of harsh responses to disrespect or outright humiliation, such as America's counterproductive isolation of Cuba and Iran after the Bay of Pigs disaster and the 1979 hostage crisis, the highly emotional escalation of the transatlantic conflicts over the 2003 Iraq invasion (Pond 2003; Szabo 2004, chaps. 2 and 3), China's harsh responses to all kinds of face threatening acts (Gries 2004, chaps. 3 and 4; Shirk 2008, chaps. 6 and 8), Russian self-isolation in the wake of NATO's enlargement and the Kosovo intervention (Ambrosio 2005, chaps. 4–6; Pouliot 2010, chaps. 4–6), and India's persistent reluctance to enter cooperative projects with partners that failed to recognize its unique cultural achievements (Narlikar 2006) – to mention but a few. On the other hand, recent trends in American–Indian relations also demonstrate the beneficial effects of respect. Thus, President Clinton's highly acclaimed visit in 2000 not only gave him the status of a 'rock star' (Fareed Zakaria) in India, but it also paved the way for a dramatic rapprochement between the two powers (Talbott 2006; Zakaria 2008, 226). For instance, the Indian government reversed its position on the US request for an FBI residence in New Delhi. Up to that point, an institutionalized presence of American police agents had been seen as an unacceptable infringement of Indian sovereignty and independence. In the wake of the visit, however, Indian elites came to regard it as a useful means to improve intelligence cooperation in the common fight against violent extremism (Mohan 2000a, 2000b). Apparently, a shift to a more respectful foreign policy can sometimes make a real difference in bilateral relations. Therefore, minimizing disrespect is not only a moral obligation for decision-makers. It is also a prudent policy for promoting cooperation at the expense of conflict.

## The costs and drawbacks of respectful behavior

Given all these benefits of mutual respect and the risks inherent in acts of disrespect, one may be excused for wondering why disrespectful behavior has not altogether vanished. What prevents persons, groups, and states from creating a cooperative world by treating each other in a more respectful manner? Sometimes, misunderstandings or a lack of tact may play a role. However, given the substantial benefits of respectful conduct, more persistent obstacles must also be involved. Apparently, showing a respectful attitude also implies costs – and sometimes such costs are quite substantial.

First of all, duly appreciating other nations' achievements, perspectives, or importance consumes time, which could also be used for other purposes. Giving others our thorough attention reduces the attention available for third parties or other issues. Presidents and prime ministers cannot pay extensive visits to all key countries year after year, let alone to all nations which consider themselves part of this league. Sometimes, the pressure of unfolding events can simply overburden decision-makers' capacities. Thus, during the Asian financial crisis of 1997, Indonesians, Koreans, and Thais were deeply offended by the almost dictatorial manner in which the International Monetary Fund (IMF) imposed dramatic changes in long-standing national economic policies. In some cases, a handful of IMF experts, who had never been to the country before, had spent just three frantic days in the national capital before they practically dictated a wide-ranging adjustment program. Under those circumstances, there were hardly any consultations with the affected national representatives, let alone with local interest groups. On the other hand, the intensity of capital flight and currency speculation created an enormous pressure (and thus a countervailing obligation) to speed up the process (Blustein 2003, chap. 5; Higgott 2000).

Second, fully respecting other countries' rights and needs often involves material costs. One need not think of the consequences of climate change to realize that respecting some countries' basic needs can be very expensive, indeed.

Third, respecting other actors, even when it just means paying attention to them, further opens one to their influence. Taking someone seriously and giving due notice to her views also affects her social expectations. It may not only increase her trust in us, but will also make her anticipate that her positions will actually be taken into account. Mere professions of respect can quickly appear as 'cheap talk.' To appear genuine, respect ultimately must have some tangible consequences. A 'costly signal' of respect will always be more credible than mere rhetoric.

Fourth and related, showing greater respect for someone else can lead to misunderstandings concerning the relative rank of the actors involved. Emphasizing another nation's achievements, virtues, and overall importance can even encourage an inflated self-esteem well beyond the level intended by the respecting actor. Hence, it may inadvertently blur status differences and thus complicate negotiations or multilateral decision-making. In extreme cases, showing too much respect could thus even provoke unintended status conflicts (Gould 2003; Wohlforth 2009).

Fifth, showing more respect for a particular state can offend its international competitors as the latter may come to see this greater consideration as an implicit lowering of their own status. For instance, Japanese elites may resent enhanced Western recognition for China, or Pakistanis might feel disregarded by increased US respect for India.

Finally, satisfying another state's respect expectations may run counter to the prestige ambitions or enemy images of domestic groups and thus might compromise the executive's domestic standing.

In light of all these potential drawbacks, national leaders often are right to be choosy as regards the objects of their public expressions of respect. Just as ordinary persons who know that politeness can achieve a lot with some people but may be totally wasted on others, responsible officials must carefully assess which governments are likely to reciprocate a more respectful treatment at a given point in time. Decision-makers must not give more respect to governments which might just 'pocket' its benefits without subsequently adjusting their own attitudes and behavior. If, for instance, these executives deem their state or nation far more worthy or important than does the rest of international society, it can be extremely difficult (or costly) to satisfy their appetite for appreciation. Under these circumstances, enhanced recognition might just reinforce that government's self-righteousness or arrogance and thereby even instigate it to further raise its expectations concerning the 'adequate' level of 'due' respect. Consequently, any foreign policy aimed at making use of the beneficial potentials of respect must be based on sound analysis of foreign expectations.

## Making better use of respectful gestures in foreign policy

So what can Western leaders and diplomats do to make better use of the potential benefits of respect without paying too high a price? Are there any practical suggestions going beyond guidelines firmly established in the realm of conventional wisdom, such as: do not needlessly trample on others' rights, do not humiliate, be humble and polite, pay attention to diplomatic protocol, etc.? Is there anything which diplomats and politicians still can learn from psychologists or IR scholars? In fact, there are some valuable lessons which go beyond the obvious. Some of them relate to the fact that even today respect remains an underappreciated factor. Others take into account psychological insights about inexpensive ways to express respect or to avoid disrespectful behavior.

### *Increase your efforts to study the identities and perceptions of other nations and their elites*

Adequate knowledge of foreign perspectives is the sine qua non of more respectful policies. To respect others effectively, we need to know precisely what they want to be respected for. Often, we have some broad ideas about foreigners' symbolic needs but are unaware of specific qualities or achievements they want to see appreciated. Or we underrate their sensitivity to statements or policies which they understand as condescending or even insulting. This seems especially likely in the context of East–West encounters where Western officials need special expertise to grasp the symbolic connotations of certain gestures and postcolonial legacies. Absent such historical sensibility, they tend to underestimate Asian desires for visible symbols of full equality. Thus, Western representatives profoundly misjudged the enduring impact of their refusal to accommodate a Japanese request to inscribe the principle of racial equality into the covenant of the League of Nations (Aydin 2007, chap. 6; Iriye 1974, 257–261). Just like everyone else, government officials tend to underestimate cultural differences. Inevitably, they take some perceptions, interpretations, norms, and values for granted, simply because they are not contested within their own societies. Besides, cultural variations are reinforced by the tendency known as 'social creativity': everyone is inclined to give more weight to those kinds of qualities or virtues where s/he compares favorably to her/his social environment. For both reasons, foreign governments and publics can hold very different views on the significance of certain status dimensions and on the relative ranks nations occupy in this regard. Moreover, in the 'target' state itself, elite views might differ from those held by the broader public, and an incoming administration's ideas may sometimes differ significantly from those of its predecessor. Naturally, such shifts and ambiguities will be even more pronounced in societies undergoing rapid economic and cultural change, such as the dynamic nations in Asia.

Because of these potential gaps in perception, governments should provide for additional in-house expertise on the relevant perspectives of foreign governments, intellectual elites, and publics. Currently, most embassy officials and foreign service desk officers are just too preoccupied with pressing practical issues. They simply lack the time (and often also the expertise) to give serious thought to such questions. By the time they have achieved a more nuanced understanding of the host country, they tend to be transferred to yet another station where they need to start allover again. Academics or think-tank analysts may be more qualified in this regard. Yet, they often do not have the access required for timely warnings or interventions. Governments, therefore, need to make room for both more ongoing in-house studies of foreign sensibilities and more regular contacts between relevant officials and external experts with in-depth knowledge on foreign cultures and historic memories. Particular attention must be given to ideas about the nation's unique achievements or merits (see later).

### *Identify appropriate relationships and situations*

Respectful gestures need to be made when they really can make a difference. They will achieve little in distributive conflicts that chiefly concern material resources as such. Nor will they help in disputes instigated by incompatible interests of powerful domestic groups. Under such circumstances, respectful behavior may only promote a more sober atmosphere for bargaining, in as much as it helps to avoid emotionalizing the material conflict. However, to achieve a salient effect, such gestures need to be targeted on issues that primarily concern status aspects. And even when such symbolic aspirations predominate, respectful motions must be made at the right moments, that is, when the foreign audience is open for a new perspective of the bilateral relationship. Audiences with firmly entrenched stereotypes and conflict norms (see earlier) may just distrust any sincere expression of respect. All this makes it even more imperative that diplomats and country experts closely study foreign identities and the status perceptions they imply. In addition, they also need to pay close attention to domestic cleavages and power struggles, lest they 'waste' an initiative on an unreceptive leadership.

### *Do not hesitate to ask foreigners about their identity and related respect expectations*

At times, it may be very useful to address foreign officials personally to find out about their views on their country's place in world history and contemporary affairs – provided such an inquiry is made in a tactful and circumspect manner. Given the hazards of misperception mentioned earlier, it is quite likely that such a direct inquiry will uncover some new aspects which even long-time country experts had been unaware of. Such efforts are especially instrumental in interactions with Asian nations with lively collective memories of Western colonization, as various policy-makers and influential domestic groups may have quite different views on past interactions and their contemporary relevance. Sometimes a face-to-face exchange could make it easier to differentiate between authentic status views and other claims which are made for purely tactical reasons. What is more, clarifying a government's sense of its nation's place in global society might even establish a common baseline for status issues. In this manner, countries like China or India might be induced to present more consistent opinions on their international rank, rather than vacillating between self-presentations as great powers, regional powers, or developing countries (Shambaugh 2013, 153). This in turn would help to stifle status conflicts which otherwise could be provoked by ambiguous or slowly escalating status ambitions.[6] Finally, the sheer act of making a sincere effort to understand the counterpart's perspective and identity might be much appreciated as a sign of ascribed value and importance.

### *Listen and grant voice opportunities*

Getting a chance to express one's views is one of the crucial preconditions of feeling respected. It conveys that one 'counts' in the eyes of the interlocutor. In addition, being listened to also indicates that one's particular views are taken seriously (even where they fail to persuade). Of course, such effects are somewhat undermined when consultations do not bring about a modification of an unwelcome policy. However, a credible effort to understand critical views will always be appreciated. In fact, as psychologists have established, even consultations that are held *after* an unwelcome decision has already been taken make the latter more acceptable to parties that are negatively affected (Lind, Kanfer, and Earley 1990). Hence, it often makes sense to resume consultations after such a controversial option has been chosen by going back to affected governments and explaining the reasons which eventually overruled their opposite advice. To convey additional respect, envoys can also express official regret and point out the exceptional quality of the situation.

### *Find inexpensive ways to effectively express your respect*

As pointed out earlier, respecting foreign rights and needs can be quite costly. Of course, this should not be seen as an excuse for disregarding them. In many situations, giving full respect to particular rights and needs is not only a prudent policy but also a moral obligation. Going beyond that by verbally expressing respect for additional rights and needs, however, may not be a useful way to inspire more goodwill as mere words will hardly suffice in such situations. Consequently, it may be more efficient to focus on others' past achievements, collaborative efforts, virtues, or on ideas both sides share. For instance, it might have made a great impression on the Iraqi people if, right after the toppling of Saddam Hussein, high ranking US officials had conspicuously articulated their great admiration for the rich history and unique cultural heritage of that country. Paying a high-profile visit and labeling the region the cradle of urban civilizations (which it actually is) would have cost the Bush administration hardly anything. Yet, it could have meant a great difference for a population facing temporary occupation by a superpower with a different cultural background. Expressing respect in this way would not have undercut US influence in Iraq. Instead, such gestures might have put the relationship with the subject population on a sounder footing by saving part of its dignity.

## *Make efficient use of special gestures of recognition*

Chief executives and heads of state can convey respect through extended state visits or by offering well-tailored invitations to foreign counterparts. Sometimes, hosting a prime minister at a special retreat, such as Camp David or Chequers, or at private estates is seen as an indication of special esteem. For other nations, China again being a good example, official state dinners and meticulously performed welcoming ceremonies signify the highest form of respect (Bader 2012, 110, 126–127; Indyk, Lieberthal, and O'Hanlon 2012, 54; Shambaugh 2013, 56–57). Similarly, the opportunity to address a national parliament, such as the US Congress, is considered a great honor in many countries. Often, such gestures are awarded to underscore the amiable nature of a particular relationship. As such, they are certainly appreciated by foreign dignitaries. However, from the perspective of respectful diplomacy, such invitations come close to a wasted effort. For instance, US presidents have often granted these special invitations to the representatives of close allies, such as Britain or Australia, at times when their bilateral relations were rather friendly and stable. Under these circumstances, they may have further increased personal bonds, yet cannot have made a big impact on the overall relationship. This could have been different if invitations had been granted to representatives of very status sensitive countries whose elites and publics are particularly interested in *obtaining* the respect of an influential Western country. Accordingly, it seems more sensible to extend such invitations primarily to representatives from countries like Indonesia or India than to Canadian or Dutch prime ministers. The same principle applies to official state visits which could be more focused on countries with more problematic or volatile relationships, while consultations and negotiations with closer allies could be increasingly conducted through high-level envoys or in the form of video conferences.

## *Do not hesitate to take part in fair dialogs on relative status*

At some point, it may become apparent that two nations hold conflicting views on their relative status. When such differences affect ongoing negotiations – for instance, by lending a prestige dimension to a distributive issue – it is likely that any possible settlement will be perceived as disrespecting by at least one of the parties. Under these circumstances, representatives should not necessarily shy away from engaging their foreign counterparts in open dialogs on status criteria and assessments. Obviously, such talks cannot bring about immediate results. Even if national leaders themselves could reconcile their *personal* perceptions through direct dialog, they often would face severe domestic penalties should they abruptly lessen their publics' status aspirations. Still, such an exchange can be useful to convince at least the foreign leadership that one's demands are based on a sincere and deeply engrained national status conception which makes sense in one's own specific perspective – rather than on arrogant ignorance of another country's rightful position.

## Discuss complaints about the use of double standards

Dialogs about perceived status positions can also be helpful for clarifying complaints about double standards. After all, such charges are based on the perception that an actor's judgment is biased by an unjustified attribution of unequal ranks, which makes an actor apply a given norm in a discriminatory manner to actors who actually may deserve equivalent treatment. Such allegations need to be carefully addressed by the accused party – not only to ensure that truly discriminatory behavior can be corrected as soon as possible but also to elucidate unfounded charges which are due to misunderstandings of pertinent norms or circumstances. For instance, according to Gries (2004, 67), many Chinese harbor a veritable 'Nobel Prize complex', a resentment that Chinese achievements have been denied their rightful confirmation by the West, because (to date) no Chinese economist has been awarded the Nobel Prize for the country's economic miracle. As Nobel Prizes are meant to recognize personal scientific accomplishments rather than national economic achievements, the Swedish Academy can hardly be accused of applying double standards in this case. Likewise, many Chinese accuse the US of undue interference in the South China Sea disputes. They see it as high-handed meddling of an extra-regional power which supposedly claims a unique right to participate in regional conflict settlement (Bader 2012, 105; Lieberthal and Jisi 2012, 14, 18). Even though an explicit exchange about such charges will not always result in a common perspective, it may at least enhance the aggrieved party's understanding of the other actor's reasons and motives.

## Make intelligent use of public diplomacy

Sometimes, governments should directly address foreign publics. Doing so can be especially useful when other governments misrepresent one's own policies and attitudes. For instance, weak governments with questionable democratic legitimacy are frequently tempted to shore up their domestic support by depicting foreign nations as arrogant adversaries. To correct such dangerous myths, leaders must look for effective ways to convey respect for that nation (but not necessarily for its rulers). Up to now, such efforts too often focused on high-level contacts with dissidents or opposition leaders. However, publicized meetings with the latter might be easily portrayed as opportunistic efforts to split a nation or tarnish its image, instead of appearing as genuine appreciation of its talents, values, or achievements. And often, authoritarian rulers are quite successful in framing Western political critique as biased disregard directed against the nation as a whole (Qingguo 2005, 20; Tan 2011, 229; Wang 2012, 120, 229). A safer method to convey respect for an oppressed nation may therefore focus on the celebration of its contemporary artists and scientists or of its past cultural achievements. Where high-level meetings with unpopular dissidents seem useful or morally required, they could be matched by well-publicized contacts with highly respected public intellectuals.

## Do not expect quick results!

While open contempt or humiliation can immediately poison a relationship, a single gesture of respect will hardly ameliorate a strained relationship with a long history of mutual estrangement. Of course, such a move can loosen up the other side and make it curious about the next steps. Thus, president Obama's overtures to the Islamic world (together with his family's Muslim background) probably have instigated some hopes that the US would actually show greater concern for Islamic nations' views and ambitions. However, by themselves alone, these words could hardly erase decades of resentment and suspicion. Memories of alleged US double standards are still ready to pop up as soon as Washington relaxes its pressure on the Israeli government to stop constructing settlements in the West Bank and fully implement the Road Map. To have a beneficial effect on such a relationship, the shift to respect must appear genuine, sincere, and lasting. Ultimately, it may bring about mutual accommodation, but only if the other side believes in a profound transformation of the relationship. This may take particular time when diplomats and political leaders must also consider public moods and perceptions. Hence, officials should be prepared for long-term efforts consisting of a whole sequence of gestures which sooner or later need to be followed by practical steps with material consequences.

**The growing importance of international respect**
The diplomacy of respect will not become the silver bullet for foreign policy problems, neither for those of the US nor for those of any Western other country. Yet, as argued earlier, if applied with discretion, it can help promote international cooperation and, even more important, control the escalation of some conflicts. The current US administration deserves credit for having realized that diplomacy needs to pay greater attention to that neglected dimension of international affairs. Given the damage the US image has suffered during the preceding administration, attaining this insight may have been easier for American officials than for those of other Western countries. However, the latter would be mistaken were they to assume that giving more respect to other nations is a lesson to learn for American officials alone. Rather, profound economic and political transformations in the global arena make it imperative for decision-makers everywhere to reflect on the growing importance of international respect.

Globalization will further promote contacts between people with diverse cultural backgrounds. Increasingly not only elites will interact, but also ordinary citizens will meet, talk, and negotiate with foreigners from faraway countries. As a result, nations and cultural communities can less and less cultivate their identities behind the 'protective bars' of local discourses. Rather, they will have to cope with a growing number of articulations which challenge their positive self-images. While such exchanges will certainly enrich the knowledge and understanding of many people, they will also promote misunderstandings, unpleasant arguments, and the experience of disrespect. As it will become more difficult to ignore the divergent views of strangers, citizens will increasingly call upon their political representatives to defend the dignity or status of their community.

These trends will be further enhanced by the ongoing shifts of power and status. Managing the ongoing power transition and the necessary adaptation of international institutions will be difficult enough on its own. It will require great diplomatic skills and tact to find common ground and to build enough trust in the durability of the new arrangements. Yet, the dramatic rise of non-western powers, such as China, Brazil, and India, is bound to challenge not only the established power hierarchies but also the dominance of occidental norms, values, and world views. Rising states will not just raise their voice more often to articulate their own outlooks on the basis of their special understanding. They will also demand more influence, more attention for their points of view, and more status. As a result, the current status hierarchy is bound to become more fluent and ambiguous, thereby giving rise to conflicting claims, misunderstandings, and hurtful feelings. In this demanding political setting, leaders and diplomats must do their utmost both to avoid the impression of arrogance or neglect and to contain any feelings of resentment. Hence, they will be well advised to look for effective ways to show their respect for foreign leaders and their peoples. Making proper use of such opportunities will not put an end to conflict and competition among nations and their political elites. Yet, it can go a long way in making political disagreements less tense so that they can be more easily settled by pragmatic bargaining.

## Notes

1. According to a recent opinion survey, almost 60% of the Chinese think that their country is not receiving the international treatment it deserves, while 65% consider their nation disrespected by the US (Jung 2012, 7, 13).
2. Of course, in organizational decision-making, carefully designed institutions can mitigate such effects, especially when leaders feel accountable to their supporters. Emotions, however, can easily travel within groups which share a strong collective identity. Hence, even well-informed leaders can 'catch' the angry mood of populations and thereby be impaired in their strategic calculations (Haidt 2013, 88–89; Mackie, Smith, and Ray 2008).
3. Not surprisingly, many Asian intellectuals reacted to Western imperialism with counter-narratives that stressed Western moral decline, Asian virtues, and a strong desire for retaliation (Mishra 2012, chap. 6; Aydin 2007, chaps. 5 and 6).
4. For a more extensive discussion of these issues, see Wolf (2011, 2012) which this section builds upon.
5. In his first encounter with President Obama, Vladimir Putin reportedly complained for almost an hour about the disrespectful treatment he had received from George W. Bush and Condoleezza Rice (Mann 2012, 186).
6. For instance, David Shambaugh (2013, 262–266) reports in his book *China's Global Presence* that he often heard Chinese officials complaining about perceived Western disrespect for Chinese national conditions, policies, or ways of doing things. Typically, these officials attributed Western 'prejudice' and 'arrogance' to a lack of Western understanding. However, when asked about the precise nature of these alleged misunderstandings, Shambaugh's interlocutors could not provide any examples of disputes which in fact had resulted from Western ignorance or misperceptions. It always turned out that mere disagreement with specific Chinese policies was seen as sufficient evidence of disrespect. In this manner, policy differences were confused with status disagreements. Exchanges about status positions would help to avoid such misperceptions and thus help to 'downgrade' indignation about 'Western disregard' to normal political differences.

## References

Abrams, D., M. Wetherell, S. Cochrane, M. A. Hogg, and J. C. Turner. 1990. "Knowing What to Think by Knowing Who You Are: Self-Categorization and the Nature of Norm Formation, Conformity and Group Polarization." *British Journal of Social Psychology* 29 (2): 97–119. doi:10.1111/j.2044-8309.1990.tb00892.x.

Ambrosio, T. 2005. *Challenging America's Global Preeminence: Russia's Quest for Multipolarity*. Aldershot: Ashgate.

Ames, R. T. 1997. "Continuing the Conversation on Chinese Human Rights." *Ethics & International Affairs* 11 (1): 177–205. doi:10.1111/j.1747-7093.1997.tb00027.x.

Anderson, B. R. O. G. 1983. *Imagined Communities: Reflections on the Origin and Spread of Nationalism*. London: Verso.

Assmann, A. 2006. *Der lange Schatten der Vergangenheit: Erinnerungskultur und Geschichtspolitik* [The Long Shadow of the Past: Practices of Remembrance and the Politics of Memory]. Munich: CH Beck.

Aydin, C. 2007. *The Politics of Anti-Westernism in Asia: Visions of World Order in Pan-Islamic and Pan-Asian Thought*. New York: Columbia University Press.

Bader, J. A. 2012. *Obama and China's Rise: An Insider's Account of America's Asia Strategy*. Washington, DC: Brookings Institution Press.

Bloom, W. 1993. *Personal Identity, National Identity and International Relations*. Cambridge: Cambridge University Press.
Blustein, P. 2003. *The Chastening: Inside the Crisis that Rocked the Global Financial System and Humbled the IMF*. New York: Public Affairs.
Clinton, H. 2011. "America's Pacific Century." *Foreign Policy* 189 (1): 56–63.
Congressional Research Service. 2012. "Pivot to the Pacific? The Obama Administration's "Rebalancing" Toward Asia." http://www.fas.org/sgp/crs/natsec/R42448.pdf
Cremer, D. D. 2002. "Respect and Cooperation in Social Dilemmas: The Importance of Feeling Included." *Personality and Social Psychology Bulletin* 28 (10): 1335–1341. doi:10.1177/014616702236830.
Deng, Y. 2008. *China's Struggle for Status: The Realignment of International Relations*. New York: Cambridge University Press.
Dillon, R. S. 2007. "Respect: A Philosophical Perspective." *Gruppendynamik und Organisationsberatung* 38 (2): 201–212. doi:10.1007/s11612-007-0016-5.
Druckman, D. 1994. "Nationalism, Patriotism, and Group Loyalty: A Social Psychological Perspective." *Mershon International Studies Review* 38 (1): 43–68. doi:10.2307/222610.
Farhi, F., and S. Lotfian. 2012. "Iran's Post-Revolution Foreign Policy Puzzle." In *Worldviews of Aspiring Powers: Domestic Foreign Policy Debates in China, India, Iran, Japan, and Russia*, edited by H. R. Nau and D. M. Ollapally, 114–145. Oxford: Oxford University Press.
Fathi, N. 2009. "Nuclear Offer on the Way, President of Iran Says." *New York Times*, April 15. http://query.nytimes.com/gst/fullpage.html?res=D03E5DF1431F935A25757C0A96F9C8B63.
Feather, N. T., and K. Nairn. 2005. "Resentment, Envy, Schadenfreude, and Sympathy: Effects of Own and Other's Deserved or Undeserved Status." *Australian Journal of Psychology* 57 (2): 87–102. doi:10.1080/00049530500048672.
Feather, N. T., and R. Sherman. 2002. "Envy, Resentment, Schadenfreude, and Sympathy: Reactions to Deserved and Undeserved Achievement and Subsequent Failure." *Personality and Social Psychology Bulletin* 28 (7): 953–961. doi:10.1177/014616720202800708.
Frank, R. H. 1986. *Choosing the Right Pond: Human Behavior and the Quest for Status*. New York: Oxford University Press.
Frank, R. H. 2010. *Luxury Fever: Weighing the Cost of Excess*. Princeton, NJ: Princeton University Press.
Fraser, N., and A. Honneth. 2003. *Redistribution or Recognition? A Political–Philosophical Exchange*. London: Verso.
Gellner, E. 1983. *Nations and Nationalism*. Ithaca, NY: Cornell University Press.
Giesen, B. 1999. *Kollektive Identität: Die Intellektuellen und die Nation* [Collective Identity: The Intellectuals and the Nation]. Frankfurt/M.: Suhrkamp.
Gould, R. V. 2003. *Collision of Wills: How Ambiguity About Social Rank Breeds Conflict*. Chicago, IL: University of Chicago Press.
Gries, P. H. 2004. *China's New Nationalism: Pride, Politics, and Diplomacy*. Berkeley, CA: University of California Press.
Haidt, J. 2013. *The Righteous Mind: Why Good People are Divided by Politics and Religion*. New York: Vintage Books.
Haidt, J., and C. Joseph. 2004. "Intuitive Ethics: How Innately Prepared Intuitions Generate Culturally Variable Virtues." *Daedalus* 133 (4): 55–66. doi:10.1162/0011526042365555.
Haslam, S. A., C. McGary, and J. C. Turner. 1996. "Salient Group Memberships and Persuasion: The Role of Social Identity in the Validation of Beliefs." In *What's Social about Social Cognition? Research on Socially Shared Cognition in Small Groups*, edited by J. L. Nye and A. M. Brower, 29–56. Thousand Oaks, CA: Sage.
Heins, V. 2008. *Nongovernmental Organizations in International Society: Struggles over Recognition*. New York: Palgrave Macmillan.
Higgott, R. 2000. "The International Relations of the Asian Economic Crisis: A Study in the Politics of Resentment." In *Politics and Markets in the Wake of the Asian Crisis*, edited by K. Jayasuriya, H.-R.K. Beeson, and R. Robison, 263–285. London: Routledge.
Honneth, A. 1996. *The Struggle for Recognition: The Moral Grammar of Social Conflicts*. Cambridge, MA: MIT Press.
Horowitz, D. L. 1985. *Ethnic Groups in Conflict*. Berkeley: University of California Press.
Hudson, S. D. 1980. "The Nature of Respect." *Social Theory and Practice* 6 (1): 69–90. doi:10.5840/soctheorpract19806112.

Indyk, M. S., K. G. Lieberthal, and M. E. O'Hanlon. 2012. *Bending History. Barack Obama's Foreign Policy*. Washington, DC: Brookings Institution Press.

Iriye, A. 1974. "The Failure of Economic Expansion. 1918–1931." In *Japan in Crisis: Essays on Taisho Democracy*, edited by B. S. Silberman and H. D. Harootunian, 237–269. Princeton, NJ: Princeton University Press.

Jung, J.-Y. 2012. *Rising China and the Chinese Public's Security Perceptions*. EAI Asia Security Initiative Working Paper 23. Seoul: East Asia Institute.

Kymlicka, W. 2001. *Politics in the Vernacular: Nationalism, Multiculturalism, and Citizenship*. Oxford: Oxford University Press.

Laden, A. S., and D. Owen, eds. 2007. *Multiculturalism and Political Theory*. Cambridge: Cambridge University Press.

Larson, D. W., and A. Shevchenko. 2010. "Status Seekers: Chinese and Russian Responses to U.S. Primacy." *International Security* 34 (4): 63–95. doi:10.1162/isec.2010.34.4.63.

Lebow, R. N. 2008. *A Cultural Theory of International Relations*. Cambridge: Cambridge University Press.

Lerner, J. S., and D. Keltner. 2001. "Fear, Anger, and Risk." *Journal of Personality and Social Psychology* 81 (1): 146–159. doi:10.1037/0022-3514.81.1.146.

Liao, N. 2013. "Dualistic Identity, Memory-Encoded Norms, and State Emotion: A Social Constructivist Account of Chinese Foreign Relations." *East Asia* 30 (2): 139–160. doi:10.1007/s12140-013-9194-7.

Lieberthal, K., and W. Jisi. 2012. *Addressing US–China Strategic Distrust*. John L. Thornton China Center Monograph Series 4. Washington, DC: Brookings Institution.

Lind, E. A., R. Kanfer, and P. C. Earley. 1990. "Voice, Control, and Procedural Justice: Instrumental and Noninstrumental Concerns in Fairness Judgments." *Journal of Personality and Social Psychology* 59 (5): 952–959. doi:10.1037/0022-3514.59.5.952.

Lindemann, T. 2010. *Causes of War: The Struggle for Recognition*. Wivenhoe Park: ECPR Press.

Lindemann, T. 2012. "Concluding Remarks on the Empirical Study of International Recognition." In *The International Politics of Recognition*, edited by T. Lindemann and E. Ringmar, 209–225. Boulder, CO: Paradigm.

Lindemann, T., and E. Ringmar, eds. 2012. *The International Politics of Recognition*. Boulder, CO: Paradigm.

Mackie, D. M., T. Devos, and E. R. Smith. 2000. "Intergroup Emotions: Explaining Offensive Action Tendencies in an Intergroup Context." *Journal of Personality and Social Psychology* 79 (4): 602–616. doi:10.1037/0022-3514.79.4.602.

Mackie, D. M., E. R. Smith, and D. G. Ray. 2008. "Intergroup Emotions and Intergroup Relations." *Social and Personality Psychology Compass* 2 (5): 1866–1880. doi:10.1111/j.1751-9004.2008.00130.x.

Malone, D. 2011. *Does the Elephant Dance? Contemporary Indian Foreign Policy*. Oxford: Oxford University Press.

Mann, J. 2012. *The Obamians: The Struggle Inside the White House to Redefine American Power*. New York: Viking.

Miller, D. T. 2001. "Disrespect and the Experience of Injustice." *Annual Review of Psychology* 52 (1): 527–553. doi:10.1146/annurev.psych.52.1.527.

Miller, M. C. 2013. *Wronged by Empire: Post-Imperial Ideology and Foreign Policy in India and China*. Stanford, CA: Stanford University Press.

Mishra, P. 2012. *From the Ruins of Empire: The Revolt against the West and the Remaking of Asia*. London: Allen Lane.

Mohan, C. R. 2000a. "Govt. Hails Clinton's Message to Pak." *The Hindu*, March 25.

Mohan, C. R. 2000b. "FBI Director Coming to Strengthen Ties." *The Hindu*, March 30.

Narlikar, A. 2006. "Peculiar Chauvinism or Strategic Calculation? Explaining the Negotiating Strategy of a Rising India." *International Affairs* 82 (1): 59–76. doi:10.1111/j.1468-2346.2006.00515.x.

Obama, B. 2009a. "All This We Will Do (Presidential Inaugural Address)." *New York Times*, January 21, section P, 2.

Obama, B. 2009b. "Obama Extends to Iran Olive Branch on Videotape." *New York Times*, March 10, 10.

Obama, B., and J. Biden. 2008a. "A Stronger Partnership with Europe for a Safer America." Accessed April 23, 2009. http://www.barackobama.com/pdf/Fact_Sheet_Europe_FINAL.pdf

Obama, B., and J. Biden. 2008b. "Barack Obama and Joe Biden's Plan to Secure America and Restore our Standing." http://origin.barackobama.com/issues/foreign_policy/

Oldmeadow, J. A., and S. T. Fiske. 2012. "Contentment to Resentment: Variation in Stereotype Content Across Status Systems." *Analyses of Social Issues and Public Policy* 12 (1): 324–339. doi:10.1111/j.1530-2415.2011.01277.x.

Ollapally, D. M., and R. Rajagopalan. 2012. "India. Foreign Policy Perspectives of an Ambiguous Power." In *Worldviews of Aspiring Powers: Domestic Foreign Policy Debates in China, India, Iran, Japan, and Russia*, edited by H. R. Nau and D. M. Ollapally, 73–113. Oxford: Oxford University Press.

Onea, T. A. 2014. "Between Dominance and Decline: Status Anxiety and Great Power Rivalry." *Review of International Studies* 40 (1): 125–152. doi:10.1017/S0260210512000563.

Petersen, R. D. 2002. *Understanding Ethnic Violence: Fear, Hatred, and Resentment in Twentieth-Century Eastern Europe*. Cambridge: Cambridge University Press.

Pond, E. 2003. *Friendly Fire: The Near-Death of the Transatlantic Alliance*. Washington, DC: Brookings Institution Press.

Pouliot, V. 2010. *International Security in Practice: The Politics of NATO-Russia Diplomacy*. Cambridge: Cambridge University Press.

Qingguo, J. 2005. "Disrespect and Distrust: The External Origins of Contemporary Chinese Nationalism." *Journal of Contemporary China* 14 (42): 11–21. doi:10.1080/1067056042000300754.

Ringmar, E. 1996. *Identity, Interest, and Action: A Cultural Explanation of Sweden's Intervention in the Thirty Years War*. Cambridge: Cambridge University Press.

Ringmar, E. 2012. "The International Politics of Recognition." In *The International Politics of Recognition*, edited by T. Lindemann and E. Ringmar, 3–23. Boulder, CO: Paradigm.

Rosen, S. P. 2007. *War and Human Nature*. Princeton, NJ: Princeton University Press.

Shambaugh, D. L. 2013. *China Goes Global: The Partial Power*. New York: Oxford University Press.

Shirk, S. L. 2008. *China: Fragile Superpower*. Oxford: Oxford University Press.

Suzuki, S. 2008. "Seeking 'Legitimate' Great Power Status in Post-Cold War International Society: China's and Japan's Participation in UNPKO." *International Relations* 22 (1): 45–63. doi:10.1177/0047117807087242.

Szabo, S. F. 2004. *Parting Ways: The Crisis in German–American Relations*. Washington, DC: Brookings Institution Press.

Talbott, S. 2006. *Engaging India: Diplomacy, Democracy, and the Bomb*. Washington, DC: Brookings Institution Press.

Tan, Q. 2011. "The Change of Public Opinion on US–China Relations." *Asian Perspective* 35 (2): 211–237.

Taylor, C. 1995. "The Politics of Recognition." In *Philosophical Arguments*, edited by C. Taylor, 225–256. Cambridge, MA: Harvard University Press.

Tully, J. 2004. "Recognition and Dialogue: The Emergence of a New Field." *Critical Review of International Social and Political Philosophy* 7 (3): 84–106. doi:10.1080/1369823042000269401.

Turner, J. C., M. A. Hogg, P. J. Oakes, S. D. Reicher, and M. S. Wetherell. 1987. *Rediscovering the Social Group: A Self-Categorization Theory*. Cambridge, MA: Basil Blackwell.

Tyler, T. R., and S. L. Blader. 2000. *Cooperation in Groups: Procedural Justice, Social Identity, and Behavioral Engagement*. Milton Park: Psychology Press.

Tyler, T. R., and S. L. Blader. 2001. "Identity and Cooperative Behavior in Groups." *Group Processes & Intergroup Relations* 4 (3): 207–226. doi:10.1177/1368430201004003003.

Van Den Brink, B., and D. Owen, eds. 2007. *Recognition and Power: Axel Honneth and the Tradition of Critical Social Theory*. Cambridge: Cambridge University Press.

Van Kleef, G. A., E. Dijk, W. Steinel, F. Harinck, and I. Beest. 2008. "Anger in Social Conflict: Cross-Situational Comparisons and Suggestions for the Future." *Group Decision and Negotiation* 17 (1): 13–30. doi:10.1007/s10726-007-9092-8.

Wang, Z. 2012. *Never Forget National Humiliation: Historical Memory in Chinese Politics and Foreign Relations*. New York: Columbia University Press.

Wendt, A. 2003. "Why a World State is Inevitable." *European Journal of International Relations* 9 (4): 491–542. doi:10.1177/135406610394001.

Wohlforth, W. C. 2009. "Unipolarity, Status Competition, and Great Power War." *World Politics* 61 (1): 28–57. doi:10.1017/S0043887109000021.

Wolf, R. 2011. ""Respect and Disrespect in International Politics: The Significance of Status Recognition." *International Theory* 3 (1): 105–142. doi:10.1017/S1752971910000308.

Wolf, R. 2012. "Prickly States? Recognition and Disrespect between Persons and Peoples." In *The International Politics of Recognition*, edited by T. Lindemann and E. Ringmar, 39–56. Boulder, CO: Paradigm.

Wolf, R. forthcoming. "Respecting Foreign Peoples: The Limits of Moral Obligations." *Journal of International Relations and Development*. doi:10.1057/jird.2014.10.

Wright, R. 1994. *The Moral Animal: Evolutionary Psychology and Everyday Life*. New York: Vintage Books.

Xiang, L. 2012. "China and the 'Pivot'." *Survival* 54 (5): 113–128. doi:10.1080/00396338.2012.728349.

Yan, X. 2001. "The Rise of China in Chinese Eyes." *Journal of Contemporary China* 10 (26): 33–39. doi:10.1080/10670560123407.

Zakaria, F. 2008. *The Post-American World*. New York: W. W. Norton.

# REPLY

## Treating Asian nations with respect: promises and pitfalls of status recognition: a reply to Reinhard Wolf

Michael Clarke

*Griffith University, Nathan, QLD, Australia*

This is a reply to:

Wolf, Reinhard. 2014. "Treating Asian nations with respect: promises and pitfalls of status recognition." *Global Discourse*. 4 (4): 462–480. http://dx.doi.org/10.1080/23269995.2014.947064

Reinhard Wolf (2014) has made a thoughtful and provocative contribution to a largely constructivist literature on the role of trust, respect and status in international relations. Wolf's major contribution lies in two areas: (1) his elucidation of a well-developed conception of 'respect' and its relationship to the politics of status recognition and (2) the application of this model to the Wests' (primarily the United States) diplomatic relations with China, India and Iran.

Wolf's conception of respect builds on insights derived from literatures concerned with the 'politics of recognition' across the fields of social psychology, political science and international relations. While recognising the important contributions of previous studies in this sphere (e.g., Charles Taylor 1995), Wolf accurately notes that although 'most of these contributions assume that actors engage in these struggles to achieve social recognition of their specific identities', they 'have little to say about actors' desire to be treated as consequential members of society which deserve to taken seriously irrespective of any specific identity claims'.

Wolf seeks to correct this oversight by demonstrating that actors such as China, India and Iran very clearly deploy what could be termed status/respect-oriented foreign policy discourses to have their claims to being consequential and legitimate regional and international actors recognised by the West. The use of China, India and Iran as examples of highly status-conscious states that believe they are not receiving due recognition from the West (and especially the United States) are well chosen to demonstrate the relevance of respect and status recognition in contemporary international politics. Each of these states have constructed much of their post-colonial identity around a national narrative of humiliation by, and ultimately emancipation from, Western imperialism/colonialism – e.g., China's well-worn discourse regarding its 'one hundred years of national humiliation' at the hands of rapacious Western and Japanese imperialism. One only has to note China's recent sabre-rattling over the South China Sea or recall Ahmadinejad's bellicose rhetoric regarding Iran's 'right' to nuclear technology to recognise the long-shadow that such status-oriented discourse throws over contemporary Chinese and Iranian foreign policy.

The core argument of the paper – that the 'engine' of much inter-state tension, particularly between Western and Asian states, is the interaction between respect/disrespect and status recognition – is not entirely novel. Realists from Thucydides to Morgenthau have, of course, noted the constant roles played by human passions – be they honour, fear or greed – in stimulating violent inter-state conflict throughout the centuries. Respect, defined in Wolf's contribution as 'an attitude expressing adequate recognition for another actor's status', is in many respects a cognate of honour. Yet, Wolf's clear point of departure with such realists is to insist that the 'politics of recognition' need not be conceived of as a static and unchanging element of international relations but rather conceived of as a socially constituted and dynamic factor shaping international relations.

The clear implication of such a conception is that the 'politics of recognition' can be positively manipulated to decrease the likelihood for status-derived conflicts. In this context, the author draws our attention to the Obama administration's seemingly intuitive understanding of the status-oriented imperatives of Chinese, Indian and Iranian diplomacy. From the author's perspective, while the extension of President Obama's 'open hand' during his first term was not reciprocated by states such as China and Iran, the United States should nonetheless strive to make better use of 'respectful gestures' in its diplomacy with these states.

Yet, the core problem here is that while the author has amply demonstrated how the 'politics of recognition' have often lay at the centre of much Chinese, Indian and Iranian foreign policy rhetoric in recent times, it is difficult to identify such rhetoric as a *cause* of conflict between such actors and the West/United States. For example, how would the granting of 'voice opportunities' mitigate the South China Sea dispute or the continuing North Korean nuclear impasse? Are there not situations in which we must accept that parties to a conflict have irreconcilable security and national interests? In another instance let us consider the current state of Sino–US relations. How can we expect Washington to engage in respectful treatment of Beijing, mindful of its status-oriented imperatives, when it is reasonably clear that Beijing is intent on challenging US hegemony in Asia? This could not only be taken as a clear challenge to US security interests by Washington but could also, ironically, be taken as a threat to America's own status-oriented imperatives as a global leader.

In contrast to Wolf, I think President Obama, after the concerted and respectful 'charm offensive' of his first term, would be prudent to heed Thucydides' advice that 'Men naturally despise those who court them, but respect those who do not give way to them'.

## References

Taylor, C., ed. 1995. "The Politics of Recognition." In *Philosophical Arguments*, 225–256. Cambridge, MA: Harvard University Press.
Wolf, R. 2014. "Treating Asian Nations with Respect: Promises and Pitfalls of Status Recognition." *Global Discourse* 4 (4): 462–480. doi:10.1080/23269995.2014.947064.

# Interest, passion, (non)recognition, and wars: a conceptual essay

Thomas Lindemann

*University of Versailles (UVSQ), Sciences Po, Paris, France*

> This contribution will outline the limits of utilitarian models to the comprehension of interstate war and defend the idea that behind the concepts of interests are always hidden conceptions of (non)recognition between Self and Other. Thus, to pursue objectives such as territorial aggrandizement by war supposes a certain minimization of the 'Other' as a simple instrument to obtain something. The hidden normative condition of war underlying the 'war for oil' or 'war for power' is the framing of Others as inanimate or inferior. Thus, from the point of view of recognition theory, international conflicts are fought when the 'Self' holds minimized presentations of Others which are the condition of possibility for the famous war for interest. This article is the first conceptual stage in a larger research project that will examine the basis of nonrecognition, war, and the 'minimization of the Other' as a motivation for conflict.

## Introduction

Most studies focusing on war favor utilitarian and positivist approaches organized around realist and liberal paradigms (Art and Cronin 2003; Mearsheimer 2001; Wendt 1999; Achen and Snidal 1989; Fearon 1995; Organski and Kugler 1980; Blainey 1973). The reduction of war to the quest for security, power (*homo politicus*), or profit (*homo economicus*) made by utilitarian theories does not only apply to realist or liberal approaches but also to the Copenhagen Schools' constructivism (Buzan, Waever, and de Wilde 1998), which implicitly begins with the premise of *homo strategicus* ensuring his domination through *speech acts* and *securitization moves*. Overall, most theorists in international relations seem to have repeated the Hegelian dichotomy, assuming that once a state is internationally and formally recognized, its behavior must be analyzed in terms of pursuing a rationally defined, strategic, and material interest (Hegel 2013, paragraphs 331–340).

The issue of recognition, developed by several scholars during the last decades (Ringmar 1996; Wendt 1999; O'Neill 2004; Lebow 2008, 2010; Lindemann 2010; Wolf 2011; Honneth 2012; Lindemann and Ringmar 2012), has hinted on an alternative logic of war more attentive to emotional and moral dynamics such as revenge, hatred of Others, or restoration of justice. These emotions are aroused by a nonrecognition of the Self, that is to say, an actor's perception that his proclaimed self-image is greater than that which is returned by the Other. Such denials of recognition are directly capable of producing belligerent effects by encouraging offended leaders or political entities to restore their self-esteem through violent actions against those who offend them (Saurette 2006). Even for Clausewitz, the most virtually destructive wars, the 'absolute war' (Clausewitz 1989, Book 1, Chapter 1), imply the existence of strong hatred and honor issues. The idea that war is necessary to preserve one's honor against an evil and ruthless opponent has undoubtedly been a motivation for belligerent populations in major wars such as the Thirty Years War, the Napoleonic Wars, or World War I and II. So, unlike these reductionist perspectives, the study of recognition makes the 'expressive' assumption that the leaders and/or the ruled populations of a political entity often reflect strong emotions when seeking to enforce a certain image of themselves and of their communities (*homo symbolicus*) (Lindemann and Ringmar 2012).

However, this literature on recognition has also several shortcomings. The most serious one is its inability to take into account the strategic dimension of 'wars' (Vennesson 2001). Principally, recognition scholars, when faced with 'strategic issues', choose two options. The first is one of denial: for some scholars, 'expressive' considerations seem to always take precedence over 'instrumental-strategic' ones. This attitude has some empirical problems, especially when it has to explain what Clausewitz calls 'limited war options', such as small-scale interventions where logics of 'punishment' are secondary and clearly subordinated to 'instrumental' ambitions such as seizing territory or energy resources. The analysis of expressive dynamics must therefore be supplemented by a further analysis, more attentive to the role of strategic and material interests in triggering wars. Thus, the second option, apparently wiser, is to concede that strategic logics may in some situations prevail over expressive ones. However, the risk with this option is turning recognition into nothing more than a 'residual' variable, limited to explaining situations where 'normal' assumptions of rationality do not work.

I will question the prevailing strong dichotomies of 'strategy/interest' on the one side and 'recognition/expressivity' on the other. By bringing in the study of recognition to understand wars, I am attempting to unveil the mechanisms that make a war 'cold' for the purest possible interest. This type of war corresponds to Clausewitz's limited war, waged for a specific political goal (Clausewitz 1989). My main thesis is that war for a cold interest is only possible when emotions of compassion are neutralized by the nonrecognition of the Other: 'People go to war because of how they *see, perceive, picture, imagine* and *speak of* others' (Der Derian 2002, 5). This 'non-recognition' of the Other is often much more discrete than 'hatred', usually framing the Other as being 'insignificant' rather than being 'evil'. Far from wanting to replace the instrumental paradigm of war by an 'expressive' *doxa*, I recognize that there are wars which are subjectively led for a tangible 'interest', such as the cabinet wars of the eighteenth century, the colonial wars in the nineteenth century, or some more limited interventions such as the United States in Panama or the Soviet Union in Afghanistan in the twentieth century.

However, the material interest and strategic calculus[1] is not sufficient, on its own, to explain the use of armed force. Its bellicose expression depends on a condition of possibility which has to 'deliver' this interest from social and moral constraints (Price 2008). Most often, violence is associated with a social taboo (Price, Tannenwald, and Katzenstein 1996), and the use of force for pure profit has not been considered legitimate in contemporary international relations at least since the end of World War II. Furthermore, individuals are capable of empathy and even compassion for Others, and few people are able to bear witnessing a killing before their eyes without some prior emotional framing. In other words, the realization of a material interest by use of force requires the prior neutralization of any feeling of guilt through the nonrecognition of the Other, or more precisely the framing of the Other as having negligible or at best a purely instrumental value. Overall, the warlike interest is always dialogical because it must take the Other into account.

Thus, I defend the thesis that, even when they trigger wars for cold 'interests', elites are influenced by cognitive frames pertaining to the nonrecognition of Others, neutralizing their empathy and compassion. In the first section, I will argue that even in purely interest-driven wars, nonrecognition is crucial to enhance violence because it anesthetizes the actors' compassion for the 'target'. In the second section, I highlight that strategically motivated decision-makers need to take into account their audience's moral expectations and that they must at least 'manufacture' the nonrecognition of the Other in order to legitimize war. The last section outlines the contribution of the study of nonrecognition for understanding the 'motivation' of decision-makers themselves when they engage in war for material interests.

## Compassion, nonrecognition, interest, and war

Most theories of *homo economicus* and *homo politicus* believe in the tradition of Machiavelli and Hobbes that the elite's interest for maximizing goods is something that is obvious regardless of others (Honneth 1992, 10; Epstein 2013). However, this essentially 'monadic' vision of interests is far from being clear, especially if the satisfaction of such interests involves the manipulation or the elimination of the Other (Arendt 2001).[2] In human societies, the act of killing is often a taboo that must first be overcome. In rational choice theories, *homo economicus* is actually far from being a 'natural' man; he seems more autistic. The purely instrumental view of war neglects the fact that before armed forces can be used, empathy or compassion for Others must be neutralized, even for decision-makers. As we shall see, denying recognition to Others is an important mechanism for bringing people to define their interest in a completely 'monadic' way.

In this section, I first show that most studies on the causes of political violence dismiss the emotion of compassion as a resource for pacification of social relations. Instead, emotions are found guilty of the deadliest violence if they are not totally ignored. I will then present an alternative train of thought, emphasizing the virtually pacifying role that emotions like empathy and compassion toward Others can play. As such, the lack of empathy which is assumed to be 'natural' by war studies must first be explained and accounted for.

The study of international violence often ignores emotions (Goldgeier and Tetlock 2001). This can probably be explained by the difficulty to combine the study of emotions with behaviorist ideals of 'measurement and operationalization' (Crawford 2000, 120–122; Saurette 2006). There is a strange consensus among authors having studied the role of emotions in the outbreak of violence that only the taming of emotions could be expected to moderate violence.

According to Albert Hirschman, there has been a tendency among political thinkers since the seventeenth and eighteenth centuries to consider the passions as a source of war with reference to the seminal works of Machiavelli/Hobbes and to the state of nature, where man, responding to his whims, is a wolf to man. Emotions such as pride are identified as harmful to human survival and already opposed to reason. This sets up a whole body of thought on how 'evil' passions such as 'pride' can be tamed. From Hobbes's Leviathan to the writings of Burke and Gustave le Bon, thinkers have sought to devise the virtues of an authority able to curb the irrational, 'savage' and destructive instincts of the crowd in order to ensure civil peace.

Some thinkers, however, like Montesquieu as well as Hobbes himself, recognize 'peaceful' passions to counteract the destructive ones: 'The passions that incline men to peace are fear of death, desire of things necessary for commodious living, and a hope by their industry to obtain them' (Hobbes 2010, section 13.14). Gradually, the bourgeois 'passion' – greed – must come to counteract, as the result of a rational 'material' quest, the excesses of passions. The passion for gain – *pleonexia* – takes over from the excessive pursuit of glory and therefore hinders it.

However, the thinkers of the seventeenth and eighteenth centuries never established thought of reason, rationality, and economic interests on equal terms. The 'eclipse of reason' (Horkheimer 2007), or the forgetting of a collective rationality (common good) greater than the purely subjective aspirations of survival and well-being, is more recent and undeniably associated with the development of capitalism in the industrial era. Instrumental rationality (Weber) in the nineteenth and early twentieth centuries is reflected in both the Clausewitzian controlled war and the *Staatsraison* with its *Realpolitik* radicalization (Ludwig von Rochau) in the Bismarckian era. The terminological change of the pejorative concept of 'passion of gain' into a simple 'interest' and then into notions of 'reason' and 'rationality' ends with the econometric models that were particularly popular within social science departments of some American universities interested in economy and rational choice theory. The former 'compensatory passion' capable of overcoming the ravages of honor eventually becomes a pure rationality underlying all human behavior: 'Indeed, I have come to the position that the economic approach is a comprehensive one that is applicable to all human behavior...' (Becker 1986, 112).

Concerning its interpretation of violence, this anti-emotional model of rationality has led us to ignore the pacifying role of certain emotions. The most common theories, such as those of Norbert Elias or, more recently, Steven Pinker (2011), on peace processes have reintroduced the idea of an emotional control over dominating or sadistic passions. According to Norbert Elias (2000), the 'containment' of emotions via mechanisms of monopolization and complex interdependencies could be a source of peace. Elias considers the development of courtesy and the refinement of manners as psychosocial consequences of the process of state monopolization. For Elias as well as for Freud, 'civilization' presupposes a 'consciousness of guilt' which is the result of a weakening of the instinct of aggression by placing it under the supervision of an inner body, the superego (Freud 1985, 89).

Elias's theory overemphasizes the virtues of 'instinctual repression'. The 'superego' – incorporating moral values of a significant Other – is not necessarily a pacifier. Identification with an external 'violent' force is still imaginable (Glad 2002). As Jacques Lacan noted, the father figure not only serves the purpose of repression (the superego), but also of sublimation, the ego ideal (Lacan 1984). Thus, in Nazi Germany, the father figure was built by identifying it with an aggressive and manly behavior encouraging attacks against the weakest, while compromise was associated with weakness, helplessness, and femininity (Dicks 1950; Loewenberg 1975). Authority alone is therefore not able to lead to peace. It requires a 'benevolent' hegemon ruling with the rule of law (Battistella 2006). Freud himself indicates an alternative path to peace through the mobilization of the *Eros*, believing that a sense of community can mitigate violence (Freud 2010). Repression of instinctual economy, and in particular of sexuality, can itself be a source of aggression as demonstrated by the ideology of 'racial purity'. (Reich 2003, Chapter 3; Marcuse 1963, Chapter 11).

Another alternative and less broadly shared philosophical tradition has highlighted the possible role of empathy and compassion in the pacification of social relations. Rousseau formulated the theory that mercy is a natural law and an obstacle to violence:

> It is therefore certain that pity is a natural sentiment, which, by moderating in every individual the activity of self-love, contributes to the mutual preservation of the whole species. It is this pity which hurries us without reflection to the assistance of those we see in distress; it is this pity which, in a state of nature, stands for laws, for manners, for virtue, with this advantage, that no one is tempted to disobey her sweet and gentle voice; it is this pity which will always hinder a robust savage from plundering a feeble child, or infirm old man, of the subsistence they have acquired with pain and difficulty… (Rousseau 2009, 32)

For Rousseau, man is not 'greedy' and 'thirsty' for power by nature. What is truly revolutionary with Rousseau is that there is a kind of primary innate recognition: 'Consult your own happiness with as little prejudice as you can to that of others' (Rousseau 2009, 69). Even Adam Smith, who is originally regarded as the founding father of economic interest, admits in *The Theory of Moral Sentiments* (1759) that the principle of 'sympathy' is in man's heart, because it allows the existence of social ties. Defined as the ability to be sensitive to the feelings of others, sympathy allows for moderate judgments, complying with the hypothetical impartial spectator to which each and everyone refers (Smith 2004, 18).

The most recent research confirms the existence of some kind of original capacity for empathy in humans, regardless of their material interests (Hewstone and Wolfgang Stroeb 2001). This empathic capacity is particularly high when an individual feels a similarity with an actual or alleged victim of physical violence. In one experiment, nearly 80% of individuals feeling a 'similarity' with the victim are willing to help a 'friend' who is apparently receiving electric shocks, even if this victim can easily escape from such a situation (Batson 2011). This experiment demonstrates first that empathy and compassion are possible and second that these feelings are 'channeled' by a recognition of the Other (a recognition which is more or less strong), in the sense that one identifies the Other as one's own Self.

More recently, Andrew Linklater drew our attention to the possibility of activating the potential of empathy in a broader international society to counteract violence: 'Detecting the existence of feelings of mutual identification and perhaps above all, the capacity to empathize at the level of the global society; attributes which are essential to counteract the harm that exists in world politics' (Linklater 2011, 194). At the same time, the pursuit of material interests through violence clearly requires disabling such an original empathy. This is performed through the nonrecognition of the Other (Schiff 2014) and the virile framing of the 'Self'.

This nonrecognition framing can take two forms which we will treat in the following sections: the hero-protector idiom and the existential and statuary minimization of the Other.

## Self-recognition as a hero-protector: a strategy to seduce domestic audiences in wars of interest

Several major models for analyzing the behavioral mechanisms in warfare studies can be distinguished. They share a minimization of traditional moral and emotional reasoning put forward by the paradigm of recognition. However, even those paradigms are not able to explain wars without referring to some 'legitimation' process enabling war. It is not sufficient to 'want' war, it is also important to be 'able' to make it. While opposing their reductionism, the paradigm of recognition does not exclude instrumental approaches. Recognition and nonrecognition shape strategic consideration in a decisive war.

Based on the paradigm of instrumental rationality, materialist analyses of interstate wars view instrumental approaches as the manifestation of the power of states, as the expression of a struggle between their respective interests, and as an effect of the desire for economic and strategic gains or the desire to avoid such losses. They thus offer a utilitarian interpretation of the origins of armed violence (Levy and Thompson 2010, chapter 2). The rationality of actors – supposedly seeking to maximize their 'assets' (Mearsheimer 2001) – is reduced to its material dimension, that of a 'war for security', a 'war for hegemony', or an 'imperialist war'. These analyses assume that actors systematically compare the costs and benefits of the use of armed force (Fearon 1995; Huth and Russett 1993; Blainey 1973; Organski and Kugler 1980; Waltz 1979). Therefore, they share the conviction that actors do not engage in a war where the enemy may inflict costs which are disproportionate to the expected benefits. These premises regarding the peacekeeping virtues of deterrence were refined by studies on international crises. Consequently, problems of engagement, of communication, of threat proportionality, and of credibility have been discussed with a view to ensure a more 'effective' deterrence in managing these crises (Huth and Russett 1993). However, these rationalist perspectives have completely neglected the issue of legitimation. Crudely speaking, such an analysis suggests that once the elite has decided to wage a war, it has no particular difficulty legitimizing it. This assumption is quite doubtful; for instance, the Bush Administration was unable to engage in war against Iran in 2007 because the legitimacy of such an engagement was problematic.

On the contrary, critical constructivist authors are more attentive to the process of legitimation. The widely cited study by Buzan, Waever, and de Wilde (1998) demonstrates how actors securitize issues instead of asking *why* they securitize (Buzan, Waever, and de Wilde 1998, 25). Most importantly, the school of securitization suggests that legitimization is only referring to threats and not to moral issues such as 'recognition'. Ronald Krebs and Jennifer Lobasz's study of the US war against Iraq illustrates the instrumental vision of identities (Krebs and Lobasz 2007). The authors suggest that the Bush administration in 2002/2003 virtually forced the Democratic opposition to accept the war against Iraq by presenting it as a vital threat. The Republican rhetoric of war against terrorism and its acceptance in the media effectively defused opposition to the war. It was almost impossible to express opposition to the war against Iraq without being branded as weak or even complicit with regard to terrorism.

These studies, made in a more critical vein, have opened stimulating new approaches but neglect the importance of 'non-recognition' in the legitimation process. Positively, recognition – a valued identity of the Other – is important for elites. Even strategic calculations in a competitive environment are made in a context where these elites must take into account the moral expectations of other actors and populations in order to not lose their self-esteem with regard to Others and to themselves. Manipulating elites need to preserve their symbolic capital (Bourdieu 1972, 2003). State actors that lose face after a military intervention which is perceived as strongly illegitimate may quickly become perceived as rogue states, such as Iraq after its 'intervention' in Kuwait in 1990. A politically depreciated entity – such as Iraq in 2001 or Libya in 2011 – can be more easily attacked than a more legitimate entity such as Luxembourg. Thus, even those in power concerned exclusively with material gains need to justify and legitimize the wars in which they engage. Policymakers who ignore the moral and emotional expectations of the international community may lose face and encourage, as a material consequence, the formation of a powerful counter-coalition.

Roughly speaking, elites have two narrative options at their disposal to justify war: one is the 'cold' legitimization variant, which I will present in the next section, and the other is the hero-protector narrative, which I will discuss here. This narrative of dramatization is basically dichotomous, insofar as the Self is made into the hero while the Other is construed as evil (Dower 1987; Farrell 2002). In this case, the acceptance of war is triggered by two factors: a feeling ('outrage') of nonrecognition *of the Self* and the neutralization of compassion by nonrecognition *of the Other*. This double effect is produced by two oppositions: the sharp opposition between an innocent victim and a perverse aggression ('outrage') and between the 'coward' and the 'hero-protector'. The legitimization of the Iraqi war by the Bush administration in 2002/2003 is an excellent illustration of this dramatized narrative. The 'Weapons of Mass Destruction' threat argument, conforming to the perspective of securitization, was just as potent as the moral condemnation of Saddam Hussein's 'evil' regime and the appeal to the 'honor-related' duty to help innocent victims.

The theme of the 'innocent' and 'pure' victim crying out for 'protection' stands out conveniently. In the State of the Union address of 29 January 2002, Bush asserted that torture in Iraq was a widespread and systematic method: 'Iraq continues to flaunt its hostility toward America and to support terror. The Iraqi regime has plotted to develop anthrax and nerve gas and nuclear weapons for over a decade. This is a regime that has already used poison gas to murder thousands of its own citizens, leaving the bodies of mothers huddled over their dead children…This is a regime that has something to hide from the civilized world' (Bush 2002). Concerning the vicious 'villain', Saddam Hussein was explicitly presented as a sadist killer. The news channel *CBS* broadcasted in its 'Primetime Thursday' edition a testimony from Saddam's alleged mistress, Parisoula Lampsos. She described him 'as a Viagra-fueled lover who enjoyed watching The Godfather and tapes of his enemies being tortured' (ABC News 2002). The traitorous coward is also very present in the speeches of the Bush administration. To contrast with this, the United States painted themselves in a more heroic and virile way. One neoconservative thinker, Robert Kagan, co-founder of the now-defunct neoconservative political organization *Project for the New American Century*, famously stated that 'Americans are from Mars, Europeans from Venus'. In contrast with the unmanly, distrustful 'coward' and old Europe, American decision-makers presented themselves as the masculine, valiant and honor-championing protectors of liberties. The fact that Iraq was practically the only state in the world not to condemn the attacks comforted the vision of American leaders. In his address on the 9/11, Bush proclaimed: 'America was targeted because it is the brightest beacon of liberty and progress in the world' (Ritter 2002). On 1 May 2003, Bush presented himself in uniform after landing with his jet on the aircraft carrier USS Abraham Lincoln, for his 'mission accomplished' speech. It was the first time since Teddy Roosevelt that an American president in function had worn a military uniform. The more recent Western interventions in Kosovo (1999), Libya (2011), Mali (2013), and the Central African Republic illustrate the power of moral mechanisms, crystallizing the contrast between the figure of the innocent victim (children, women, elderly, and ordinary men) and an evil aggressor who knows no compassion for his victims. The underlying alternative to this narrative framing in many Western media was either intervene or lose your dignity.

Another narrative, linked to nonrecognition and international violence, is more characterized by the minimization of the Other. In substance, this second narrative 'banalizes' and 'minimizes' the opponent as well as the use of violence. While this narrative of minimization can be a manipulation tool for the 'elite' manipulation (Bigo 2011), it also serves to frame the minds of decision-makers.

## The minimization of the Other: the hidden 'non-recognition' mentality of elites as a necessary condition for war of interests

The nonrecognition framing that accompanies the subjective interest-driven motivation is necessarily less spectacular than is the execration of the Other as an evil aggressor or public enemy. Too negative a focus on the Other would lead to a different motivation for war more explicitly linked to an expressive dynamic such as revenge or the desire for annihilation (Crettiez 2006; Cashman 2013). Negating the Other, by the satisfaction of an interest through the use of violence, relegates the Other's existence as a being with needs to the background of considerations. This is a somewhat corrupted and rather disparaging vision of the Other, making it possible to instrumentalize the Other in the pursuit of 'material' goals. Minimization of the Other allows for disengagement (Goffman 1999), which designates the absence of any emotional involvement in the existence of the Other.

Minimization in the most basic *existential* sense means denial of the Other's *agency*. Others are not 'identified' as actually existing as free actors (Bartelson 2013) and are often portrayed as 'purely passive waiting for Western technology and aid to show up' (Ahmed 2011, 20–22). They may not be considered as 'free' because they do not really affect in a visible manner one's own life, due to geographical or relational distance. For Adam Smith, one's sympathy for the Other is selective and depends mainly on the density of a given relationship, such as a national/foreigner relationship. Geographical and 'imaginary' remoteness (Benedict Anderson) immunizes against empathy, as evidenced by the very partial interventions of 'Europeans' for human rights in the world.

More subtly, minimization of the Other's agency can be presented as an 'objectification' of the Other (in the sense of not recognizing the Other as a being with needs and capabilities for reaction). This latter form of minimization is also referred to as 'reification', which is the act of considering the Other as a mere object or an inanimate thing, and this is the most obvious manifestation of instrumental nonrecognition. Reification can occur following a market-based logic. This purely instrumental disposition toward the Other is conditioned by a vision of the world that involves a reification of the Self and of the Other as well as a trivialization of violence in the name of any law of necessity, market, national security, or the future of nations. Already, Montesquieu blames trade for the 'transformation it operates in all human relationships, making everything about money and dropping into oblivion the virtue of hospitality as well as these other moral virtues which prevent people from always discussing their interests with rigidity' (quoted by Hirschman (1997 55)). This reification can occur with the penetration of 'market' mechanisms in all spheres of society (Marx, Lukacs), as with the increasing technicality of the world and the triumph of instrumental reason (Adorno, Horkheimer). While 'instrumental' and 'objectified' relationships with the Other are inevitable, reification in the stricter sense refers to the act of forgiving the Other's living existence beyond a particular situation (Honneth 2012, 41).

Furthermore, the minimization of the Other can be partial and refer to the 'reduction' of his *status*. The *existence* of the Other can be recognized, but compared to the Self, the Other is perceived as being hierarchically or morally inferior. The perception of the Other's 'inferiority' weakens our compassion for them while the perception of Other's superiority strengthens it: 'The man of rank and distinction, on the contrary, is observed by all the world. Everybody is eager to look at him, and to conceive, at least by sympathy, that joy and exultation with which his circumstances naturally inspire him' (Smith 2004). The master of Hegel is not responsive to the needs of the 'slave' and the Other exists only as a support for an idealized image of the Self. In the *Phenomenology of Spirit*, Hegel suggests that the unbridled pursuit of the 'consumption' of goods, that is, the master's pure consumption (*reine Genuss*), implies a negation of the Other (Hegel 1970: B IV). Even the pursuit of gains implies a dialogical relationship and more precisely a purely instrumental view of the Other, making it possible to anesthetize one's emotions.

I will now detail here empirically the argument that even wars between political units that are most commonly interpreted in terms of interest actually entail a 'minimizing' nonrecognition of the opponent.

### *Existential minimization as a necessary condition for wars for interest*

The possibility for some forms of violence is facilitated when they are no longer perceived as constituting real wars. The most recent 'Western interventions' present themselves at best as rescue missions and at worst as necessary surgeries. Symbolic and discursive issues of recognition in the context of the Russian–Chechen conflict show how the concept of recognition *of the war* itself is a central issue in the recognition – and denial of recognition – process among actors in conflict (Merlin and Huérou 2012).

Abstraction minimization is a framework for regulating emotions. The closer a victim is, the more emotion the victim evokes (national and religious similarity, in-group versus out-group). As such, after 9/11, the lives of those who died were presented in detail in daily news and therefore they felt very close (Butler 2004). In contrast, the pure abstraction of the Other facilitates violence. The 'outsiders, the noncitizens are always misrecognized by the fact that they are not mutually recognizable as insiders' (Brincat 2009a, 51; see also Brincat (2009b)). Everything happens as though the Other had never lived. Christophe Wasinski's study on civilians killed by US forces in Iraq and Afghanistan reveals how technical discourse on the 'clean' war are likely to produce an abstract, distanced, and reified representation of the Other, therefore establishing a process of nonrecognition that legitimizes the use of armed violence (Wasinski 2012). Carol Cohn states: 'Defense analysts talk about "countervalue attacks" rather than about incinerating cities' (Cohn 1987, 492). Furthermore, the absence of intervention in humanitarian affairs seems to be explained by a lack of economic and political interest. However, it also implies an 'indifference' toward the suffering of others, whose very *existence* becomes secondary. We can consider that the policy of economic sanctions, which most often affects people and not the regime, aims to exonerate the non-interventionists, allowing them to maintain a good image with little cost (Sindjoun 2002).[3]

Another form of existential minimization of the Other is the framing of the Other as an abstract *force*. Even authors who believe that wars are triggered by security dilemmas or transition cycles (Organski, Kugler, Gilpin) often tacitly assume the denial of the other regime or its government's officials. The definition of a threat cannot be reduced to pure physical capacity; it must involve projecting a 'harmful' intent (Wendt 1999). While the hostile intent may be real, the security dilemmas are often 'narrative'. More often than not, they involve the presentation of the Other as a reified and naturally aggressive power. To explain security dilemmas or transition dilemmas, we must understand why an opponent *today* must remain an opponent *tomorrow*. 'Securitization' is a reifying mechanism. The more the Other is perceived as a threat, the more the Other seems small and inanimate. At the root of the theory of transition is the very scientific idea that the opponent is a unified entity, determined by an irresistible *logos* of expansion, independently of individual wills. Everything happens as though the 'actors' were moved by anonymous and irresistible forces. The mechanical representation of China's aggressiveness, 'spurred on' by its own potential, is an example of 'scientistic' objectification: 'What makes a future Chinese threat so worrisome is that it might be far more powerful and dangerous than any of the potential hegemons that the United States confronted in the twentieth century...A wealthy China would not be a status quo power but an aggressive state determined to achieve regional hegemony' (Mearsheimer 2001, 401). This form of offensive realism is not as neutral and applicable to all states as one may be inclined to believe. When Mearsheimer discusses US policy, he repeatedly criticizes its 'misguided policy of engagement' with regard to China. In sum, the intentions of US policy are less dependent on their position of power and less offensive than those of China. The attribution of harmful intent from an abstract force, coupled with a social-Darwinian vision that dates back to the nineteenth century, influenced some German leaders to engage in a policy of brinkmanship in 1914. Given the Russian population growth of three million, the German Chancellor and his advisor Riezler, inspired by Ratzel's theory, believed that Russia would need more *Lebensraum*. In addition, theories of transition and their reification of the Other as a 'force' often lead to an overestimation of the enemy unit and its future potential. Everything happens as if the actors were not able to innovate or react. Such scientism produces a 'neutralizing' effect on compassion toward Others. Thus, those responsible for the crisis of July 1914 often referred to fate in order to clear themselves of any responsibility and guilt: 'Control had been lost and the stone had started rolling' (Bethmann Hollweg, 30 July 1914, quoted by Lindemann (2001).

In addition, the propensity to engage in armed aggression between political units is higher when there is an 'affective' distance between them, and especially when they each believe that the Other, insofar as they are politically or religiously different, represents a threat in terms of identity. The reductive nature of an exclusively strategic interpretation of wars appears when we consider the counter-factual reasoning which could occur if the protagonists had mutually recognized each other and identified with each other. For instance, when the Czarina Elizabeth died in 1762 and Peter II ascended the throne, he withdrew from the alliance with France and Austria, thus saving his hero Frederick II from a desperate situation. Empirical research on the causes of war suggest that states sharing the same political system are much less likely to engage in war than those with different or opposing political organizations. Consequently, peace between democracies (Cashman 2013; Huth and Russett 1993) may not so much be due to the inherent properties of these political structures as to the perception of dealing with a 'similar' Other in the context of the confrontation with the Soviet Union. The awareness of sharing a similar vision of the world becomes especially significant when it is challenged, that is, in the face of ideological heterogeneity. Monarchical solidarity had no meaning in the eighteenth century when it cements the States of the Pentarchy, threatened by the 'revolution'. It must therefore be concluded that when there is no identification with the Other, the use of armed force is compatible with a valued image of the Self and with the definition of interests which disregard the Other (Lindemann 2010, 36).

The existential minimization of the Other, by framing the Other as having only a purely instrumental value framing, is often hidden. At first sight, the paradigm of the rational actor maximizing the interests of power seems particularly well suited to the dynamics of the cabinet wars or mercenary wars of the eighteenth century. As such, the War of the Spanish Succession (1701–1714), the War of the Polish Succession (1733–1738), the annexation of Silesia by Frederick II in 1740, the War of the Bavarian Succession (1778–1779), and the Prussian wars against Denmark (1864) and Austria (1866) have been interpreted in terms of pure strategic interests. These dynastic wars occur in a power vacuum caused by the death of a monarch and his replacement by a weak monarch struggling to secure defensive alliances (Blainey 1973, 69). Even some more contemporary Western interventions, like the US invasions of Iraq in 1991 and 2003, were analyzed as the result of the United States' hegemonic interests exploiting the void left by the soviet downfall. Far from being natural, the instrumental view of war is grounded on a hidden contempt for the Other. All these wars are made possible in part by several forms of contempt by elites which are more or less 'soft' and which make it acceptable to sacrifice human lives for an objective 'interest': first there is a form of nonrecognition toward the enemy regime, then there is a nonrecognition of the opposing population, and then finally a possible contempt for one's 'own' people.

*Statuary minimization and wars for interests*

Judith Butler (Butler 2004) explains that there are hierarchies among lives in terms of how much they are worth weeping over, conditioned by interpretive frameworks that regulate the influence of affects and indignation: the more the Other is perceived as a slave, the less one is likely to feel empathy (Patterson 1982). The actor's power and legitimacy are strong regulators of affects. The violence of a 'recognized' state is perceived as less shocking than the violence of a less recognized or 'irregular' actor. Most of the time, a statuary depreciation precedes the outbreak of war, as was the case for instance when people started referring to Saddam Hussein as simply 'Saddam' or as a component of the axis of evil. Contempt for the enemy regime and its leaders encourages a government to defend its interests by the use of armed force against regimes which are deemed 'inferior'. When the other regime is demonized, it is easier to justify the war and neutralize the paralyzing effect of compassion.

Dynastic quarrels were based on a hardly concealed contempt of monarchs for their subjects and for the subjects of rival powers. As such, the first partition of Poland (1772) between Russia and Prussia cannot be exclusively interpreted as the result of geopolitical (making the Prussian territory more round) or economical interests, but as depending also on a certain vision of the Poles as an 'exploitable' people. The anti-Polish rhetoric was widespread in Europe and especially in Prussia where, after the conquest, Frederick used the comparison of the Canadian Iroquois. As for the colonial wars, often attributed to economic interests or social imperialism (the desire to assuage popular aspirations), they imply a disregard for the subjected populations. Patricia T. Young and Jack S. Levy believe that the War of Jenkin's Ear (1739–1748) between Great Britain and Spain would never have happened without the presence of a possibly xenophobic public coupled with the offense that the severed ear of Captain Jenkins (by a Spanish captain) caused to British officials (Young and Levy 2011).

Statuary nonrecognition can even be extended to one's own population. The term *Kanonenfutter* (food for powder) was popularized to describe the action of the infantry during the trench warfare of the World War I and refers to the 'cynical' use of soldiers by strategic leaders for suicidal missions. One of the most widely cited theories in the literature on the origins of the war is the theory of the scapegoat. It assumes that a regime threatened by internal difficulties is often tempted to displace these problems via an external diversion. From the Hundred Years War to the Vietnam War all the way to the US invasion of Iraq, the scapegoat theory has been widely used in academic literature (Cashman 2013, chapter 6; Schumpeter 1951). However, the scapegoat theory assumes a purely instrumental relationship between the rulers and the ruled. Even advocates of this theory often admit that a warlike instrumentalization is probabilistic and that it is the making of a particularly amoral authoritarian government.

## Conclusion

Far from suggesting that the 'material' interest counts for nothing in the onset of armed conflict, I have tried to demonstrate the thesis that the 'monadic' interest alone is not enough to explain the use of armed force between political units. I have argued that the material interests – questions of security, material profit, or political legitimacy – can lead to war only if the Other is minimized, in existential or statutory terms. In an ideal-typical way, we can identify four main situations concerning interest, emotional framing, and recognition of the Self and the Other. According to a first configuration, the actors feel offended and hate each other, and we can assume that they will consider the use of military force even if the strategic or economic interest is unclear. Such confrontations characterize the wars of extermination of the Other such as the Thirty Years War or the World Wars. According to a second ideal-typical configuration, the actors feel generally recognized by significant Others in international relations, are motivated by an interest, and show indifference toward Others without much hatred. The type of war that corresponds to this state of affairs is the cabinet wars of the eighteenth century. Finally, there are two peaceful complements to these two ideal-typical wars: first is the peace between democracies, where actors feel recognized, recognize Others, and maintain peace despite opposite economic and strategic interests. Second is a conditional peace where the protagonists perceive each other in a minimized way but do not have an interest to go to war.

## Notes

1. My 'target' in terms of war theories is twofold: rationalism and materialism. I assert that both the instrumental 'rational' acts of humans and the quest for 'profit' by eliminating others presuppose, first, a framing of the Other as being 'insignificant'.
2. Arendt's banality of evil thesis is not far from mine but she is more interested in 'hierarchy-killing' than in 'interest-killing'.
3. I would like to thank Luc Sindjoun for this suggestion.

## References

ABC News. 2002. "Ex-Mistress Recalls Ruthless Man." Accessed September 12, 2002. http://www.Abcnews.go.com
Achen, C., and D. Snidal. 1989. "Rational Deterrence Theory and Comparative Case Studies." *World Politics* 41: 143–169.
Ahmed, M. 2011. "White Hero, Brown Villain: Symbolic Violence in the Misrepresentation of Pakistani Flood Victims by British Newspapers." MA, Methods of Social Research, University of Kent.
Arendt, H. 2001. *Eichmann in Jerusalem*. New York: Penguin's Classic.
Art, R. J., and P. et Cronin, eds. 2003. *The United States and Coercive Diplomacy*. Washington, DC: United Nations Institute of Peace.
Bartelson, J. 2013. "Three Concepts of Recognition." *International Theory* 5 (1): 107–129. doi:10.1017/S175297191300002X.
Batson, D. 2011. *Altruism in Humans*. New York: Oxford University Press.
Battistella, D. 2006. *Retour a l'état de guerre*. Paris: Armand Colin.
Becker, G. 1986. "Economic Approach to Human Behaviour." In *Rational Choice*, edited by J. Elster, 108–122. New York: University Press.

Bigo, D. 2011. "Pierre Bourdieu and International Relations: Power of Practices, Practices of Power." *International Political Sociology* 5 (3): 225–258. doi:10.1111/j.1749-5687.2011.00132.x.
Blainey, G. 1973. *The Causes of War*. New York: Free Press.
Bourdieu, P. 1972. *Esquissse d'une théorie de la pratique*. Paris: Droz.
Bourdieu, P. 2003. *Raisons Pratiques*. Paris: Seuil.
Brincat, S. 2009a. "Hegel's Gesture to Radical Cosmopolitanism." *Journal of Critical Globalisation Studies* 1 (1): 47–65.
Brincat, S. 2009b. "Reclaiming the Utopian Imaginary in IR Theory." *Review of International Studies* 35 (3): 581–609. doi:10.1017/S0260210509008663.
Bush. 2002. "State of the Union Address." CNN.com, January 29, 2002.
Butler, J. 2004. *Precarious Life*. London: Verso.
Buzan, B., O. Waever, and J. de Wilde. 1998. *Security. A New Framework for Analysis*. Boulder, CO: Lynne Rienner.
Cashman, G. 2013. *What Causes War*. New York: Rowman-Littlefield.
Clausewitz, C. 1989. *On War*. Princeton, NJ: Princeton University Press.
Cohn, C. 1987. "Sex and Death in the Rational World of Defense Intellectuals." *Signs: Journal of Women in Culture and Society* 12 (4): 687–718. doi:10.1086/494362.
Crawford, N. 2000. "The Passions of World Politics." *International Security* 24 (4): 116–156.
Crettiez, X. 2006. *Violence et Nationalism*. Paris: Fayard.
Der Derian, J. 2002. "The War of Networks." *Theory and Event* 5 (4). http://muse.jhu.edu/journals/theory_andevent/v005/5.4derderian.html
Dicks, H. V. 1950. "Personality Traits and National Socialist Ideology: A War-Time Study of German Prisoners of War." *Human Relations* 3: 111–154. doi:10.1177/001872675000300201.
Dower, J. 1987. *War without Mercy. Race and Power in the Pacific War*. New York: Pantheon.
Elias, N. 2000. *The Civilizing Process*. London: Blackwell.
Epstein, C. 2013. "Theorizing Agency in Hobbes's Wake: The Rational Actor, the Self, or the Speaking Subject?" *International Organization* 67 (2): 287–316. doi:10.1017/S0020818313000039.
Farrell, T. 2002. "Memory, Imagination and War." *History* 87 (285): 61–73. doi:10.1111/1468-229X.00214.
Fearon, J. 1995. "Rationalist Explanations for War." *International Organization* 49: 379–414. doi:10.1017/S0020818300033324.
Freud, S. 1985. *Civilization and Its Discontents*. New York: Norton.
Freud, S. 2010. *Why War? A Correspondence between Albert Einstein and Sigmund Freud*. New York: Sequoia Free Press.
Glad, B. 2002. "Why Tyrants Go Too Far: Malignant Narcissism and Absolute Power." *Political Psychology* 23 (1): 1–2. doi:10.1111/0162-895X.00268.
Goffman, E. 1999. *The Presentation of Self in Everybody*. New York: Life.
Goldgeier, J. M., and P. E. Tetlock. 2001. "Psychology and International Relations Theory." *Annual Review of Political Science* 4: 67–92. doi:10.1146/annurev.polisci.4.1.67.
Hegel, G. W. F. 1970. *Phänomenologie des Geistes*. Frankfurt a.m.: Suhrkamp.
Hegel, G. W. F. 2013. *Grundlinien der Philosophie des Rechts*. Hamburg: Meiner.
Hewstone, M., and W. Wolfgang Stroeb. 2001. *Introduction to Social Psychology*. London: Blackwell.
Hirschman, A. 1997. *The Passion and the Interests*. Princeton, NJ: Princeton University Press.
Hobbes, T. 2010. *Leviathan*. London: Yale University Press.
Honneth, A. 1992. *Kampf um Anerkennung, Francfort*. Germany: Suhrkamp.
Honneth, A. 2012. *Reification*. Oxford: Oxford University Press.
Horkheimer, M. 2007. *Zur Kritik der instrumentellen Vernunft*. Frankfurt am Main: Fischer.
Huth, P., and B. Russett. 1993. "General Deterrence Between Enduring Rivals: Testing Three Competing Models." *The American Political Science Review* 87: 61–73. doi:10.2307/2938956.
Krebs, R., and J. Lobasz. 2007. "Fixing the Meaning of 9/11: Hegemony, Coercion, and the Road to War in Iraq." *Security Studies* 16 (3): 409–451. doi:10.1080/09636410701547881.
Lacan, J. 1984. *Les Complexes Familiaux Dans la Formation de L'individu*. Paris: Navarin Éditeur.
Lebow, R. 2008. *A Cultural Theory of International Politics*. Cambridge: Cambridge University Press.
Lebow, R. 2010. *Why Nations Fight*. Cambridge: Cambridge University Press.
Levy, J., and W. Thompson. 2010. *Causes of War*. London: Wiley Blackwell.

Lindemann, T. 2001. *Les doctrines Darwiniennes et la guerre de 14*. Paris: Economica.
Lindemann, T. 2010. *Causes of War. The Struggle for Recognition*. Colchester: ECPR.
Lindemann, T., and E. Ringmar, ed. 2012. *The International Struggle for Recognition*. Boulder, CO: Paradigm, Yale Series.
Linklater, A. 2011. *The Problem of Harm in World Politics*. Cambridge: Cambridge University Press.
Loewenberg, P. 1975. "Psychohistorical Perspectives on Modern German History." *The Journal of Modern History* 47 (2): 229–279. doi:10.1086/241319.
Marcuse, H. 1963. *Eros Et Civilisation*. Paris: Minuit.
Mearsheimer, J. 2001. *The Tragedy of Great Powers*, 2001. New York: Norton.
Merlin, A., and A. Huérou. 2012. "Le conflit tchétchène a l'épreuve de la reconnaissance." *Cultures & Conflits* 87 (87): 47–68. doi:10.4000/conflits.18475.
O'Neill, B. 2004. *Honor, Symbols and War*. Ann Arbor: Michigan University Press.
Organski, A. F. K., and J. Kugler. 1980. *The War Ledger*. Chicago, IL: Chicago University Press.
Patterson, O. 1982. *Slavery and Social Death*. Cambridge, MA: Harvard University Press.
Pinker, S. 2011. *The Better Angels of Our Nature*. New York: Penguin.
Price, R., 2008. ed. *Moral Limit and Possibility of World Politics*. Cambridge: Cambridge University Press.
Price, R., N. Tannenwald, and P. Katzenstein. 1996. *Norms and Deterrence*. New York: Columbia University Press.
Reich, W. 2003. *Massenpsychologie des Faschismus*. Cologne: Kiepenheuer et Witsch.
Ringmar, E. 1996. *Identity, Interest, Action, Cambridge*. Cambridge: University Press.
Ritter, S. 2002. *War in Iraq*. New York: Context books.
Rousseau, J.-J. 2009. *Discourse on the Origin of Inequality*. Oxford: Oxford University Press.
Saurette, P. 2006. "You Dissin Me? Humiliation and Post 9/11 Global Politics." *Review of International Studies* 32 (3): 495–522. doi:10.1017/S0260210506007133.
Schiff, J. 2014. *Burdens of Political Responsibility*. Cambridge: Cambridge University Press.
Schumpeter. 1951. *Imperialism and Social Classes*. Translated by H. Norden. New York: Kelley.
Sindjoun, L. 2002. *Sociologie Des Relations Internationals Africaines*. Paris: L'Harmattan.
Smith, A. 2004. *The Theory of Moral Sentiments*. New York: Kessinger.
Vennesson, P. 2001. "Bombarder Pour Convaincre." *Culture Et Conflits* 37: 23–59.
Waltz, K. 1979. *Theory of International Politics*. Reading, MA: Addison-Wesley.
Wasinski, C. 2012. "Reconnaître l'absence et Dire les responsabilités : Le cas des civils tués par les forces armées Américaines en Afghanistan et en Irak." *Cultures & Conflits* 87 (87): 97–118. doi:10.4000/conflits.18482.
Wendt, A. 1999. *Social Theory of International Politics*. Cambridge: Cambridge University Press.
Wolf, R. 2011. "Respect and Disrespect in International Politics: The Significance of Status Recognition." *International Theory* 3 (1): 105–142. doi:10.1017/S1752971910000308.
Young, P. R., and J. S. Levy. 2011. "Domestic Politics and the Escalation of Trade Rivalry: Explaining the War of Jenkins' Ear, 1739–1748." *European Journal of International Relations* 17 (2): 209–232.

# REPLY

## Recognizing non-recognition: a reply to Lindemann

Brent J. Steele

*University of Utah, Salt Lake City, UT, USA*

This is a reply to:

Lindemann, Thomas. 2014. "Interest, passion, (non)recognition and wars: a conceptual essay." *Global Discourse.* 4 (4): 483–496. http://dx.doi.org/10.1080/23269995.2014.926734.

Lindemann's article is a key example of a creative and innovative but also well-informed argument of international theory, reminding me of Tarik Kochi's (2009) seminal book that also deals with recognition. Like Kochi, Lindemann draws on Hegel but also an equally impressive diversity of philosophical, theoretical and interdisciplinary resources. Lindemann consults these studies and arguments to posit a factor, or step, in conflict situations so far overlooked by theorists on war – that there is a moment, necessarily so, of 'non-recognition' that takes place before war. This is the case, Lindeman suggests, even (especially?) in wars driven by so-called material or rational interest. The Other must be non-recognized in a process that leads to war. Lindemann's arguments may be most valuable for their heuristic value – his framework of 'abstraction-minimization' is notable for its potential propositions and hypotheses ('The closer a victim is, the more emotion the victim evokes'). Thus, Lindemann's provocations should lead to further investigations regarding the plausibility of such 'existential minimization' being, as he puts it, a 'necessary condition for wars of interest'.

My only issue is epistemic – how do we *know* or how might we sense that it is 'non-recognition' that helps lead to war? Lindemann is engaging in what I have termed a politics (or analysis) of 'interiority' (Steele 2013), the effectiveness of which rests upon the analyst's or theorist's ability to persuade (rather than demonstrate) that something we cannot see or observe but still intuit or divine is behind the phenomenon we are trying to explain – in this case, war. Take notice of his subtitle to one section – there is a 'hidden "non-recognition" mentality of elites' that is doing not only some of the work, but the *necessary* work, for Lindemann's argument. 'Hidden' and 'mentality' – those are powerful, even transcendental and mystical, terms. What is the method that Lindemann uses to substantiate his certainty here? Such certainty trusts there being not only a non-recognition move, but also an almost too-clean sequence of non-recognition of the enemy regime (and 'then opposing population … then possible contempt for one's "own" people'). We have some quotes here or there, as well as some historical references, which indeed suggest the plausibility of Lindemann's sequencing – but there is no prior step that indicates just what, besides another argument (albeit one vividly informed by theory), which justifies to the reader some knowledge about a process that is really, *necessarily*, happening 'out there' in the world of global politics, either now or historically.

Lindemann should not be singled out in this respect – most studies (including, regrettably, some of my own earlier works, see Steele 2008) on war engage in this analysis via (or of) interiority. Much of the work Lindemann critiques in this article indeed falls into that same trap of references to interiority. I remain today much more circumspect about analysts' abilities to formulate via the 'hidden' and 'mental' some process (whether it is primary or secondary in its influence) that may be responsible for any explanandum.

But this is important for another reason, and that is the distinction Lindemann makes between his 'non-recognition' of the Other and the 'recognition' of similar Others (like two democracies), a distinction that implicates the related term of 'misrecognition' used by Shannon Brincat in his referenced (and incredibly persuasive) studies (Brincat 2009a, 2009b). Much like the Jervis concept of 'misperception' assumes that there is one correct, quasi-Archimedean point from which accurate *perception* occurs (Jervis 1976), Lindemann's argument is that such a process of correct 'recognition' is really out there, and it is only when this is negated or in error that conflict occurs. Maybe, instead, there's simply always recognition? It can be manifested in peaceful ways (as it is amongst, apparently, democracies), or in ways where one recognizes the Other but seeks to completely destroy its 'centre of gravity' in violent and often gendered ways, as Peet and Sjoberg (2011) suggest in explaining the targeting of women and civilians in warfare.

Lindemann's argument is nevertheless extremely provocative, and it may generate future study that forcefully accounts for how we might recognize what non-recognition 'looks like' in public.

**References**

Brincat, S. 2009a. "Hegel's Gesture to Radical Cosmopolitanism." *Journal of Critical Globalisation Studies* 1: 47–65.
Brincat, S. 2009b. "Reclaiming the Utopian Imaginary in IR Theory." *Review of International Studies* 35: 581. doi:10.1017/S0260210509008663.
Jervis, R. 1976. *Perception and Misperception in International Politics*. Princeton, NJ: Princeton University Press.
Kochi, T. 2009. *The Other's War: Recognition and the Violence of Ethics*. Abingdon: Birkbeck Law Press.
Peet, J., and L. Sjoberg. 2011. "Targeting Civilians in War: Gender and Intentional Civilian Death." In *Feminist International Relations: Conversations about the Past, Present, and Future*, edited by J. A. Tickner and L. Sjoberg. New York: Routledge.
Steele, B. 2008. *Ontological Security in International Relations*. London: Routledge.
Steele, B. 2013. *Alternative Accountabilities in Global Politics: The Scars of Violence*. London: Routledge.

# (Dis-)respect and (non-)recognition in world politics: the Anglo-Boer war and German policy at the turn of the nineteenth/twentieth century

Lena Jaschob

*Department of Political Science, Goethe-University Frankfurt/Main, Frankfurt am Main, Germany*

> This article argues that (dis)respectful behavior and (non-)recognition can have a greater impact on political decisions than considerations of power. To demonstrate this, I analyze Anglo-German interactions during the Anglo-Boer War of 1899–1901, especially the 'Bundesrath-Affäre' around the turn of the year 1899/1900. To begin with, the German position concerning the South-Africa question will be examined. The German political shift from initial support for the Boers to later neutrality, which obviously privileged the British position, will be examined next. Specifically, this article asks to what extent questions of status and (dis-)respect motivated German policy towards Great Britain. Contrary to German expectations, the British Government did not recognize German policy as a move in the greater status game. As a result, the German leadership felt disrespected and embarked on a new naval act, which in turn intensified the naval antagonism between the German Empire and Great Britain in the years to come.
>
> The Anglo-German relationship was characterized by misunderstandings, feelings of nonrecognition, and disrespectful behavior on both sides. Problems occurring around the Anglo-Boer war can highlight the consequences of disrespectful behavior and nonrecognition in this special relationship. By reconstructing the 'Bundesrath-Affäre,' the political consequences of such behavior will be shown: The Royal Navy seized three German mail boats in the winter of 1899–1900 without any explanation or legitimization. This provoked a diplomatic crisis between the German Kaiserreich and Great Britain. The German leadership felt severely disrespected by the British policy of nondisclosure, and as a consequence, feelings of being inadequately recognized erupted in German society. Although the diplomatic crisis was quickly resolved, the underlying perceptions of disrespect and nonrecognition had a persisting negative effect on the Anglo-German relationship. These subjective experiences dominated political actions on the German side, and classical power-political interests faded into the background.

## Introduction

After the death of Wilhelm I in March 1888 followed by the death of the 99-day-emperor Friedrich III in June 1888 and the coronation of his young and inexperienced son Wilhelm II, the German Kaiserreich, founded in 1871, searched for a new position in the changing international system. Coming from a great position of power – as it was determined after the Congress of Vienna in 1814–1815 – the Kaiserreich strove for position of world power. Because of huge economic growth and prosperity, a strong position in research and development, and imperialist and social-Darwinian thinking, the German Kaiserreich wanted to expand its reach. Wilhelm II was the head of and the driving force behind this movement.

The relationship between the German Kaiserreich and Great Britain played a crucial role here. First, there were very strong family ties between the German and British monarchy. Second, Great Britain was the greatest world power of the time and therefore the first country from whom Germany wanted acceptance as a world power. Third, Great Britain possessed the things Germany wanted to have: colonies and a large battle fleet. Therefore, it is hardly surprising that the German Kaiserreich focused on Great Britain and that it reacted so sensitively to British behavior. One of the first expressions of this was the German response to the British engagement in South Africa.

In a first step, I will lay down my theoretical framework. Focusing on status as a concept in International Relations and Social Identity Theory, this article will deal with status as a structural phenomenon in the international system. Second, I will examine the German response to Great Britain – especially on the South-African question. A short overview of the German–British relationship in the early 1890s will be given here, followed by a description of the German–British conflict over South Africa. The focus lies on the Krüger-Telegram and its surroundings as well as on the German position during the Anglo-Boer war of 1899–1901. The crucial shift from supporting the Boers to a neutral position in the war is a key element here. This article asks how this political shift was motivated and what effects it had on the German–British relationship. Third, this article demonstrates the German sensitivity towards British behavior during the Anglo-Boer war. By processing the 'Bundesrath-Affäre' of 1899–1900, the article argues that German behavior was motivated by status-seeking. As a consequence, the German leadership felt disrespected by the British crisis management and reacted with hasty attempts to re-establish the status of which it subjectively felt deprived. For this reason, the limited diplomatic problem over three German mail boats had consequences for German naval policy – the main political element of Germany's world-political ambitions.

## The concept of status and (dis-)respect in international relations and beyond

The theoretical framework of this article is generated by adapting social-psychological findings about status to the field of International Relations (Wolf 2012) and by combining it with realistic elements. While the concept of status is quite overlooked in most theoretical approaches of International Relations (Larson and Shevchenko 2010, 66), the term 'status' is well established in the realist field of International Relations. Realist conceptions of status and prestige focus on the relevance of material capabilities (Morgenthau 1954) or on the differences in power structures (Paul and Nayar 2003). All these concepts deal with status in terms of 'hard power' – status can be measured in absolute terms. Then status is – like military strength or economic superiority – another commodity for states to acquire on the international market to demonstrate power and strength. Status thus can be understood as the rank and also the power of a nation in the international system in an abstract way (Weber and Winckelmann 1980, 531–533) or as a very ambiguous concept of hierarchy, because it says very little about the concrete claims of, for example, being a world power or an economic power. But the problem is that status can be expressed in various ways – some states focus on their achievements in civilization (Fikenscher, Jaschob, and Wolf 2012), some on their big naval program (Jaschob 2012), and others on different kinds of power. This complexity cannot be fully mapped by the above-mentioned concepts.

Social-psychological findings expect that status is related to an agent's social rank. Status is therefore defined as 'a ranking or hierarchy of perceived prestige' (Tajfel and Turner 1979, 37). This concept assumes that other groups accept the agent's achievements and characteristics, because the latter are relevant enough to grant it a specific role in the overall social framework. Status cannot then be reached by accumulating 'hard power', as in realist approaches. It can only be earned by an agent by demonstrating that it deserves it. Elements of this concept were picked up by Axel Honneth (1996). Based on the concepts from philosophical literature, he marked status as a social need. Directly linked to this understanding of status is the concept of respect (Wolf 2008, 2012).

With these two different approaches in mind, I will conceptualize status as a structural element in the international system and therefore as an element that affects all nations in this system. This means that the demand for status recognition is not only an obsession of a single state or group of states, but a structural setting which determines political action. The distribution of status as a structural feature in the international system is directly linked to the concept of respect (Wohlforth 2009). Respect, in this regard, can be understood as the adequate recognition of one's subjectively deserved status. As a result, a status mismatch can occur, which can increase the antagonism between these actors and can finally lead to a serious conflict (Wolf 2011). Thus, experiencing disrespectful behavior through a subjectively relevant actor can increase one's wish for higher status and recognition.

States as the relevant units in the international system compete for high ranks in the system. But to achieve a desired position of power in the international system, states not only need material capabilities, they are also dependent on recognition by other states – their status capabilities have to be accepted and respected by the others. Thus, status becomes a structural element because, on the one hand, a state has to demonstrate that it deserves the desired status, and on the other hand, the international community has to respond to this demonstration by respecting or disrespecting the other's status. If the desired status is not respected by other states, a status mismatch can occur (Wolf 2011). Such a status mismatch directly affects the structure of the international system, because in the short term it can lead to a conflict, and in the long term it can bring the hierarchy of the system into question. Status therefore plays a crucial role in the struggle for power in the international arena. While it could be linked to classical elements of power politics such as military or economic strength, it can also be linked to 'soft power,' diplomacy, or the personal feelings of important statesmen (see below). Because of its structural nature, status affects all political arenas in the international system, but it is not bound to specific items of power and therefore is not measurable in an absolute way. It is a relational good that is one brick in the house of the international system: If a state's status is recognized and respected by others, this does not mean that another state's status has to be lowered. There is no defined quantity of status available in the international system; there is an unlimited amount, which could be expressed in various ways. Thus, the acquisition of status works differently than the acquisition of material capabilities; it cannot be gained unilaterally. One's status only exists as it is recognized and respected by others.

## The German Kaiserreich on its way to world power and the upcoming of the Anglo-Boer war

With the appointment of Bernhard von Bülow as State Secretary of Foreign Affairs and Alfred von Tirpitz as State Secretary of the Reichsmarineamt in mid-1897, the German Kaiserreich began a systematic attempt to attain the position of a world power. The famous speech about the German right to become a world power, given by Bülow in December 1897, was one of the first steps in implementing this political program:

> We must demand that the German missionary and the German entrepreneur, German goods, the German flag and German ships in China are just as respected as those of other powers. We are finally very willing to give recognition to the interests of other Great Powers in East Asia, in the certain prospect that our own interests will likewise find the credit that they are due. In a word: we don't want to put anyone in the shadow, but we too demand our place in the sun. In East Asia as in the West Indies, we will endeavour, true to the traditions of German policy, without unnecessary sharpness, but also without weakness, to defend our rights and interests.
> (Quoted in Hewitson 2004, 148)

Since 1897, Europe had been divided into two systems of alliances: the 'Zweibund', containing France and Russia, and the 'Dreibund', containing the German Kaiserreich, Austria–Hungary, and Italy. Great Britain was not part of this system; the British crown and government preferred a policy of 'Splendid Isolation' (Massie 1993, 19) because they were convinced that noninterference would be the best way to secure the Empire. Even though this system was characterized by these two blocks, it was open for change; the blocks were not as solid as they seemed to be (Brechtken 2006, 356). With the German plans for becoming a world power, the increasing German High Seas Fleet (Fremont-Barnes 2003, 77), and the Anglo-Boer war, beginning in fall 1899, the system was set in motion.

In 1886, gold deposits were discovered in Witwatersrand, a region that belonged to Transvaal, which got its full internal independence under a British suzerainty in 1881.[1] This discovery raised economic interest among the British, and as a consequence, nearly 100,000 people, mostly British, immigrated to Transvaal. These immigrants were called 'Uitlanders' and soon the first conflicts arose between Great Britain and the Boers: the Boers became a minority in their own country and therefore the integration of the Uitlanders was problematic (Nasson 2010, 47–48; Steele 2000, 6). The major topic was the material interests of some British capitalists in the Rand region. They were convinced that a modern state under British rule was most suitable for their economic interests (Mommsen 2001, 1). Beside these economic interests, the British policy towards South Africa changed. Uniting South Africa under a British protectorate as a 'South African Confederation' led by self-governing white settlers was the main goal of this new policy, guided by Gladstone as the new Prime Minister and Chamberlain as Minister of Colonies. As a reaction, the Boers insisted strongly on their independence (Bender 2009, 52). This was the framework for the Anglo-Boer war, which could then be understood as an economically motivated war, on the one hand, and a war about the rights of the Uitlanders in particular and the supremacy over South Africa in general, on the other hand (Henshaw 2001, 17–18; Nasson 2010, 17; Chap. 2).

The German–Boer relationship had strengthened since 1894 and culminated in the Krüger-Telegram.[2] This Telegram was, on the one hand, the peak of German support for the Boers, and on the other, it was the turning point of the German–Boer relationship (Kröger 2001, 30). Since 1896, not only had trade decreased significantly, but German policy had also distanced itself from the Boers. With the German–British contract over South Africa (Angola treaty) in 1898, the change in the German–Boer relationship was complete. From a German perspective, this was a kind of Realpolitik. The German leadership wanted to be involved in the British–Portuguese negotiations over the future of the Portuguese colonies. Owing to political pressure, the German leadership succeeded in participating in these negotiations. This political step signaled an indirect acceptance of the British policy on South Africa (Rosenbach 1993, 98).[3] To avoid a political dilemma, the German leadership tried to induce Krüger, president of the Transvaal, to negotiate with Great Britain. The aim was to prevent a war between Great Britain and the Boer Republic, and therefore, the German leadership had to maintain neutrality (Bender 2009, 137). This tactical action failed, and as a result, the war broke out. To solve its political dilemma, the German leadership decided to stay neutral through the conflict (Rosenbach 1993, 186–190). This allowed for further Anglo-German negotiations about colonial territories in Africa and Asia, and it signaled concessions to German society, which was mainly pro-Boer (Geppert 2007). The German neutrality thus had two functions. On the one hand, it allowed Germany to cursorily stay out of the struggles in South Africa. On the other hand, it was meant to pave the way for a strong German bargaining position. Both aims failed. The British government quickly unmasked the German neutrality: the German desire for colonial compensation was too obvious (Rosenbach 1993, 192).

In the course of the war, the then renewed outbreak of Anglo-German antagonism was mainly characterized by a press war. Both governments tried to influence their press systems to mitigate the harsh and hostile articles (Geppert 2007, 142–145). But these attempts failed: Anglophobia and, respectively, Germanophobia, controlled the masses. On the political scene, the German government tried to use the initial defeats of the British troops in South Africa to restore the German position and to get far-reaching compensations (Bender 2009, 140). But because of the dominant press war and because of clumsy German behavior, these political attempts failed too. Until the 'Bundesrath-Affäre' occurred, there were no real chances for the German government to benefit from the difficult British position in the war.

The 'Bundesrath-Affäre' was the most important episode of the Anglo-Boer war for the German Kaiserreich. This diplomatic crisis lasting for about two weeks substantially worsened the Anglo-German relationship and demonstrated the implications of the Anglo-German status mismatch for the first time. It was not the crisis itself that became the problem, but the manner of addressing it and the tone of the dispute (Kröger 2001, 37). The first German mail boat 'Bundesrath' was seized by the British Royal Navy on 29 December 1899. There was no visible reason for this act; the British suspicions about weapons transport or other suspicious supplies for the Boers could not be proved. The British Government reacted immediately to the German request for an explanation: they were also not informed about the action of the Royal Navy, but they would clarify this and then respond (Lepsius, Mendelssohn Bartholdy, and Thimme 1924, No. 4414). On 4 January 1900, a second German mail boat was seized and the German Government renewed its request for clarification of the situation. The third and last German mail boat was seized on 6 January 1900. Up until this incident, the German Government had received no definite answer from the British Government about the reasons for these actions (Lepsius, Mendelssohn Bartholdy, and Thimme 1924, Nos. 4420–4430). To the German Government, British behavior seemed tactical and a willful nonrecognition of German demands (see below). On the tenth of January 1900, the German Ambassador in London, Count Hatzfeldt, transmitted the British apology to Bülow, the State Secretary of Foreign Affairs. The German Government now accepted the British course of action and dissociated from its previous position. This quick shift in German behavior – from linking the seizing to questions of status and respect, to an attitude of nearly full cooperation with the British – is hard to understand, but if one looks at these incidents from a broader perspective, it could be seen as a tactical step to reach the desired position of world power.

## The Krüger-Telegram and its implications on the German–British relationship

The dismissal of Bismarck in 1890 set German foreign policy in motion. Caprivi, as Bismarck's successor, tried to carry on a calm and contained foreign policy. He used trade agreements to stabilize Germany's position on the European continent and wanted to establish a unique European economic area to attain a hegemonic German position in a peaceful manner. He pursued no worldwide political ambitions. For him, German power and strength were located on the European continent (Ullrich 2000, 31). Hohenlohe-Schillingsfürst, chancellor since 1894, also supported the German 'Großmachtstatus.' Like Caprivi, he had no world political ambitions, but because of his age – he was 73 at the time he was appointed chancellor – and because of his scant interest in foreign policy, Kaiser Wilhelm II could now succeed in trying to implement his own world political dreams.

After Caprivi's resignation from office, German foreign policy became more and more erratic and hasty. There was no clear strategic plan, and the policy was determined by a zig zag course (Ullrich 2000, 32). In particular, the relationship with Great Britain was in decline. Partly because of the rising colonial antagonism between the Kaiserreich and Great Britain, the relationship was more and more characterized by irritability and misunderstandings (Schieder 1977, 277). A first low point was reached in January 1896 when the German Kaiser supported the Boers in South Africa against the British colonial power with his famous Krüger-Telegram:

> I express to you my sincere congratulations that you and your people, without appealing to the help of friendly powers, have succeeded, by your own energetic action against the armed bands which invaded your country as disturbers of the peace, in restoring peace and in maintaining the independence of the country against attack from without. (van der Poel 1951, 135)

At this point, the rising Anglo-German antagonism erupted (Nasson 2010, 52) and two mass hysterias clashed together. The British leadership understood the Krüger-Telegram as an affront to their policy against the German Kaiserreich and to their geopolitical position as the one and only world power. Germany was about to become one of the leading economic powers, and therefore, Great Britain regarded the Krüger-Telegram as an offensive political move to challenge British supremacy (Nasson 2010, 60; Ullrich 2000, 32). From the British perspective, the telegram suggested the support of an unacknowledged statesman and for that reason the British Government formulated a harsh reaction to the Krüger-Telegram, which led to an outbreak of nationalist feeling in Germany because the political voice of the Kaiserreich in the world seemed to be in great danger (Schieder 1977, 278).

But why did the limited Anglo-Boer conflict have such importance for the Kaiserreich? The history of the Anglo-German struggles over South Africa, especially the incidents just before the Krüger-Telegram, could shed light on this. In 1894, the crisis over the Transvaal (northeast of the British Cape Colony) reached its first peak. Great Britain demonstrated its naval superiority over the Kaiserreich by rejecting a German request for access rights to the Delagoa Bay. By doing this, Great Britain limited German trade ambitions in South Africa and taught Germany a lesson about colonial expansion (Canis 1997, 142–143).[4] The German Kaiserreich wanted to use the Transvaal as its own sphere of influence and to put pressure on the British colonial empire to win colonial concessions in other parts of Africa (Canis 1997, 177). But after the British demonstration of sea power, the situation escalated because Great Britain never agreed to the German proposals for negotiations. Marshall, German State Secretary of Foreign Affairs, wrote that Salisbury, British Prime Minister, would create 'To the cost of well known special German interests a purely egoistic policy, which would never been endured by Germany' (N.N. 1896, 10–11).

The German leadership felt highly disrespected and inadequately recognized by the British government and therefore searched for an opportunity to retaliate. The Krüger-Telegram, as a reaction to the illicit Jameson Raid, must therefore be understood as the conclusion of the lesson taught by the Germans (Canis 1997, 180). With his congratulations on the successful defeat of the British troops, Kaiser Wilhelm II openly supported the Boer struggle for independence, and thus he brought the German Kaiserreich into an anti-British position. As I have shown above, the Krüger-Telegram led to a low point in the Anglo-German relationship. The Jameson Raid and its aftermath were the reasons for the upcoming Anglo-Boer war.

## The 'Bundesrath-Affäre' as a case of disrespect

This diplomatic crisis was provoked by civil merchant shipping (Bender 2009, 187). Right after the start of action, maritime control was aggravated through the Royal Navy. Great Britain wanted to hinder the delivery of arms to the Boers and destroy their channels of supply. As a reaction to the early defeats of the British army, the Royal Navy established a naval blockade on the South-African coast because the initial victories of the Boers seemed due to their naval supply channels (Bender 2009, 187).

On 29 December 1899, the Royal Navy seized the German mail boat 'Bundesrath' on its way to the South-African coast. This seizure was made without any explanations. Chancellor Bülow commissioned Ambassador Paul von Hatzfeldt to determine the reasons for the seizure and to demand strongly the surrender of the 'Bundesrath,' otherwise substantial damage would occur (Lepsius, Mendelssohn Barholdy, and Thimme 1924, No. 4412). In the first instance, the British government responded in cooperative manner because they were themselves astonished by the course of action of their Royal Navy in South Africa (Lepsius, Mendelssohn Barholdy, and Thimme 1924, No. 4414). The German government could not accept this – in its eyes – unsatisfactory answer. As I have shown above, there were strong anti-British tendencies in German public opinion. Therefore, Bülow cabled to Hatzfeldt, German neutrality was an enormous political accomplishment. British society had always been hostilely disposed against the Germans, and because of the British actions in the run-up to the Anglo-Boer war, it would be impossible to suddenly demand pro-British society (Lepsius, Mendelssohn Barholdy, and Thimme 1924, No. 4397). As a consequence, German ship owners were heavily annoyed by the British actions, and they worried about detention reapplications of more German ships. If this came to pass, then German ship owners would demand full restitution because of their economic losses (Lepsius, Mendelssohn Barholdy, and Thimme 1924, No. 4413). On 1 January 1900, Bülow stated to Hatzfeldt that the 'Bundesrath' had not transported contraband or any other suspicious supplies, and therefore he hoped for a replacement and argued that the Royal Navy violated international law intentionally to prevent shipping (Lepsius, Mendelssohn Barholdy, and Thimme 1924, No. 4416). One day later, he put his accusations in concrete terms: for him it was highly questionable whether it would be generally possible to seize neutral ships without any suspicion (Lepsius, Mendelssohn Barholdy, and Thimme 1924, No. 4417). As Hatzfeldt answered that the British government again affirmed its intention to solve the question quickly, Bülow instructed Hatzfeldt to hand over an official memorandum. Hatzfeldt should make it clear that the seizure of the 'Bundesrath' was illegal in terms of international law and that the German demands must now be aggressively pursued because of the absence of an explicit and official British statement (Lepsius, Mendelssohn Barholdy, and Thimme 1924, No. 4419). Already in this early stage of the crisis, Bülow felt subjectively disrespected by British official behavior. To him, British behavior seemed tactical and disrespectful, because they did not recognize German demands and rights. The British government stated several times that they were interested in a quick and uncomplicated solution. In fact, they needed to clarify the situation for themselves because they were as surprised as the Germans, but Bülow did not see this point. He wanted to make an example to enhance German status and standing. Of course, the seizure of a neutral mail boat was an infringement, but as German boats were not the only ones seized, there was no need to exploit this incident as a full diplomatic crisis. Bülow wanted to use this second-order conflict for two reasons. First he wanted to demonstrate a strong German position while he insisted on German rights. Second he wanted to use this incident to push the new naval act, which was adopted in March 1898, and to promote the upcoming amendment of the naval act in June 1900 (Jaschob 2012).

In addition to Bülow, Kaiser Wilhelm II also felt disrespected and wanted to affirm German status. Therefore he stated:

> In view of the pronounced unkindness – not to say hostility – by the British which is among other things characterized by seizuring German ships, I take for true to stress *intensively* our *neutrality*. Thus it would be recommended to forbid apriori the export of each item of war material, shells, artillery by Krupp etc. [...] ordered by the British. Then again, Italy must be reminded that it is a power of the 'Dreibund' and therefore it has no competence [!] to help Great Britain through sending mules or even through the occupation of Egypt in order to free the local British garrison which should be sent to the cape." (Wilhelm II 1900, emphasis in original)

This outburst by Wilhelm II was a snapshot. He acted against his own government; they did not want to expand this incident into a full diplomatic crisis (Rosenbach 1993, 232). But just a few days later, the German government swung over to the course of Kaiser Wilhelm II because of the seizure of a second mail boat. Now there was a new level of conflict: with the second seizure and the harsh German reactions, the former legal dispute evolved into a question of prestige.

The second German mail boat was seized on 4 January 1900. In a harsh reaction, Bülow instructed Hatzfeldt to hand over a second memorandum and to demand the immediate release of the two ships; otherwise grave entanglements would be the consequence (Lepsius, Mendelssohn Barholdy, and Thimme 1924, No. 4420). Again the British government assured a quick process and stated that they were annoyed about the situation, but incapable of saying something concrete about the incidents (Lepsius, Mendelssohn Barholdy, and Thimme 1924, No. 4423). Now Bülow was convinced that Salisbury underestimated the situation. To him, it was impossible not to be informed of the reasons for seizuring neutral German mail boats and, because of an imminent meeting of the Reichstag, he could no longer remain silent (Lepsius, Mendelssohn Barholdy, and Thimme 1924, No. 4424). Internally, he argued that the British government did not want to solve the problem quickly because they viewed the Kaiserreich as dependent. In his eyes, this was not the case. The Kaiserreich had acted with great restraint during the Samoan tangle because it was strongly interested in a good relationship. Thus, the British proceeding concerning the neutral German ships would be a 'systemic inconsideration.'

The German government would no longer allow itself to be insulted by the British government without any consequences. Now questions of honor would be questions of life, and therefore important questions of interest would recede into the background if the British government did not deal with the German government in an appropriate manner (Lepsius, Mendelssohn Barholdy, and Thimme 1924, No. 4425). Bülow emphasized an insufficient consideration of German positions, and that therefore Hatzfeldt should insist on the release of the ships and charge that, in terms of international law, the German government had been right. He assumed that the British government wanted to harm German trade and had not wanted to engage with the Boer policy towards neutral civil shipping (Lepsius, Mendelssohn Barholdy, and Thimme 1924, No. 4426).

On 7 January 1900, when the message that a third German mail boat had been seized reached the German government, the situation was on the brink of collapse. Now German interests were seriously damaged, and the systematic approach by the British was clear to the German government. At this point, the Kaiser entered the game. He demanded the immediate appointment of a commission to investigate the incidents (Lepsius, Mendelssohn Barholdy, and Thimme 1924, No. 4427). Bülow seconded him by stating that the Hague Peace Conference had just decided to implement a court of arbitration for solving international problems (Lepsius, Mendelssohn Barholdy, and Thimme 1924, No. 4428). After repeated consultations with the British government, Hatzfeldt reported to the Ministry of Foreign Affairs that Salisbury was still strongly interested in a quick solution. He was not willing to accept the German legal point of view but he accepted the German demands for indemnity. Salisbury pointed out that the 'General' (the mail boat that was seized on 4 January 1900) had already been released and the 'Herzog' (seized on 6 January 1900) would soon follow. Only the 'Bundesrath' had to be brought in front of a prize court because it was likely that this boat had transported contraband (Lepsius, Mendelssohn Barholdy, and Thimme 1924, No. 4430). These statements made Bülow furious. One can see on his remarks to Hatzfeldts telegram that he was frustrated by the still unreleased evidence for contraband on the 'Bundesrath'. He emphatically demanded this evidence and furthermore a quick solution to the incidents.

But just one day later, on 9 January 1900, Bülow calmed down and accepted Salisbury's point of view. He cabled to Hatzfeldt that he now understood the British position, but that obviously the German public opinion was still highly aroused and therefore another delay of the meeting of the Reichstag was becoming more and more difficult. He commissioned Hatzfeldt to point out that Germany demanded an end to the seizures and that the Kaiserreich was still interested in a good Anglo-German relationship (Lepsius, Mendelssohn Barholdy, and Thimme 1924, No. 4431). In his answer, Salisbury welcomed Bülow's attempts to delay the debate in the Reichstag and made it absolutely clear that he would solve the problem as soon as possible and do everything in his power to prevent further incidents. In addition, he was also strongly indignant with the administration in Durban because he had still not received any information about the 'Bundesrath' and possible contraband (Lepsius, Mendelssohn Barholdy, and Thimme 1924, No. 4433). This telegram could be understood as an excuse note. Salisbury gave in to the German position. He wanted to calm down the situation as he was not interested in an international quarrel or a war-like dispute with the Kaiserreich. In the aftermath of Salisbury's apology, Bülow and Salisbury exchanged a few more telegrams in which they told each other how politely and easily the crisis had been solved (Lepsius, Mendelssohn Barholdy, and Thimme 1924, Nos. 4434–4451). Bülow's feeling of disrespect was now as good as blown away. But why did the German government not insist on full compensation and an official apology, which would reestablish German prestige?

After the seizure of the 'Bundesrath,' the German government was truly annoyed by British behavior. But soon they saw the opportunity to use these incidents to further their own interests. The Reichsmarineamt, supported by Wilhelm II, planned to bring a new naval law before the Reichstag. The 'Bundesrath-Affäre' seemed to be a good opportunity to secure the process and demonstrate the necessity of a large German navy to the public (Bender 2009, 195). Tirpitz (State Secretary of the Reichsmarineamt) wanted to use the feelings of disrespect and humiliation to promote his naval policy in the Reichstag as well as in public (Massie 1993, 209). Also, the declaration of neutrality has to be viewed under these conditions. The German government needed a calm foreign situation, and especially a good Anglo-German relationship, to develop their battle fleet without any opposition (Reinermann 2001, 205). In the short run, it seems that the German government exploited the 'Bundesrath-Affäre' for internal political ends, but in the long run, it was used to advance German ambitions for status as a world power. By demonstrating the seeming nonrecognition by the British government, the German government could embark on an enlargement of the German navy. A powerful navy was seen as one of the major features of world power status, and therefore the 'Bundesrath-Affäre' was used as an exploitation of disrespect in order to the desired and demanded position of world power. The 'Bundesrath-Affäre,' then, was gratefully received by the German press (Bender 2009, 189). They sensationalized the incidents into questions of honor and prestige, and as a result, a wave of indignation rolled through German society. The press assumed that Great Britain would undermine German trade interests, that it had its own colonial designs on the harbors, and thus it would not give way to German colonial claims (Bender 2009, 191).

For both sides (the Kaiserreich and Great Britain), the 'Bundesrath-Affäre' was also a question of prestige. Even though the 'Bundesrath-Affäre' was used to promote a new naval act as one expression of the strategic plan to become a world power, it was seen as a question of national prestige because it directly pointed to the residual status mismatch between the German Kaiserreich and Great Britain. The Anglo-German relationship was burdened by these incidents and nearly everyone felt disrespected and wounded in their honor (Fröhlich 1990, 218): 'What was so awkwardly perceived here was not so much our point of view, but rather the abruptness in how it was represented' (Metternich 1924).

Count Metternich, the later German Ambassador in London, pointed out that it was not the crisis itself that was responsible for German feelings of nonrecognition, but the way in which it was handled by the two governments. The question of status evolved not out of the material facts, but arose from the status mismatch and the German feelings of having been treated in a disrespectful manner.

## Conclusion

The decline of the Anglo-German relationship – beginning with the Krüger-Telegram in 1896 – came to one of its low points in the 'Bundesrath-Affäre.' As I have shown above, the German government felt highly disrespected by British behavior at the beginning of the 'Bundesrath-Affäre.' In the aftermath of the crisis, anti-British sentiments were thoroughly established in German public opinion. Also the 'Bundesrath-Affäre' can be understood as a question of prestige. Both sides – the German government as well as the British – declared this limited conflict to be a question of honor, and nobody wanted to give in first. Nevertheless, the crisis ended quickly because the German government needed a good Anglo-German relationship for their naval program, and the British government was not interested in a long and tricky legal dispute because they needed all their power to defeat the Boers. Beside these two possible understandings of the 'Bundesrath-Affäre,' it could also be understood as a case of political exploitation of second-order conflicts to high politics.

Right after the Krüger-Telegram in January 1896, Kaiser Wilhelm II stated that the German Kaiserreich had now reached the position of a world power. The unequivocal British reaction to his support for the Boers brought home to him that it was not so easy to get recognition for his desired status as a world power. He looked jealously on British sea power and supremacy, and therefore he tried to achieve diplomatic power and respect through a powerful naval presence (Clark 2008, 181–182). Germany needed a large battle fleet to cope with this world power status. For Kaiser Wilhelm II, world policy was the corollary of the foundation of the Reich in 1871 (Mommsen 2002, 95). But not until the appointments of Bernhard von Bülow as State Secretary of Foreign Affairs and Alfred von Tirpitz as State Secretary of the Reichsmarineamt in summer 1897 did world policy become a realistic option for German policy. In the mind of Kaiser Wilhelm II, the Krüger-Telegram was quite a good opportunity to launch his strategy for a large German battle fleet (Mommsen 2002, 89), but time was not ripe for an overarching German world policy. First, the ideas of imperialism, nationalism, and socio-Darwinian thinking needed time to penetrate German society (Berghahn 1971). After the first German colonial expansion to China, and the Bülow-speech demanding Germany's place in the sun in 1897, these ideas fell on fertile ground and slowly the idea of Germany as a world power became accepted (Canis 1997, 233–234). The 'Bundesrath-Affäre' was one of the first expressions of this newly conceived plan.

But the German Kaiserreich also depended on a good Anglo-German relationship to establish itself as a world power: according to my theoretical framework, it wanted to be recognized by Great Britain as a relevant and rising power that wanted to become a world power. Therefore, the German government decided to stay neutral in the Anglo-Boer war, but during the 'Bundesrath-Affäre,' this position was on trial. The German government – also driven by an upset, anti-British society – tried to use this diplomatic affair to (re)-establish German prestige. The government and society felt highly disrespected by British actions, and thus they tried to get compensations – symbolically and materially. The government operated within a narrow range between strengthening its own position and worsening the Anglo-German relationship. For two reasons they finally decided to accept the British apology. First, it was obvious that this affair could not be used to achieve substantial colonial gains, and second, the German government wanted to exploit the affair to enlarge the naval program as an indirect means to recognition as a world power.

The 'Bundesrath-Affäre' as one of the early peaks in Anglo-German antagonism shows the dynamics that could be triggered by a status game. The German government, and especially the Kaiser, felt highly disrespected in their demanded status and therefore they overreacted at the beginning of this diplomatic crisis. The second-order question of seizing ships evolved into a general debate on status in the international system of the time. The German Kaiserreich started from the assumption that it had to be respected as a world power and that Great Britain did not accept and respect this assumption. As a result, the limited crisis became an international one, and a question of national honor. The status mismatch between the German Kaiserreich and Great Britain became clearly visible, and in the long term, this status mismatch threatened the entire system.

## Acknowledgement

I would like to thank Reinhard Wolf, Sven-Eric Fikenscher, Carsten Rauch and Jack Hymans for their helpful comments on an earlier version of this article.

## Funding

This work was supported by the German Research Foundation (DFG) [WO 797/8-1].

## Notes

1. As a consequence of the first Anglo-Boer war (1880–1881), the British Government retreated finally from the Transvaal in 1881 (Steele 2000, 6). The conditions of suzerainty were fixed in the Pretoria Convention from 1881 and were supplemented by the London Convention from 1884. Great Britain exerted control over Boer relations with foreign powers, frontier zones, and the issue of African rights (Nasson 2010, 43). Both Conventions were highly unclear and inconsistent and gave room for speculations and conflicts.
2. As a demonstration of the newly gained Boer wealth, Transvaal established diplomatic relations with the German Kaiserreich (Nasson 2010, 49). German politicians and the German public were strongly convinced of great economic expectations in the Transvaal region, and therefore their interest in the fate of the Boer republic was aroused (Canis 1997, 177). The German government linked German support for the Boers to extended economic concessions for German economy and trade (Pfeil 1895). The Kaiserreich was intensely interested in an independent Boer republic because this would secure German economic interests and could be used as leverage for German diplomatic and territorial interests against Great Britain (Canis 1997, 177). Since 1886, economic and especially trade relations between the German Kaiserreich and the Transvaal increased significantly. The Kaiserreich acted as a political and economic adviser and in return German enterprises were privileged in the Transvaal (Kröger 2001, 27).
3. Being part of the negotiations and the establishment of a British–German contract were seen by the German Government as first steps in the right direction. Substantially, the Angola treaty was not this outstanding as it seems to be; only future options on the Portuguese Colonies were made. But for Great Britain, this treaty was very valuable: it did not need to make clear concessions, German expansionist efforts were distracted from British colonial territory, and Great Britain got a promise of German nonintervention in a future war over South Africa (Mommsen 2001, 4–5).
4. In spite of the fact that the German Kaiserreich had no clear access rights to the Delagoa Bay, it tried to secure its sphere of influence in an indirect manner. In 1884–1895, the Delagoa Railway was finished: it was built with German capital and against British pressure (Canis 1997, 166; Nasson 2010, 49). For Great Britain, this was a clear sign of German support for the Boers, and the congratulatory telegram send by the German Kaiser was understood as a prelude to an aggressive, anti-British German policy.

## References

Bender, S. 2009. *Der Burenkrieg und die Deutschsprachige Presse. Wahrnehmung und Deutung zwischen Bureneuphorie und Anglophobie 1899–1902*. Paderborn [u.a.]: Schöningh.

Berghahn, V. R. 1971. *Der Tirpitz-Plan. Genesis und Verfall einer Innenpolitischen Krisenstrategie unter Wilhelm II*. Düsseldorf: Droste.

Brechtken, M. 2006. *Scharnierzeit 1895–1907. Persönlichkeitsnetze und Internationale Politik in den deutsch-britisch-amerikanischen Beziehungen vor dem Ersten Weltkrieg*. Mainz: von Zabern.

Canis, K. 1997. *Von Bismarck zur Weltpolitik. Deutsche Aussenpolitik 1890 bis 1902* (*Studien zur internationalen Geschichte, Bd. 3*). Berlin: Akademie-Verl.

Clark, C. M. 2008. *Wilhelm II. Die Herrschaft des letzten deutschen Kaisers*. München: Deutsche Verl.-Anst.

Fikenscher, S.-E., L. Jaschob, and R. Wolf. 2012. "Seeking Status Recognition through Military Symbols: German and Indian Armament Policies between Strategic Rationalizations and Prestige Motives." Paper prepared for the workshop "The Problem of Recognition in Global Politics", Frankfurt am Main, Juni 21–22.

Fremont-Barnes, G. 2003. *The Boer War 1899–1902 (Essential Histories, Band 52)*. Oxford: Osprey.

Fröhlich, M. 1990. *Von Konfrontation zur Koexistenz. Die deutsch-englischen Kolonialbeziehungen in Afrika zwischen 1884 und 1914*. Bochum: Brockmeyer.

Geppert, D. 2007. *Pressekriege. Öffentlichkeit und Diplomatie in den deutsch-britischen Beziehungen (1896–1912)*. München: Oldenbourg.

Henshaw, P. 2001. "The Origins of the Boer War. The Periphery, the Centre and the 'Man on the Spot'." In *The International Impact of the Boer War*, edited by K. M. Wilson, 8–24. New York: Acumen.

Hewitson, M. 2004. *Germany and the Causes of the First World War*. Oxford, New York: Berg.

Honneth, A. 1996. *The Struggle for Recognition. The Moral Grammar of Social Conflicts (Studies in Contemporary German Social Thought)*. Cambridge, MA: MIT Press.

Jaschob, L. 2012. "Ursachen und Auswirkungen von Respekt und Missachtung auf das Politische Geschehen. Die deutsch-britischen Beziehungen zur Kaiserzeit." *Representation and Contexts* 1: 1–23. http://www.wissens-werk.de/index.php/rac/article/viewFile/98/90; 25.4.2012.

Kröger, M. 2001. "Imperial Germany and the Boer War. From Colonial Fantasies to the Reality of Anglo-German Estrangement." In *The International Impact of the Boer War*, edited by K. M. Wilson, 25–42. New York: Acumen.

Larson, D. W., and A. Shevchenko. 2010. "Status Seekers: Chinese and Russian Responses to U.S. Primacy." *International Security* 34 (4): 63–95.

Lepsius, J., A. Mendelssohn Bartholdy, and F. Thimme, Hrsg. 1924. *Die Grosse Politik der europäischen Kabinette 1871–1914. 15. Band: Rings um die Erste Haager Friedenskonferenz*. Berlin: Deutsche Verlagsgesellschaft für Politik und Geschichte m.b.H.

Massie, R. K. 1993. *Die Schalen des Zorns. Grossbritannien, Deutschland und das Heraufziehen des Ersten Weltkrieges*. Frankfurt am Main: S. Fischer.

Metternich, P. G. V. 1924. "Metternich an Hohenlohe, 24.02.1900." In *Die Grosse Politik der europäischen Kabinette 1871–1914. 15. Band: Rings um die Erste Haager Friedenskonferenz*, Hrsg. J. Lepsius, A. Mendelssohn Bartholdy, and F. Thimme, 4458. Berlin: Deutsche Verlagsgesellschaft für Politik und Geschichte m.b.H.

Mommsen, W. J. 2001. "Introduction." In *The International Impact of the Boer War*, edited by K. M. Wilson, 1–7. New York: Acumen.

Mommsen, W. J. 2002. *War der Kaiser an allem schuld? Wilhelm II. und die Preussisch-deutschen Machteliten*. Berlin: Propyläen-Verl.

Morgenthau, H. J. 1954. *Politics among Nations. The Struggle for Power and Peace*. New York: Knopf.

Nasson, B. 2010. *The War for South Africa. The Anglo-Boer War 1899–1902*. Cape Town: Tafelberg.

N.N. (4.01.1896): Bericht aus Berlin, 4.01.1896, in: MdÄ, PA III, Nr. 147, 10 ff.

Paul, T. V., and B. R. Nayar. 2003. *India in the World Order. Searching for a Major-Power Status*. Cambridge: Cambridge University Press.

Pfeil, J. V. (13.11.1895): Pfeil an Hohenlohe 13.11.1895, in: PA Bonn, Afrika Gen. Nr. 13, Bd. 1, Bl. 40ff.

Reinermann, L. 2001. *Der Kaiser in England. Wilhelm II. und sein Bild in der britischen Öffentlichkeit*. Paderborn: Schöningh.

Rosenbach, H. 1993. *Das deutsche Reich, Grossbritannien und der Transvaal (1896–1902). Anfänge deutsch-britischer Entfremdung*. Göttingen: Vandenhoek & Ruprecht.

Schieder, T. 1977. *Staatensystem als Vormacht der Welt. 1848–1918*. Frankfurt am Main: Propyläen-Verl.

Steele, D. 2000. "Salisbury and the Soldiers." In *The Boer War. Direction, Experience and Image*, edited by J. Gooch, 3–20. London, Portland, OR: Cass.

Tajfel, H., and J. C. Turner. 1979. "An Integrative Theory of Intergroup Conflict." In *The Social Psychology of Intergroup Relations*, edited by W. G. Austin and S. Worchel, 33–47. Monterey, CA: Brooks/Cole.

Ullrich, V. 2000. "Zukunft durch Expansion? Die Wilhelminische Weltpolitik." In *Otto von Bismarck und Wilhelm II. Repräsentanten eines Epochenwechsels?*, Hrsg. L. Gall, 27–39. Paderborn: Schöningh.

van der Poel, J. 1951. *The Jameson Raid*. Oxford: Oxford University Press.

Weber, M., and J. Winckelmann. 1980. *Wirtschaft und Gesellschaft. Grundriss der verstehenden Soziologie*. Tübingen: Mohr.

Wilhelm II. (2.01.1900), in: PA, R 14723, Berlin.

Wohlforth, W. C. 2009. "Unipolarity, Status Competition, and Great Power War." *World Politics* 61 (01): 28–57. doi:10.1017/S0043887109000021.

Wolf, R. 2008. "Respekt. Ein Unterschätzter Faktor in den Internationalen Beziehungen." *Zeitschrift Für Internationale Beziehungen* 15 (1): 5–42. doi:10.5771/0946-7165-2008-1-5.

Wolf, R. 2011. "Respect and Disrespect in International Politics: The Significance of Status Recognition." *International Theory* 3 (01): 105–142. doi:10.1017/S1752971910000308.

Wolf, R. 2012. "Prickly States? Recognition and Disrespect between Persons and Peoples." In *The International Politics of Recognition*, edited by T. Lindemann and E. Ringmar, 39–56. Boulder, CO: Paradigm.

# REPLY

# (Dis-)respect and (non-)recognition in world politics: the Anglo-Boer War and German policy at the turn of the nineteenth/twentieth century: a reply to Lena Jaschob

Bill Nasson

*Department of History, University of Stellenbosch, Stellenbosch, South Africa*

This is a reply to:

Jaschob, L. 2014. "(Dis-)respect and (non-)recognition in World Politics: The Anglo-Boer War and German Policy at the Turn of the Nineteenth/twentieth Century." *Global Discourse*. 4 (4): 499–512. http://dx.doi.org/10.1080/23269995.2014.917028

Germany's relationship with empire overseas was fairly complex in terms of the wider history of colonial projects, not least on account of continuing historical arguments over the issue of whether predatory German imperialism was a significant contributory cause of the First World War. In that formulation, Otto von Bismarck's uncertain acquiescence in the establishing of a small fistful of German colonies overseas towards the end of the nineteenth century and Bernhard von Bulow's championing of a robust *Weltpolitik* are often cited as the dangerous fuses that lit a crackling road towards global conflagration. In that titanic clash with other older European empires, Germany's greatest rival was, inevitably, Britain. In seeking to construct a navy and to assert a maritime power to reflect its rising colonial aspirations, Berlin could not avoid locking horns with the imperial metropole that it most yearned to emulate and ideally to eclipse – London (Jones, 2014; Mulligan 2010).

As this article (Jaschob 2014) illustrates, Southern Africa was one flashpoint in a gathering crisis over mutually respectful recognition and common regard between contending Anglo-German seaborne interests. Drawing primarily on a rich range of German sources and following a minor maze of diplomatic twists and turns, it seeks to provide a theoretical and contextual explanation of a version of a gunboat episode, only this time a show not between empire and subject but between empire and empire. With the scene set by touchy Anglo-German interaction during the Anglo-Boer War of 1899–1902, we are treated to a probing examination of a prickly diplomatic furore between the German *Kaiserreich* and imperial Britain at the turn of the century. This was provoked by the seizure by the Royal Navy, which was blockading the South African coast to choke off supplies to the Boer republicans, of several neutral German mailships.

In itself, it amounted to a few acts of high-handed opportunism by 'men on the spot' (or, to be more exact, 'men on the sea'). Higher up and caught with their pants down, in a sense, both sides sought to extract themselves from a collision that was poisonous to the Anglo-German relationship. What was critical was not to lose face while doing so. As the study concludes, interestingly, this shipping dispute was not *allowed* to become the tipping point of some larger and more decisive international crisis of high politics. Wanting to be left to get on with its naval expansion programme, the German government had no wish to see an offshore crisis in South Africa run out of control, whipping up the waters of Anglo-German relations that it wished to keep calm. Britain, for its part, wanted to avoid being distracted from its major preoccupation in 1900, the crushing of an independent Boer republicanism.

With the matter of honour key to the equation, both great powers stepped back, with an indignant Germany demanding an end to violations of its merchant shipping freedoms, and Britain undertaking to avoid future inflammatory incidents. As the author notes, the British prime minister, Lord Salisbury, had no wish to pursue an international quarrel or to see his country sucked into a war-like dispute with the aggrieved Germans. So, exchanges of polite telegrams resolved a diplomatic crisis that had looked to be close to boiling over.

But, at an underlying level, expressions of even-tempered statesmanship did little more than to paper over a widening crack. For below it left a simmering entanglement of subjective attitudes and positions between mutually wary parties which came to infect Anglo-German relationships in crucial ways – one being the role of the crisis caused by the seizure of ships in implanting anti-British feeling more deeply in German public opinion. Ultimately, an accidental big fuss over small ships and the despatch of a few cheeky or impetuous diplomatic messages fuelled a far more momentous process of nervously evolving imperial power. With Germany not being accorded the respect it considered to have been its due as a global power, an essentially limited behavioural crisis turned into a pressing question of national honour.

Left unsettled, the issue of an Anglo-German mismatch in status would, in turn, pose a grave strategic threat to the global system of Great Power ordering.

Conceptually and creatively, what became the contentious 'Bundesrath' affray in the unfolding status competition between Berlin and London provides a telling historical vignette, a pinhead of antagonism upon which weighty international power issues of respect, honour, face and saving face came to turn.

The point about status – which runs through the arguments here like a golden thread – is well made. Status only acquires meaning through its being acknowledged and respected by others in the international system, and the securing of status recognition is not synonymous with the acquisition of material capacities. In other words, it is relational rather than something that can be gained unilaterally. Yet this is something which should perhaps not be pressed too far in the instance of Anglo-German tensions around Southern Africa in the 1890s. There were also real unilateral material considerations, hinted at here with reference to German press assumptions that Britain was out to undermine German trade interests and to exclude its commerce from port facilities. If anything, it may have been more the case of it being the other way around.

After all, Britain considered itself to have been top dog in its Southern African sphere of influence. It was Germany which looked to be sniffing in hungrily, eyes on the richest prize in the region, the gold-rich *Zuid-Afrikaansche Republiek* or Transvaal. As the Boer republicans looked towards slipping the leash of Britain, it was not insignificant that the formation by Paul Kruger in 1894 of an independent ZAR National Bank was aided by the eager deposit of German capital. Three years later, there was further British disquiet over German business development of Portuguese East African Delagoa Bay, aimed at elbowing into a humming Boer republican market at British imperial expense.

London's further worry over 'continental' technicians, managers and businessmen in the Transvaal economy spelled, for the most part, a worry over Germany. One should not, then, lose sight of the remorseless convergence of political, strategic and *economic* imperatives in this decisive moment. Bulow's famous 1897 demand for Germany to have its place in the sun could have extended to a spot in an increasingly 'cosmopolitan' republican Transvaal (Nasson 1999, 39; Trapido, 2011, 93). For Britain, having to swallow a nationalist Boer state was bad enough. Having a *Mittelboer* ally of Germany's African expansion may have been no less indigestible. The peremptory seizure of those German mail-boats in December 1899 and January 1900 may have had as much to do with an overriding assertion of place as with any international upholding of face.

**References**

Jaschob, L. 2014. "(Dis-)Respect and (Non-)Recognition in World Politics: The Anglo-Boer War and German Policy at the Turn of the Nineteenth/Twentieth Century." *Global Discourse* 4 (4): 499–512. http://dx.doi.org/10.1080/23269995.2014.917032.
Jones, H. 2014. "The German Empire." In *Empires at War, 1911–1923*, edited by R. Gerwarth and E. Manela. Oxford: Oxford University Press.
Mulligan, W. 2010. *The Origins of the First World War*. Cambridge: Cambridge University Press.
Nasson, B. 1999. *The South African War, 1899–1902*. London: Arnold.
Trapido, S. 2011. "Imperialism, Settler Identities and Colonial Capitalism: The Hundred Year Origins of the 1899 South African War." In *The Cambridge History of South Africa*, Vol. 2, edited by R. Ross, A. K. Mager, and B. Nasson. Cambridge: Cambridge University Press.

# Killing without hatred: the politics of (non)-recognition in contemporary Western wars

Mathias Delori

*Sciences Po Bordeaux, Centre Emile Durkheim, Bordeaux, France*

> As pointed out by military historian Joanna Bourke, 'the characteristic act of men at war is not dying, it is killing'. This simple observation has led to some important literature on how soldiers relate to the suffering and deaths they cause. This literature has shown that military consent for killing does not have its origins in a pre-discursive biological nature. Rather, it is mediated by powerful meaning structures – such as nationalist narratives or demonized representations of the enemy – that state which lives should be recognized as livable, and which lives should remain excluded from this economy of compassion. This article investigates how military consent for killing is constructed in the context of contemporary Western wars. It does so by focusing on a particular case study: those French soldiers who participated in the war in Libya in 2011. The analysis – based on 40 semi-structured interviews with military leaders and fighter aircraft pilots – reveals a framing of war where enemies are neither framed as an object of hatred nor of ritual sacrifice nor as anything else. They are 'ungrievable lives' as expressed by Judith Butler: 'they are, ontologically, and from the start, already lost and destroyed, which means that when they are destroyed in war, nothing is destroyed'. The article reviews the ideas and materialities that lead to this spectacular case of misrecognition.

## Introduction

Killing other people is not a trivial activity. It is forbidden by most moral and legal codes, and it is something most people do not do in their everyday life. Yet this general observation admits of one notable exception – soldiers – whose job or duty implies that they may infringe this moral command (Bourke 1999). Consequently, a literature has emerged that tries to understand how consent for killing is constructed. This literature has showed that it does not have its origins – contrary to what Freud assumed (Freud and Einstein 1932) – in a biological, trans-historical or pre-discursive 'human nature'. Rather, it is a social construct whose content has to be studied historically. This article addresses the question of the social construction of the military's consent for killing in the context of contemporary humanitarian and technological wars, i.e., those wars which do not rely explicitly on the 'logic of self-defense' (Kaufman 2009). It is based on a sociological enquiry focusing on those French aircraft pilots who waged the war in Libya in 2011. The article tries to understand how they make sense of the act of killing, how they relate to the suffering they cause, and what this tells us about how war is waged in concrete terms.

The literature on this issue appears strongly divided. On the one hand, mainstream scholars argue that the trend is towards greater respect for the enemy and greater control of violence. They point out, to begin with, that the biological racism, which contributed to shaping the 'culture of violence' (Audouin-Rouzeau 2002; Mosse 2000) of the two World Wars, has disappeared or, at least, receded. Besides, they argue that *jus in bello* – the law which regulates the conduct of war – has become more constraining in the context of 'humanitarian' wars, and that Western military organizations spend heavily in order to equip their personnel with precision weapons.

On the other hand, critical war studies have deconstructed this optimistic interpretation. In the first place, post-colonial studies have provided ample evidence of the discursive continuity between colonial wars and present-day ones. They have shown, in particular, that the 'cultural racism' (Hobson 2007) which gave meaning to colonization – the 'civilized/non-civilized' dichotomy – plays a central role in present-day Western wars. Parallel to this, other critical authors have argued that one does not need to frame the enemy as biologically or culturally inferior in order to feel able to kill him (Mariot 2003/2004). Dehumanization is sufficient and it is perfectly achieved – so the argument goes – by modern technologies of war, which construct a 'reified' (Honneth 2007) representation of the enemy.

In this politically- and normatively charged context, it seems advantageous to adopt an empirical approach. I will do so by focusing on one particular case: the war waged by NATO forces in Libya in 2011. This case is interesting because it displays two dynamics which are central to the contemporary Western way of war: the framing of war as humanitarian on the one hand and the use of new technologies on the other. As regards the first dynamic, NATO forces officially intervened in order to check the massacre of civilian populations, which President Gadhafi was said to be committing. To do so, the NATO made extensive use of guided missiles, drones, and high-tech fighter jets. This use of new technologies had the result that NATO forces could kill without exposing themselves to their enemy's retaliation. Indeed, while the number of people killed by NATO remains unknown (as we shall see in the fourth section of this article), we know that not a single Western soldier died during this seven-month military operation.[1]

The argument put forward in this article owes a great deal to the aforementioned critical approach to war and, more precisely, to Judith Butler's comments concerning the 'ungrievability' of certain lives (Butler 2004, 2009, 2010). My point is that the two modern dynamics – the framing of war as humanitarian and the use of new technologies – help to construct a framing of war that completely erases the face of the enemy, whatever adjective one wants to put before the word 'face' (humane, animalized, totemic, etc.). My research has found, more precisely, that the victims of violence by a Western state are not framed as an object of hatred, or of ritual sacrifice, or of military strategy, or as anything else. They are 'ungrievable lives' in the sense that 'they cannot be lost, and cannot be destroyed, because they already inhabit a lost and destroyed zone; they are, ontologically, and from the start, already lost and destroyed, which means that when they are destroyed in war, nothing is destroyed' (Butler 2010, xix). This article reviews the ideas (discourses, images, narratives, etc.) and materialities (procedures, routinized actions, etc.) that shape this spectacular case of misrecognition.

The article proceeds as follows. First, I will introduce the literature on contemporary Western wars, in particular liberal and critical studies. In the second section, I present my empirical framework. This is based on two primary sources: an ethnographic study of three French Air Force bases and 40 semi-structured interviews with French soldiers who took part in the war in Libya. I elaborate on my theoretical framework and argument in the third and fourth sections.

## Review of the literature: liberal and critical approaches to contemporary Western wars

All students of war agree with the notion that Western warfare has gone through important changes since the end of the Cold War. The most obvious developments are the rise of new discourses on war (such as the discourses on the 'war on terror' and 'humanitarian war'), the professionalization of military organizations, and the use of new technologies that facilitate killing from a distance. Unsurprisingly, specialists in the field disagree when assessing how these trends affect the social construction of consent for killing and the manner of waging war. In the following paragraphs, I will review the two opposite perspectives on this issue: the liberal and the critical.

To begin with, several authors have developed a sympathetic view of present-day Western wars. They have argued that the trend is towards a more human representation of the enemy, and therefore a greater control of violence. They have put forward several arguments in order to fuel this interpretation. Most of these arguments are inspired by the liberal theory of international relations (Battistella 2008).

These authors point out, firstly, that racist depictions of the enemy do not enjoy the centrality they used to have (Audouin-Rouzeau 2008). Admittedly, those politicians willing to sell their war to the public opinion still represent the Other in a negative way. Think, for instance, of the representation of the Taliban put forward by the Bush administration before invading Afghanistan in 2001–2002 (Holland 2011) or, more generally, about the frightening and Orientalist (Said 1979) image of the 'Islamic terrorist' mobilized in the so-called 'war on terror'. Yet this kind of discourse is said to have little influence on soldiers themselves, and therefore on the practice of war. According to Le Corvisier, the reason for this lies in the fact that modern Western military organizations have learned throughout history that war is better waged 'when soldiers kill without passion, in order to win' (Corvisier 1975, 5). Since then, so the argument goes, they have spent much energy on teaching norms and values that prescribe respect for the enemy. Although this trend is scarcely a new one, it is said to have become more important with the professionalization of military organizations.

Secondly, proponents of this approach argue that *jus in bello* – the law which regulates the conduct of war – has become more effective since the end of the Cold War. Thus, Vennesson has made the point that international law has become a key component of Western military cultures and military doctrines (Vennesson et al. 2008). When this is not the case, public opinion in Western countries is said to have developed such a degree of sensitivity about the human consequences of Western state violence that military organizations are obliged to take this normative development into account (Hurrel 2002). The institutionalization of such 'international regimes' has been documented in fields as different as landmines and chemical weapons (Price 1998; Finnemore 1999).

Finally, these authors point out that the actual nature of warfare reinforces this dynamic. They argue that 'rules of engagement' regulate the use of force, thus, rendering completely outdated the prospect of 'total war' (Colonomos 2008). Besides, they observe that Western military organizations spend a lot of money on equipping their personnel with precision weapons such as GPS and laser-guided bombs. Hence, the argument states that the actual instruments of war make it possible to meet the dictates of contemporary moral norms and strategy, namely greater respect for the enemy and greater control over violence (Pinker 2011; Vennesson et al. 2008). All these developments are said to materialize in a 'fact': a decrease in the overall number of people killed during warfare.[2]

Unsurprisingly, this optimistic view has been challenged by scholars who take a more critical and reflective perspective (Brincat, Lima, and Nunes 2012; Aradau 2012; Roach

2007; Edkins and Nick 2009). Critical war and security studies do not constitute a perfectly unified paradigm. They cover research fields as different as gender studies (Enloe 2004; Blanchard 2003; Tickner and Sjoberg 2011), post-colonial studies (Amos and Parmar 2005; hooks 1995), post-structuralist approaches (Edkins 1999), etc. In spite of these differences, the proponents of these approaches share a common distrust vis-à-vis the liberals' positivist claims to produce value-free scholarship (Tickner 2005). They argue that the proponents of the liberal approach to IR condemn themselves to a certain short-sightedness when they choose to study an object – the violence of liberal states – by using 'liberal' categories of analysis. Instead, they take political liberalism as an object of investigation and try to understand how it generates its own violence (Geis and Brock 2006).

As often happens, the most frontal critique of the liberal approach has been put forward by postcolonial theorists. They have pointed out that the discourse on 'humanitarian war' is scarcely new. It has its roots in the West's neo-colonial self-representation as a 'humanity's soldier' (Chuter 1996), and the narrative of the 'civilizing mission' (Hobson 2007, 105). In some cases, such as the US war in Afghanistan of 2001–2002, the discursive continuity with colonial wars materialized in a number of precise meaning structures and symbols. Thus, Ayotte and Husain have conducted a study of the discourse, which preceded the US war in Afghanistan in 2001–2002. They found that this discourse relied on Orientalist images and narratives – like that which frame Afghan women as 'gendered slaves in need of "saving" by the West' (Ayotte and Husain 2005, 113) – which exactly echo the British and French colonial discourses of the nineteenth century.

Given the numerous discursive continuities between those wars and contemporary Western warfare, it is tempting to hypothesize that this colonial way of war – the mix of cruelty and paternalism described by Fanon (2002 [1961]) – has not completely vanished. Several empirical elements support this interpretation. For instance, current Western counter-insurgency doctrines explicitly draw upon precedents and action principles that originated in colonial wars (Olsson 2008). Besides, the disproportion between the number of victims on each side of contemporary Western wars – an approximate ratio of 1/50 according to Chaliand – recalls those colonial wars when the technological superiority of Western armies led to a complete asymmetry in the exposure of combatants to the risk of death or injury (Chaliand 2008, 62). Finally, the rare independent testimonies on actual Western warfare suggest that the 'cruelty' (Asad 2007, 94) which drove colonial wars is not over. Taking the examples of the Western and Israeli wars in Afghanistan, Iraq, Gaza and Lebanon, Asad points out that 'Western states (including Israel) have massacred thousands of civilians and imprisoned large numbers without trial; they have abducted, tortured, and assassinated people they claim are militants and laid waste to entire countries' (Asad 2007, 93).

The main argument put forward by proponents of this post-colonial reading of Western wars is that this culture of violence is neither a throwback to some pre-modern or pre-liberal time, nor a response to violence coming from outside (as liberals suggest). Rather, it 'is integral to liberalism as a political formation' (Asad 2007, 3). The reason for this lies, firstly, in the 'cultural racism' (Hobson 2007) which the 'civilized/non-civilized' and the 'liberal/non-liberal' dichotomies carry. As Butler puts it, this claim to wage war on behalf of humanity 'reveals its own barbarism (...) as it "justifies" its own violence by presuming the barbaric sub-humanity of the other against whom that violence is waged' (Butler 2010). According to Asad, this logic is central to the social construction of present-day consent for killing: 'the right to kill is the right to behave in violent ways toward other people – especially toward citizens of foreign states at war and toward the uncivilized, whose very existence is a threat to civilized order' (Asad 2007, 59).

Parallel to this, other critical scholars have put forward another argument concerning the misrecognition (Honneth 2007) that accompanies the use of violence in warfare today. This 'critical sociological approach' puts greater emphasis on the discourses and technologies associated with modernity (Mavelli 2013; Pin-Fat 2013; Seth 2013). Besides, it points out that the cultural racism accurately described by postcolonial approaches is not the only motor of the present-day consent for killing. In some cases, modern subjects kill without hatred, simply because they fail to represent and 'recognize' Alter as an Alter-Ego (Honneth 2005; Lebow 2008; Lindemann 2010).

This logic of misrecognition emerges, in particular, from the rationalization of the conduct of war, and the reifying dynamics that this process generates. The notion of 'rationalization' is understood, here, in the most classical (Weberian) sense of the term. It refers to a century-old process which includes the bureaucratization of military organizations (Bartov 1998; Arendt 1963), the development of strategy (Wasinski 2010), and the rise of technically complex instruments of war such as artillery, aviation, and more recently, computers. Critical sociologists of war argue that these *dispositifs* (in Foucault's term) introduce a greater physical and mental distance between combatants, and therefore annihilate the positive emotions (compassion, pity or sympathy, etc.) engendered by the recognition of the Other as an Alter-ego (Arendt 1963). Consequently, they erase the moral and human dimensions of war, as the world saw during the first half of the European twentieth century.

This critical approach is interesting for the subject under investigation here because the rationalization of war seems to have reached a new threshold in the context of contemporary Western wars. Indeed, the new technologies of war – drones, computers, etc. – add another series of 'layers' (Latour and Venn 2002, 251) to this process of dehumanization. By doing so, these new technologies construct a framing of war that further euphemizes violence and creates a reified image of the enemy. They do so by increasing the distance between combatants (Dubey and Moricot 2008), erasing the border between reality and fiction (Der Derian 2009; Herman and Peterson 2012), and shaping – in the case of drone operators – a 'play-station' mentality (Chamayou 2013, 153).

As we can see, the literature on modern warfare does not offer any clear answer to the questions raised in the introduction: how do soldiers make sense of the act of killing? How do they relate to the suffering they cause? And what does this tell us about how war is actually waged? While mainstream scholarship argues that a 'civilizing process' is at stake which leads to a greater control of violence,[3] this view has been strongly criticized by those authors who take a more critical and reflective approach. On the one hand, students of post-coloniality have made the point that liberal discourse carries a 'cultural racism', which materializes in a neo-colonial manner of waging war. On the other hand, critical sociologists have argued that this logic is not central to the modern economy of violence. The latter owes more to those modern institutions – in particular new technologies – which contribute towards shaping a reified image of the enemy. In this highly contested area, empirical research may offer some insights.

## Empirical framework: a sociological enquiry focusing on those French pilots who waged the war in Libya in 2011

As stated in the introduction, this article makes use of a sociological study in order to investigate how soldiers make sense of the act of killing. The study focuses on the NATO war of 2011 in Libya and, more precisely, on those French aircraft pilots who actually dropped bombs. In the following paragraphs, I explain why I chose this particular case study and how I conducted the enquiry.

The French and NATO war in Libya in 2011 is an ideal case study to explore the act of killing in present-day warfare because it illustrates two important dimensions of contemporary Western wars, their framing as 'humanitarian' and the use of new technologies which introduce a greater distance between Western soldiers and the people they kill. As regards the first dynamic, NATO forces officially intervened in order to 'preserve humanity from a greater evil' (Weizman 2012). In fact, the decision to intervene was taken at the beginning of the Libyan civil war when Western media and governments reported that the army of President Gadhafi was about to commit massacres against the population of Benghazi.[4]

Several commentators have rightly pointed out that the NATO forces went well beyond this mandate, suggesting that hidden motives lay behind this humanitarian rhetoric.[5] At the level of public discourse, however, the war remained framed as 'humanitarian' until the death of Muammar Gadhafi. In contrast to the wars in Afghanistan or Iraq, the other discourse justifying post-1990 Western wars – the 'war on terror' – did not play much of a role. Even when they emphasized Gadhafi's historical link with 'international terrorism', Western mainstream media insisted on the idea that Gadhafi and his regime were oppressive to their own people. They did so by relying on some well-known Orientalist narratives, such as the story of 'white men saving brown women from brown men' (Ayotte and Husain 2005; Spivak 1988). Typical in this regard is the *New York Times*' long report on how some members of the Gadaffi forces abducted and raped a woman named Eman al-Obeidy in March 2011.[6]

As regards the second dynamic (new technologies), this military intervention took the form of a massive air campaign against the Libyan loyalist army. NATO forces made an extensive use of those new technologies that allow killing from distance, in particular drones and high-tech fighter jets using guided munitions. It is important to highlight, in this respect, that the job of the modern fighter jet pilots in Libya is not very different from that of a drone operator. Admittedly, piloting a fighter jet is more dangerous than manipulating a joystick from a distance. However, the 'rules of engagement' adopted by NATO and France obliged the pilots to fly above the range of Gadhafi's anti-air missiles and drop bombs from this altitude. This particular means of waging war resulted in one simple fact: while the number of people killed by NATO remains unknown (as we shall see in the fourth section), we know that not one single Western soldier died during this eight-month military operation.[7]

Finally, the focus on France is justified by the fact that this country played an important role in both the decision to go to war and its conduct. Indeed, French President Nicolas Sarkozy played an important role in persuading the members of the UN Security Council to pass Resolution 1973, which authorized the NATO to use force in order to create a no-fly zone above the Libyan territory. As regards the conduct of war, the French forces claim to have been responsible for 30% of the strikes carried out by the NATO coalition.[8]

My empirical research focuses on those who concretely wage war (Sylvester 2012). It is based on two sets of primary sources. First, I conducted interviews with those soldiers who dropped bombs (and thus probably caused deaths), namely fighter aircraft pilots (23 interviews), fighter aircraft navigators (10), and members of the special forces (3). The importance given to fighter aircraft pilots and navigators reflects the reality of the French military intervention in Libya. Indeed, France does not have any armed drones. Therefore, most French strikes were carried out by fighter aircraft pilots drawn from the Air Force and the Navy.[9]

The second part of the empirical enquiry aimed at understanding the conduct of war in its most concrete aspects. Indeed, a key assumption of this study is that the soldiers' frames of interpretation do not float in the air. They are mediated by instruments, procedures, routinized practices, and *dispositifs* (van Veeren 2014; Holmqvist 2013). In order to grasp this dimension of war, I conducted three interviews with members of the French military command. In addition, I conducted a two-week ethnographic enquiry at French Air Force bases in Nancy, Montauban, and Paris.

Both the ethnographic study and the interviews were conducted between December 2012 and March 2013, i.e., about 18 months after the war.

## Theoretical approach: identifying the 'frames' (J. Butler) which mediate the actual conduct of war

It is a commonplace to state that any sociological research is the product of an interaction between two practices: the practice of collecting data, and the practice of building hypotheses. The exact nature of this interaction has led to some important epistemological debates. On the one hand, some scholars have advocated an inductive approach, which consists of moving from observations to broader generalizations (James 1981). On the other hand, other scholars have proposed the opposite, i.e., devising clear hypotheses before putting them to the test (Popper and Miller 1983). In this article, I rely on a reflective or critical epistemology which rejects both options and assumes, following Adorno and others, that research takes the form of an 'experiment' (Adorno 1969, 132), where theorization and observation 'interpenetrate each other' (Adorno 1969, 131). In this particular research, the 'experiment' took the form of a resonance and 'interpenetration' between the aforementioned empirical observations and Judith Butler's critical theory of 'frames of war' (Butler 2004, 2009, 2010).

Butler devised the concept of 'frame of war' in order to account for those meaning structures which mediate the moral and emotional relation towards violence. As noted by Zehfuss and MacLeish, Butler has not studied how these frames of interpretation take form at the level of the military (Zehfuss 2009; Macleish 2013). Her book *Frames of War* gathers together several essays on the social construction of compassion in contemporary discourse. Butler tries to understand why modern subjects tend to feel concerned by the suffering and deaths of some people (including that of people who do not belong to their community), while remaining completely indifferent to the suffering and deaths of others (Butler 2004). The cases she studied – media reaction to the 9/11 attacks, the US policy of humiliating prisoners in Guantanamo, the treatment of Muslim immigrants in Europe, etc. – are to some extent remote from my argument. Indeed, this article deals with a particular kind of warfare – humanitarian and technological wars such as that waged by NATO in Libya – and I do not claim that my findings apply to all wars studied by Butler (the 'war on terror', the 'war against immigration', etc.). Besides, she takes a philosophical stance that raises the question of the ethical response one should make to the question of the ungrievability of certain lives. Although I find this question very important, I do not claim to have any solution to offer. Rather, my interest in Butler's work is based on the following three ideas.

Firstly, Butler helps towards overcoming the materialism versus idealism debate, which has interested some International Relations (IR) scholarship. She assumes, in accordance with the most recent advocates of discourse theory (Torfing 2005), that conceiving reality as a discourse does not mean giving priority to ideas over matter (Foucault 1966), to moral values over technologies (Latour and Venn 2002), or to identities over interests (McSweeney 1999). In practice, ideas and materialities mutually constitute each other. Hence, 'discourse is defined as an empirical collection of practices that qualify as discursive in so far as they contain a semiotic element' (Torfing 2005, 7).

Applied to the question of war, this discursive approach does not 'imply that life and death are direct consequences of discourse (an absurd conclusion, if taken literally). Rather, it implies that there is no life and no death without a relation to a frame' (Butler 2010, 7).

Secondly, Butler shows – in line with the discursive approach proposed by Foucault (Foucault 1997 [1976]) – that the 'frames of war' are inseparable from relations of power. She observes that they are like 'frames' of any kind: they are 'always throwing something away, always keeping something out, always de-realizing and de-legitimating alternative versions of reality' (Butler 2010, xi). Liberal political discourse, for instance, may be more inclusive than others. It is possibly more generous than, say, the racist discourse that emerged in Germany in the 1930s (to give only one suggestive example) (Hutchison 2014). Yet this discourse firmly keeps out of the frame those who do not meet its ontology of the human: Muslim women who choose to wear the veil in France (Butler 2010, 75), immigrants who do not pass the tests of 'gay-friendliness' in the Netherlands (Butler 2010, 105), detainees held in Guantanamo (Butler 2010, 55), etc.

According to Butler, the selective character of frames of war is particularly noticeable in the way Westerners reacted to the 9/11 attacks on the one hand, and the ensuing US war on terror on the other. After observing that the victims of the former engendered an incommensurate (and legitimate) collective emotion, Butler asks about the latter: 'Why is it that we are not given the names of the war dead, including those the US has killed, of whom we will never have the image, the name, the story, never a testimonial shard of their life, something to see, to touch, to know?' (Butler 2010, 39). Butler's argument is that these lives – more numerous by far than the 2973 victims of the 9/11 attacks – remain 'ungrievable' because they are the blanks of contemporary discourse.

This last comment helps in clarifying the third (and most important) idea that I find articulates with my research findings, namely this notion of 'ungrievable lives'. As pointed out in the introduction, Butler defines ungrievable lives as 'those that cannot be lost, and cannot be destroyed, because they already inhabit a lost and destroyed zone; they are, *ontologically, and from the start* [my emphasis] already lost and destroyed, which means that when they are destroyed in war, nothing is destroyed' (Butler 2010, xix).

This notion brings an important nuance to the aforementioned critical sociological literature on contemporary Western wars. Of course, Butler would agree with those critical sociologists when they state that modern technologies of war – new weapons (Der Derian 2009), military language (Cohn 1987), military 'strategic common sense' (Wasinski 2010), etc. – distort soldiers' perceptions and shape a 'reified' (Honneth 2007) image of the enemy (see above). Yet she would probably argue, in addition to this, that those lives would likely remain invisible in the absence of such distorting instruments because the whole discourse – i.e., the whole reality we live in – contributes towards making some lives 'ungrievable'. This emerges, for instance, from Butler's study of how Israeli mainstream media participated – along with the aforementioned military *dispositifs* – in the reification of the victims of the Israeli war in Gaza in 2008–2009: 'We are asked to believe that those children are not really children, are not really alive, that they have already been turned to metal, to steel, that they belong to the machinery of bombardment, at which point the body of the child is conceived as nothing more than a militarized metal that protects the attacker against attack' (Butler 2010, xxvii).

Applied to the question under investigation, this argument implies, for instance, that the two important dynamics at stake during the war in Libya – the framing of the war as humanitarian and the use of new technologies – do not work as antagonistic forces. Following Butler, I will not contend, for instance, that the former dynamic would enlarge the military economy of compassion and that the latter would call into question this dynamic, thus, fashioning a dominant framing, which would be incompletely humanitarian or incompletely reifying. Rather, Butler's framework helps us to understand that these two dynamics come together to define the space between grievable and ungrievable lives. I elaborate further on this idea in the following paragraphs by exploring some of the concrete contours – and blanks – of this 'discursive formation' (Foucault 1969).

## Argument: when killing enemies does not count

The general argument developed in this article is that the ideas and materialities, which shaped the NATO and French war in Libya, led to the complete erasure of enemies. The latter were neither framed as an object of hatred, nor of strategy, nor of sacrifice, nor as anything else. They were 'ungrievable lives' in the sense described above: they were 'ontologically, and from the start already lost and destroyed, which means that when they are destroyed in war, nothing is destroyed' (Butler 2010, xix). Empirically, this spectacular case of misrecognition materialized in the fact that enemies 'did not count'. They did not count in the sense that they were not quantified (1). And they did not count in the sense that they had no importance (2).

### *Dead enemies are not quantified*

As pointed out by Weizman and Shaw, modern Western wars take place within the realm of mathematical reasoning (Weizman 2012; Shaw 2006). Western soldiers perform mathematical calculations at all decision-making levels: does the fact of waging war preserve humanity from a greater evil? Which technology will permit the right 'military effect' to be obtained? Is it rational to drop the bomb (and save X lives) given that the probability of causing collateral damage is Y? In the case of the war in Libya, this logic emerged from the fact that NATO provided many statistics on the actual conduct of war. NATO published very precise figures concerning the number of aerial missions (26,323), the number of bombing raids (9658), the number of bombs and missiles (7700).[10] However, NATO has not provided any figures concerning the number of Gadhafi combatants killed during the war.

The absence of statistics concerning the number of pro-Gadhafi combatants killed during this war does not simply reflect the fact that NATO does not want to communicate about it. I conducted an interview with a high-ranking French officer in charge during the war in Libya. The interview lasted more than two hours and I believe that we reached a rather high level of confidence. However, this general assured me that he too was unable to provide any order of magnitude concerning the number of Gadhafi combatants killed during this war:

[Interviewer] You tell me that there was no collateral damage. But there were casualties among the Gadhafists. Do you know how many? I could not find any number in the press …

[General X] No. I don't have any number. This is really not the kind of counting we used to do. Besides, we had no means to do it. It's important to repeat that there were no troops on the ground. (…) So I am unable … Un-a-ble. I am even unable to give you an order of magnitude.

[Interviewer] Not even an order of magnitude? I am surprised. We know that conflicts are very different in this respect. Some cause many casualties. Others much less. The Second World War, for instance, is not exactly the equivalent of the Yom Kippur war ...

[General X] No. I am unable, here, to give you any number. I don't have any idea. Honestly. Truly.[11]

This absence of counting holds true at the level of active combatants as well. When I asked the pilots how many people they had killed, most of them hesitated for a while. They did not find the question embarrassing. They did not think it was awkward. They were not surprised either (after all, this question was all the more topical given the subject of the study). They simply hesitated before answering: 'two or three', 'about ten', 'maybe a hundred'. My guess is that their initial hesitation reflected one simple thing: they had not really thought of counting before the interview took place.

It is important to add at this stage that this absence of counting is not the sole preserve of the military. The *New York Times*,[12] the *Guardian*,[13] Human Rights Watch,[14] Amnesty International,[15] and several other newspapers and NGOs carried out studies on the ground to ascertain the NATO death toll in Libya. They produced innumerable figures on this war's alleged 'collateral' victims. They have not said a word about the number of Libyan loyalist combatants killed by the 7700 NATO bombs.

This observation resonates with one of Butler's remarks: 'Even when it proves possible to know what the numbers are, the numbers may not matter at all. In other words, there are situations when counting clearly does not count. Some people are horrified to learn the number of war dead, but for others, those numbers do not matter' (Butler 2010, xx). Butler notes that this low level of interest in numbers is all the more surprising given that 'we are used to hearing, for instance, that quantitative methods reign in the social sciences, and that qualitative methods do not 'count' for very much at all' (Butler 2010, xxi). In order to understand this, she argues, one has to admit that 'certain implicit schemes of conceptualization operate quite powerfully to orchestrate what we can admit as reality; they function through ritualized forms of disavowal, so even the positivist weight of numbers does not stand as a chance against them' (Butler 2010, xxi). In the case under investigation, these 'implicit schemes' materialized in the fact that the enemies killed were of no importance.

## *Enemies killed are of no importance*

The phrase 'enemies do not count' can also be translated by 'enemies are of no importance'. By this, I do not mean that the pilots feel contempt for the people they kill. Indeed, such a statement would imply that they represent them in a negative way, an argument that would contradict all the data I have collected. Rather, I mean that the enemies are the blanks in the contemporary discourse. Indeed, military historians teach us that enemies have been represented in different ways throughout history: as dangerous others, as military objectives, as totems one honors before or after the battle, etc. Those pro-Gadhafi combatants who died in Libya were none of these. I will illustrate this by commenting on a social practice, which is less trivial than appears at first sight, namely how modern fighter jet pilots celebrate their 'successful missions'.

This celebration takes the form of a little party which brings together the pilot, his navigator, the technicians, and some of the other pilots in the detachment. They take place in a masculine and virile atmosphere similar to that described by several feminist students of war (Agathangelou 2002; Cohn 1987; Enloe 1990). The pilots and their colleagues meet over a couple of beers and comment (often coarsely) on the success of the mission.

When asked about the sense of these celebrations, the pilots put forward the following reasons. First, they emphasize that these 'successful missions' have to be celebrated because they give 'concrete expression to training'. They also highlight the need to celebrate the success collectively, i.e., 'with all the team, including the technicians who work a lot and do not have the chance to be in the cockpit'. They also point out that the French Air Force has set up a system according to which each bomb dropped leads to the award of a medal, and that 'it always feels good to be rewarded for one's job'. Finally, they explain that these parties maintain the tradition of their predecessors who celebrated their victories during air duels with other 'knights of the sky'.

Whatever the reasons for these parties, they illustrate that the contemporary way of waging war has gone through some important changes. Indeed, the tradition which consists of celebrating the death of the enemy is scarcely new. Anthropologists have described hundreds of rituals where the killing of the enemy is symbolically represented before or after the actual use of force (Girard 1972). Yet the parties I am talking about here differ from these rituals in one major aspect. Whereas the traditional sacrificial rituals display an explicit link between the enemy and its representation (the signified and the signifier, to use the linguistic terminology), the enemy is completely absent from these modern ceremonies. It is not represented as an Other, or as an evil, or in a more abstract 'totemized' way (see below). The enemy is just not there.

Instead, the whole party revolves around one single object: the bomb. Indeed, the bomb is not only the main subject of conversation. It is also represented visually in various ways. For instance, I saw several pictures where the victorious pilot had round his neck a signboard similar to those worn at stag parties but where the bomb was symbolized with a human face. On another picture, the pilots had drawn a bomb with a sexy woman riding it sidesaddle. Finally, I saw various photographs of pilots painting a little bomb on their aircraft's fuselage, just like their predecessors used to paint a little plane after each 'victory' against another 'knight of the sky'.

This last example perhaps calls for a brief history of how airmen have stopped representing their enemies. As stated above, First World War pilots counted their victories by painting little planes on their own aircraft's fuselage. With the subsequent vast increase in bombing operations, Second World War pilots began painting little buildings, factories, or bridges, depending on the mission. To a certain extent, all these paintings (planes, buildings, etc.) maintained a thread – however tenuous – with the dead enemies. Whether they were honored or hated, the dead enemies still signified, just as a dead combatant is signified in a depersonalized national obituary. Nowadays, pilots paint bombs on their planes' fuselages. Their dead enemies have lost this very last shard of recognition: being represented.

Of course, this practice of not representing enemies during the celebration of the successful missions recalls what Agamben writes about those Homo-Sacer who could be killed but not 'sacrificed' (Agamben 1998). More generally, this art of deciding over human lives resonates with what Foucault says about the change in the exercise of political power, which he associates with modernity (Foucault 1997 [1976], 2001). On the one hand, the different actors of this war – government leaders, military leaders, pilots, etc. – kill in the most classical and 'disciplinary' sense of the term. They exert a 'sovereign' power over those they actively kill (they decide to go to war, to devise a strategy which involves the death of others, to pull the trigger, etc.). On the other hand, these actors also 'make live and let die' ('faire vivre et laisser mourir') (Foucault 1997

[1976], 214) in a good biopolitical fashion. They 'make live' those they pretend to protect – Western citizens, Libyan democrats, those Libyan women abused by the pro-Gadhafi army (see above), etc., and 'let die' those whom they misrecognize at each step in the conduct of war, i.e., those who are not quantified and do not matter enough to be hated or honored.

## Conclusion

This article aimed at understanding how Western soldiers make sense of the act of killing in the context of contemporary Western wars. In order to answer this question, I carried out a sociological study of French soldiers who participated in the 2011 war in Libya. My argument is that the French soldiers and officers who waged this war are caught in a power regime, which leads to the complete obliteration of the enemy. The latter is not conceived of as an object of hatred, or as an object of strategy, or as an object of sacrifice. The dead enemy simply does not count.

I am unable to assess whether the framing of war described above applies to all contemporary Western wars. Indeed, one could fairly object that the 'war on terror' – and its associated 'targeted' and 'deliberate' killings are based on a different logic or set of principles. I am also unable to assess whether this rather biopolitical way of erasing lives is fundamentally new. Indeed, one could fairly follow Agamben when he states that biopolitics is not a product of modernity but consubstantial with political power in general (Agamben 1998).

I can argue, however, that this framing of war has found a significant form in the context of humanitarian and technological wars. Indeed, the fact that these two frames of war – the ideational frame of humanitarian war on the one hand, and new technologies on the other – emerged simultaneously is not coincidental. These two logics are part of the same discursive formation. They are 'technological morals' or 'moral technologies' (Latour and Venn 2002, 248). They rely on a common ontology of the human, i.e., a precise understanding of what a 'modern subject' is, or should be (Mavelli 2013; Seth 2013). To put this simply, one may say that the framing of war as humanitarian is an attempt to export this modern subject overseas (or to support those groups which allegedly defend this ontology of the human), and that the use of new technologies is an attempt to protect this modern subject – incarnated by the Western combatant – at all costs.

## Acknowledgements

I am grateful to Shannon Brincat, Thomas Lindemann, and the two anonymous reviewers for their accurate and stimulating comments on a previous version of this article.

## Notes

1. http://www.nytimes.com/2011/12/18/world/africa/scores-of-unintended-casualties-in-nato-war-in-libya.html?pagewanted=all
2. This point is frequently made by some liberal institutions such as the Stockholm International Peace Research Institute.
3. The notion of 'civilizing process' owes a lot to the work of Norbert Elias, although Elias – who was a direct witness of the two World Wars – never stated that this process applied to international relations. On the notion of civilizing process, see Elias (2000 [1939]). On the problem posed by the two world wars to an Eliasian theory of international relations, see Audouin-Rouzeau (2010) and Linklater (2007).

4. 'L'intervention en Libye a évité "des milliers de morts" selon Sarkozy', *Le Monde*, 25.03.2011.
5. Vinogradoff, Luc, 'L'intervention en Libye critiquée sur le fond et sur la forme', *Le Monde*, 25.03.2011.
6. http://www.nytimes.com/2011/03/28/world/africa/28tripoli.html?_r=2&
7. http://www.nato.int/nato_static/assets/pdf/pdf_2011_11/20111108_111107-factsheet_up_factsfigures_en.pdf
8. http://www.defense.gouv.fr/actualites/dossiers/operation-harmattan
9. The fact that the enquiry does not include drone operators may appear to be a limitation given the importance of this technology in modern warfare. However, it is important to repeat that the job of modern fighter jet pilots in Libya was not very different from that of a drone operator. The pilots and navigators were not exposed to the enemy's fire, with the result that the main risks they took were aeronautic and little different from training situations.
10. http://www.nato.int/nato_static/assets/pdf/pdf_2011_11/20111108_111107-factsheet_up_factsfigures_en.pdf
11. [interviewer]: On a vu qu'il n'y a pas eu de victime collatérale. Mais il y a eu des morts côté Kadhafiste. Est-ce qu'on a idée du nombre ? Je n'ai pas trouvé de chiffres.

    [General X] Non. Je n'ai pas de chiffre. C'est vraiment le type de comptabilité qu'on ne faisait pas et que, d'ailleurs, on n'avait pas les moyens de faire. Il faut quand même se rappeler qu'il n'y a pas de forces au sol ... (...) Donc moi je suis incapable ... In-ca-pa-ble. Mais je ne suis même pas capable de vous dire un ordre d'idée.

    [Interviewer]: Pas même un ordre de grandeur ? Je suis surpris. Nous savons que les conflits sont très différents sur ce point. Certains font beaucoup de morts. D'autres beaucoup moins. La Seconde guerre mondiale, par exemple, ce n'est pas la même chose que la guerre du Kippour ...

    [General X]: Non. Je suis incapable, là, de vous donner un ordre d'idées. Incapable. Très honnêtement, mais très honnêtement.
12. http://www.nytimes.com/2011/12/18/world/africa/scores-of-unintended-casualties-in-nato-war-in-libya.html?pagewanted=all
13. http://www.theguardian.com/commentisfree/2011/oct26/libya-war-saving-lives-catastrophic-failure
14. http://www.hrw.org/news/2011/10/24/libya-apparent-execution-53-Gadhafi-supporters
15. http://www.amnesty.org/en/library/info/MDE19/025/2011/en

## References

Adorno, T. 1969. "Du rapport entre la théorie et l'empirie en sociologie." *L'Homme et la Société* 13: 127–133. doi:10.3406/homso.1969.1231.

Agamben, G. 1998. *Homo Sacer: Sovereign Power and Bare Life*. Stanford, CA: Stanford University Press.

Agathangelou, A. M. 2002. "'Sexing' Globalization in International Relations." In *Power, Postcolonialism and International Relations*, edited by G. Chowdry and S. Nair, 142–169. New York: Routledge.

Amos, V., and P. Parmar. 2005. "Challenging Imperial Feminism." *Feminist Review* 80: 44–63. doi:10.1057/palgrave.fr.9400220.

Aradau, C. 2012. "Security, War, Violence – The Politics of Critique: A Reply to Barkawi." *Millennium – Journal of International Studies* 41: 112–123. doi:10.1177/0305829812451718.

Arendt, H. 1963. *Eichmann in Jerusalem: A Report on the Banality of Evil*. New York: Viking.

Asad, T. 2007. *On Suicide Bombing*. New York: Colombia University Press.

Audouin-Rouzeau, S. 2002. "La violence du champ de bataille." In *La violence de guerre*, edited by S. Audouin-Rouzeau, A. Becker, C. Ingrao, and H. Rousso, 73–97. Paris: Editions Complexe.

Audouin-Rouzeau, S. 2008. *Combattre, Une anthropologie historique de la guerre moderne (Xixe–Xxie Siècle)*. Paris: Seuil.

Audouin-Rouzeau, S. 2010. "Norbert Elias et l'expérience oubliée de la Première guerre mondiale." *Vingtième Siècle. Revue D'histoire* 106 (2): 104–114. doi:10.3917/vin.106.0104.

Ayotte, K. J., and M. Husain. 2005. "Securing Afghan Women: Neocolonialism, Epistemic Violence, and the Rhetoric of the Veil." *NWSA Journal* 17: 112–133. doi:10.2979/NWS.2005.17.3.112.

Bartov, O. 1998. "Defining Enemies, Making Victims: Germans, Jews, and the Holocaust." *American Historical Review* 103 (3): 771–816. doi:10.2307/2650572.

Battistella, D. 2008. *The Return of the State of War: A Theoretical Analysis of Operation Iraqi Freedom*. Colchester: ECPR.

Blanchard, E. 2003. "Gender, International Relations, and the Development of Feminist Security Theory." *Signs* 8 (4): 1289–1312.

Bourke, J. 1999. *An Intimate History of Killing: Face to Face Killing in 20th Century Warfare*. London: Granta Press.

Brincat, S., L. Lima, and J. Nunes. 2012. *Critical Theory in International Relations and Security Studies: Interviews and Reflections*. London: Routledge.

Butler, J. 2004. *Precarious Life: The Powers of Mourning and Violence*. London: Verso.

Butler, J. 2009. *Krieg und Affekt*. Berlin: Diaphanes.

Butler, J. 2010. *Frames of War: When Is Life Grievable?* London: Verso.

Chaliand, G. 2008. *Le nouvel art de la guerre*. Paris: L'archipel.

Chamayou, G. 2013. *Théorie du drone*. Paris: La Fabrique.

Chuter, D. 1996. *Humanity's Soldier: France and International Security, 1919–2001*. Oxford: Berghahn Books.

Cohn, C. 1987. "Sex and Death in the Rational World of Defense Intellectuals." *Signs* 12 (4): 687–718. doi:10.1086/494362.

Colonomos, A. 2008. *Moralizing International Relations: Called to Account*. New York: Palgrave.

Corvisier, A. 1975. "La mort du soldat depuis la fin du Moyen-Age." *Revue Historique* 254: 3–30.

Der Derian, J. 2009. *Mapping the Military–Industrial Media–Entertainment Network*. London: Routledge.

Dubey, G., and C. Moricot. 2008. "Trop près trop loin: Les mutations de la perception du combat par les équipages d'avions de chasse." *Les documents du C2SD* no. 99.

Edkins, J. 1999. *Poststructuralism & International Relations: Bringing the Political Back In*. Boulder, CO: Lynne Rienner Publishers.

Edkins, J., and V.-W. Nick. 2009. *Critical Theorists and International Relations*. London: Routledge.

Elias, N. 2000 [1939]. *The Civilizing Process: Sociogenetic and Psychogenetic Investigations*. Oxford: Basil Blackwell.

Enloe, C. 1990. *Bananas, Beaches and Bases: Making Feminist Sense of International Politics*. London: Pandora Press.

Enloe, C. 2004. *The Curious Feminist: Searching for Women in a New Age of Empire*. Berkeley: University of California Press.

Fanon, F. 2002 [1961]. *Les damnés de la terre*. Paris: La Découverte.

Finnemore, M. 1999. "Rules of War and Wars of Rules: The International Red Cross and the Restraint of State Violence." In *Constructing World Culture: International Nongovernmental Organizations Since 1875*, edited by J. Boli and G. Thomas, 149–165. Stanford, CA: Stanford University Press.

Foucault, M. 1966. *Les mots et les choses: Une archéologie des sciences humaines*. Paris: Gallimard.

Foucault, M. 1969. *Archéologie du savoir*. Paris: Gallimard.

Foucault, M. 1997 [1976]. "Il faut défendre la société." In *Cours au Collège de France, 1975–1976*, edited by F. Ewald and A. Fontana. Seuil: Gallimard.

Foucault, M. 2001. "Naissance de la biopolitique (1979)." In *Dits et Ecrits II, 1976–1988*, 818–825, edited by D. Defert and F. Ewald. Paris: Gallimard.

Freud, S., and A. Einstein. 1932. *Warum Krieg*. Zurich: Diogenes.

Geis, A., and L. Brock. 2006. *Democratic Wars: Looking at the Dark Side of Democratic Peace*. Basingstoke: Palgrave Macmillan.

Girard, R. 1972. *La violence et le sacré*. Paris: Grasset.

Herman, E. S., and D. Peterson. 2012. "Reality Denial: Steven Pinker's Apologetics for Western-Imperial Violence." Accessed July 17. http://www.zcommunications.org/znet.

Hobson, J. M. 2007. "Is Critical Theory Always for the White West and for Western Imperialism? Beyond Westphilian towards a Post-Racist Critical IR." In *Critical International Relations*

*Theory. 25 Years After*, edited by N. Rengger and B. Thirkell-White, 91–116. Cambridge: Cambridge University Press.

Holland, J. 2011. "'When You Think of the Taliban, Think of the Nazis': Teaching Americans '9/11' in NBC's the West Wing." *Millennium – Journal of International Studies* 40: 85–106. doi:10.1177/0305829811408680.

Holmqvist, C. 2013. "Undoing War: War Ontologies and the Materiality of Drone Warfare." *Millennium – Journal of International Studies* 41: 535–552. doi:10.1177/0305829813483350.

Honneth, A. 2005. *Verdinglichung – Eine anerkennungstheoretische Studie*. Frankfurt am Main: Suhrkamp.

Honneth, A. 2007. *Reification: A Recognition-Theoretical View*. Oxford: Oxford University Press.

hooks, b. 1995. "Feminism and Militarism: A Comment." *Women's Studies Quarterly* 23 (3/4): 58–64.

Hurrel, A. 2002. "Norms and Ethics in International Relations." In *Handbook of International Relations*, edited by W. Carlsnaes, T. Risse, and B. A. Simmons, 137–154. London: Sage Publications.

Hutchison, E. 2014. "A Global Politics of Pity? Disaster Imagery and the Emotional Construction of Solidarity after the 2004 Asian Tsunami." *International Political Sociology* 8 (1): 1–19. doi:10.1111/ips.12037.

James, W. 1981. *Pragmatism: A New Name for Some Old Ways of Thinking (1907)*. Indianapolis, IN: Hackett Publishing.

Kaufman, W. 2009. *Justified Killing: The Paradox of Self-Defense*. Lanham: Lexington Books.

Latour, B., and C. Venn. 2002. "Morality and Technology: The End of the Means." *Theory, Culture and Society* 19 (5–6): 247–260. doi:10.1177/026327602761899246.

Lebow, R. 2008. *A Cultural Theory of International Relations*. Cambridge: Cambridge University Press.

Lindemann, T. 2010. *Causes of War: The Struggle for Recognition*. Colchester: ECPR Press.

Linklater, A. 2007. "Norbert Elias, the Civilizing Process and the Sociology of International Relations." In *Critical Theory and World Politics*, edited by A. Linklater, 160–177. London: Routledge.

Macleish, K. T. 2013. *Making War at Fort Hood: Life and Uncertainty in a Military Community*. Princeton, NJ: Princeton University Press.

Mariot, N. 2003/2004. "Faut-il être motivé pour tuer? Sur quelques explications aux violences de guerre." *Genèses* 53: 154–177.

Mavelli, L. 2013. "Between Normalisation and Exception: The Securitisation of Islam and the Construction of the Secular Subject." *Millennium – Journal of International Studies* 41 (2): 159–181. doi:10.1177/0305829812463655.

McSweeney, B. 1999. *Security, Identity and Interests: A Sociology of International Relations*. Cambridge: Cambridge University Press.

Mosse, G. 2000. *La Brutalisation des sociétés européennes. De la Grande Guerre au totalitarisme*. Paris: Hachette littérature.

Olsson, C. 2008. "Afghanistan et irak: Les origines coloniales des guerres antiterroristes." In *Au nom du 11 septembre*, edited by D. Bigo, L. Bonelli, and T. Deltombe, 49–62. Paris: La Découverte.

Pin-Fat, V. 2013. "Cosmopolitanism and the End of Humanity: A Grammatical Reading of Posthumanism." *International Political Sociology* 7 (3): 241–257. doi:10.1111/ips.12021.

Pinker, S. 2011. *The Better Angels of Our Nature: Why Violence Has Declined*. New York: Viking.

Popper, K., and D. Miller 1983. "A Proof of the Impossibility of Inductive Probability." *Nature*, 302.

Price, R. 1998. "Reversing the Gun Sights: Transnational Civil Society Targets Land Mines." *International Organization* 52 (3): 613–644. doi:10.1162/002081898550671.

Roach, S. C. 2007. *Critical Theory and International Relations: A Reader*. London: Routledge.

Said, E. W. 1979. *Orientalism*. New York: Vintage Book.

Seth, S. 2013. "'Once Was Blind but Now Can See': Modernity and the Social Sciences." *International Political Sociology* 7 (2): 136–151. doi:10.1111/ips.12014.

Shaw, M. 2006. *The New Western Way of War: Risk Transfer and Its Crisis in Iraq*. Cambridge: Polity Press.

Spivak, G. C. 1988. "Can the Subaltern Speak?." In *Marxism and the Interpretation of Culture*, edited by N. Cary and L. Crossberg, 271–316. Chicago: University of Illinois Press.

Sylvester, C. 2012. "War Experiences/War Practices/War Theory." *Millennium – Journal of International Studies* 40: 483–50. doi:10.1177/0305829812442211.
Tickner, A. 2005. "What Is Your Research Program? Some Feminist Answers to International Relations Methodological Questions." *International Studies Quarterly* 49 (1): 1–21. doi:10.1111/j.0020-8833.2005.00332.x.
Tickner, A., and L. Sjoberg. 2011. *Feminism and International Relations: Conversations about the Past, Present and Future*. London: Routledge.
Torfing, J. 2005. "Discourse Theory: Achievements, Arguments, and Challenges." In *Discourse Theory in European Politics. Identity, Policy and Governance*, edited by D. Howarth and J. Torfing, 1–32. Basingstoke: Palgrave Macmillan.
van Veeren, E. 2014. "Materializing US Security: Guantanamo's Object Lessons and Concrete Messages." *International Political Sociology* 8 (1): 20–42. doi:10.1111/ips.12038.
Vennesson, P., F. Breuer, C. De Franco, and U. Schroeder. 2008. "Is There a European Way of War? Role Conceptions, Organizational Frames, and the Utility of Force." *Armed Forces & Society* 35 (4): 628–645. doi:10.1177/0095327X08317994.
Wasinski, C. 2010. *Rendre la guerre possible. La construction du sens commun stratégique*. Bruxelles: Peter Lang.
Weizman, E. 2012. *Least of Possible Evils: Humanitarian Violence for Arendt to Gaza*. London: Verso.
Zehfuss, M. 2009. "Hierarchies of Grief and the Possibility of War: Remembering UK Fatalities in Iraq." *Millennium – Journal of International Studies* 38 (2): 1–22.

# REPLY

## Killing without hatred: the politics of (non)-recognition in contemporary Western wars: a reply to Mathias Delori

Kamil Shah

*School of Political Science and International Studies, University of Queensland, Brisbane, Australia*

This is a reply to:
Delori, Mathias. 2014. "Killing without hatred: the politics of (non)-recognition in contemporary Western wars." *Global Discourse*. 4 (4): 516–531. http://dx.doi.org/10.1080/23269995. 2014.935102.

Mathias Delori (2014) seeks to investigate the ways in which Western pilots relate to the act of killing in contemporary humanitarian warfare, by looking in particular at the war waged by NATO Forces in Libya in 2011. He argues that the framing of contemporary wars through the lenses of humanitarianism and technology have the effect of erasing the enemy – that 'French soldiers operate within a regime of power' in which the enemy simply does not appear. Delori conducts a sociological and ethnographic enquiry in an attempt to understand the discourses through which consent for killing was gained in the context of French air operations in the war in Libya. It is a project Delori suggests is in line with Judith Butler's insistence for a critical engagement with those *frames of war* through which certain lives are produced as in need of and worthy of protection while others are deemed to be dangerous to humanity, their lives remaining forever *ungrievable*. Delori's intervention brings to light the manner in which ideas and materialities coalesce to produce both the *facts* of war and consent for killing. Delori's concern is that the increasing rationalisation of Western militaries and military doctrine – especially through new technologies which operate to protect combatants from direct engagement with the enemy – allows for a reading of humanitarian warfare as controlled, precise, and without excess, a reading in which the enemy is obliterated. The substantive crux of the argument seems to lay in the disinterest shown by Western States with regard to how many 'enemies' were killed in Libya during the 2011 engagement, even as statistical representations of the war and how it was carried out proliferate. Delori argues that the desire to not count the enemy dead shows that the enemy in fact 'does not count'. Indeed, he even highlights the 'enemy's' omission from post-mission ceremonies (replaced by the 'bomb'), saying that this denies the enemy other even this very last shred of recognition.

While I appreciate Delori's sense that increased use of 'play-station'-like technologies (or their equivalent in terms of French fighter pilots) accompanying humanitarian intervention has produced change in the way Western soldiers relate to killing, I nonetheless am sceptical that these aspects have been appropriately emphasised. Delori's argument seems to hinge in part on the idea that technology provides French fighter pilots, and in other cases perhaps drone operators, with unmatched levels of security under conditions of war. Indeed, they fly far overhead and remain untouchable as far as the enemy below is concerned. They launch bombs from afar, with the firing of weapons the only truly distinguishing feature when compared with practice runs. For Delori, the evidence is obvious – not a single NATO soldier was killed during the months of the intervention. While this may be true for Western pilots in the moments of live 'combat', I would nonetheless argue that contemporary Western wars (to use Delori's turn of phrase) of the post-9/11 period (and even before) have been built upon the incredible insecurity of the West. This is perhaps obvious in the retaliatory actions of the 'war on terror' but I think the argument can be made that it is equally true in many forms of 'humanitarian' intervention. Whether discussing fragile states and 'new wars' or the wilful actions of intransigent leaders, the list of threats to and enemies of the West continue to proliferate. Rather than the enemy being unrecognised, enemies are seemingly everywhere, and always a threat to the Western-led liberal world order. This, of course, is not a new story. It has a long lineage which postcolonial scholars have done well to describe. Such radical insecurity was fundamental to the colonial encounter (as discussed, for example, by Nandy in *The Intimate Enemy* and Orwell's *Shooting an Elephant*), requiring all sorts of legal formulations and fabrications, and producing an endless list of 'enemy others' within a colonial discourse of *protection*.

This, then, raises a second point. The intervention in Libya was not only grounded in a discourse of humanitarianism but also invoked the *Responsibility to Protect*, thereby leaning on the ethical obligations of the international community to act. From this perspective, we can begin to consider more critically key questions at the heart of R2P, namely *which lives are worthy of being saved*, which lives simply *don't count*, and *who decides?* On this note, it is useful to regard the manner in which R2P imagines the subjects which it must 'protect' – it assumes those populations inability to make decisions for themselves on questions of life and death, appropriating this power for the great powers of the world (Grovogui 2013, 80–81). The image of the Western military forces which Delori draws upon – fully professionalised, respectful, and fighting dispassionately – aligns with liberal discourses privileging Western military intervention and indeed conflating the West with the so-called international community. In the context of Libya, NATO was empowered to decide on behalf of the international community who should live and who could die, and such decisions could be made without reasonable accountability. The point is that a critical engagement of such relations as touched upon here may strengthen our understanding of how soldiers relate to the act of killing in contemporary Western wars.

**Reference**

Delori, M. 2014. "Killing Without Hatred: The Politics of (Non)-Recognition in Contemporary Western Wars." *Global Discourse* 4 (4): 516–531. doi:10.1080/23269995.2014.935102.

Grovogui, S. 2013. "The Missing Human: Intervention, Human Security, and Empire." In *Globalization, Difference, and Human Security*, edited by Mustapha Kamal Pasha. Abingdon: Routledge.

# Index

Note: Page numbers followed by 'n' refer to notes

9–11 attacks, the 33, 36–8, 44, 48, 127 *see also* war on terror discourses
1891 Anglo-Portuguese Treaty, the 114n3
1997 Asian financial crisis, the 73

abstraction minimization of the Other 95, 101
acculturation and exclusion 7, 51
Adorno, Theodor 16
Afghanistan war, the 43, 122, 123; as case of non-recognition 33, 36, 38–9, 41, 44
Ahmadinejad, Mahmoud 68, 85
AM (Al-Muhajiroun) 6–7, 32–3 *see also* research study of AM (Al-Muhajiroun) transformation to radical Islam
ambiguous attitude of Muslims to the 9/11 attacks 36–7, 48
Anglo-Boer War, the 106, 108, 113, 114n1
Anglo-German relations 8–9, 114n3, 117–19 *see also* Bundesrath-Affäre, the
Arendt, Hannah 15, 24–7, 98n2
armed force, use of 88–9
Asian customs and foreign trade 55

barbarian states and sovereignty 54
bifurcated nature of the world 63, 64–5
Bismarck, Otto von 117
*Bluest Eye, The* (book) 15, 21–3, 30
British policy in South Africa 106 *see also* Bundesrath-Affäre, the
Bülow, Bernhard von 105–6, 109, 110, 111, 113, 117, 119
Bundesrath-Affäre, the 104, 107–13, 117–19
Bush, President George W. 45n15, 92, 93

capacity for empathy, the 91
case study on French pilots in the 2011 Libyan conflict and its framing by the West 9, 121, 124–6, 128–31, 136–7
case study on the protection of cultural artifacts during war 56–8
celebration of missions by jet pilots 129–30

Chaplin, Charlie 25
China and international society 55, 57, 80n1; conscious of status 67, 78, 80n6, 85; foreign policy 59–60, 72; relations with the US 68, 78, 86, 95–6
colonial wars in non-European settings 57–8, 66–7 *see also* Anglo-Boer War, the
conflict and nonrecognition 8
Connolly, Dr. Julie 30
conscientious objector, the 25
costs of showing respect 73–4
critical theory and conflict between thinkers 16–17
cultural differences and foreigners' ideas of respect 74–5, 76
cultural racism 121, 123, 124

dehumanization and misrecognition 9, 31, 121, 124
depictions of the enemy in warfare 122, 129–30
Dewey, John 18
dialogue as a means of resolving conflicting views 77
dignity of the individual 2
diplomatic practice and international society 52–3, 54–5, 59, 78, 79–80
disclosure and the politics of recognition 6, 13–14, 15, 24–7, 30, 103
discourse analysis 35–6, 39–41, 49, 126–7
'discursive discovery' and 'discursive invention' 49 *see also* research study of AM (Al-Muhajiroun) transformation to radical Islam
disrespect and the inverse of social recognition 18, 34, 70–3, 79; and the 'Bundesrath-Affäre' 104, 109–10, 117–19 *see also* respect
divine recognition 42
double standards and status positions 78–9

Eastern influences on the West 64, 67
Elias, Norbert 90, 131n3

# INDEX

Ellison, Ralph 15
emotion and agency as catalysts for recognition 14–15
emotion and violence 89–91
emotions and misrecognition 15, 18–20, 22–3
English School, the 51
Eurocentrism and international society 63–5
European practices of recognition 7, 50–1; in non-European settings 57–8, 66–7, 85, 97, 106
exclusion and acculturation 7, 51
existential minimization of the Other 96–7, 101
expansion of trade and international society 53
expectation of reciprocity in practices of recognition 52

father figure and the superego, the 90
foreign policy and use of respect 74–5, 78–9
forms of recognition 13–14, 17–18
Foucauldian tradition of discourse analysis 35, 36
Foucault, Michel 130
*Frames of War* (book) 126
Frankfurt School of Critical Theory 16–17, 36
freedom of the seas 55
*Freedom's Right* (book) 14
free trade 55
Freud, Sigmund 90, 120

Gadhafi, Muammar 121, 125
German-Boer relations 106–7, 108
German Kaiserreich, the 103–4, 105–9, 113, 114n2; desire to become a world power 112, 113, 114n3–4, 117, 118
globalization and disrespect 79
Grotius, Hugo 55

Habermas, Jürgen 16
Hague Peace Conference, the 111
Hall, William E. 52
Hatzfeldt, Paul von 109–10, 111
Hegel, G. W. F. 1, 50, 51, 95
Hegelian dichotomy, the 87
Heller, Agnes 15, 20, 21
hero-protective narrative and self-recognition, the 93
hierarchical status of the current international order 79–80
Honneth, Axel 2, 6, 13, 22, 105; theory of recognition 16–18
*Human Condition, The* (book) 24, 25, 27
humiliation 34
Hussein, Saddam 93, 97

identification of ways to show respect 74–7
identity and recognition theory 2, 3–4
identity formation and mutuality 4

IEA (Islamic Emirate of Afghanistan) 35, 38, 39, 45n6
IMF, the 73
India and international society 67, 72–3
insecurity of the West and imagined enemies 137
interest-driven wars and non-recognition 89–90, 91–8, 101
interiority 101
international law: and international society 52–3, 56; and sovereignty 53, 54, 60
international relations and recognition 1–2, 7–8, 9, 105
international society, formation of 50–3, 54–5, 58, 63–5; acceptance of Turkey 51, 59; Eastern influence on 64, 67; Eurocentric construction of 63–5; practices of recognition 7, 50–1
international trade and the natural law 55
intersubjectivity 2, 42–3
*Intimate Enemy, The* (book) 64
*Invisible Man, The* (book) 15
Iran and international society 67, 68, 85
Iraq war, the 93
Islam and misrecognition 6–7, 32–3 *see also* research study of AM (Al-Muhajiroun) transformation to radical Islam

Japan and inernational society 59
Jews, the, and cultural assimilation 24–5
*Jihad,* call for 43–4
*jus in bello* 121, 122

Kafka, Franz 25
Kagan, Robert 93
*Kanonenfutter* (food for powder) 97
Kant, Immanuel 16
killing and consent in the military 9, 120, 122, 136
Kruger, Paul 118
Krüger-Telegram, the 106–7, 108, 109, 112, 113

laws of warfare 121, 122
legitimisation of campaigns by terror groups 48
liberal-humanitarian framing of war 122–3, 126–8, 131, 136–7 *see also* case study on French pilots in the 2011 Libyan conflict and its framing by the West
Libyan conflict of 2011 9
'Lieber Code,' the 57
*Life of the Mind, The* 26
loneliness 26
love-based recognition 17

Markell, Patchen 23–4
Marx, Karl 16
Master/Slave dialectic, the 1, 3, 42, 50

# INDEX

mercy as a natural law 90–1
merit-based recognition 17
military consent for killing 9, 120, 122, 136
minimization of the Other as non-recognition mentality 94–7, 98; and abstraction minimization 95, 101
misrecognition 14, 23, 128, 131; and dehumanization 9, 31, 121, 124; and human emotion 15, 18–20, 22–3; and Islam 6–7, 32–3 see also non-recognition, conceptions of
modern war technology 9, 121, 122, 124, 125, 132n9, 136–7
Mohammed, Omar Bakri (OBM) 36–7, 45n8–9
Morrison, Toni 15, 21–3
'Muslim world' as a victimized category, the 36–7, 40
mutuality and the recognition process 4–5, 7, 42–3, 50–1, 53

Napoleonic Wars, the 57
nation-states and respect 71–2
NATO 121, 125, 128, 129, 137
natural law and the need for international trade 55–6
nature of man, the 90–1
Nobel Prize, the 78
'Nobel Prize complex' 78
non-Europeans and need for recognition in international society 51, 59–60
non-recognition, conceptions of 8, 33–4, 51, 54–6, 59–60, 101–2; in interest-driven wars 89–90, 91–8, 101; in the US war in Afghanistan 33, 36, 38–9, 41, 44 see also misrecognition
Nussbaum, Martha 15, 20–1

Obama, Barack 67–8, 78, 86
Other, the see minimization of the Other as non-recognition mentality

pariahs and parvenus and cultural assimilation 24–5
peer groups and respect 71
perception of war on Islam by the West 36–8, 40
*Phenomenonology of Spirit* (book) 50, 59, 60, 94–5
philosophical thought on emotions as a source of war 89–91
Polish partitions 97
political elites and the legitimization of war 92–3, 97
politics of shame, the 20–2
post-colonialism and modern Western warfare 121, 123
practices of recognition in international society 51–3, 58–9, 85–6; in Europe 7, 50–1
psychology of emotions 18

R2P (Responsibility to Protect) 137
radicalisation of entities through discourse analysis 48–9
'rationalization' and the bureaucratization military organizations 124
recognition theory 2–6; and relations theory 1
Reichsmarineamt, the, and need for a large German navy 112, 113, 117
reification 94, 127
research study of AM (Al-Muhajiroun) transformation to radical Islam 33–44
respect 66, 68–9, 73–6, 77–8, 79–80, 85–6; and American foreign policy 67–8, 72, 76–7, 78–9; and cultural differences 74–5, 76; and social relationships 69–70; and status mismatches 8, 34 see also disrespect and the inverse of social recognition
rights-based recognition 17, 24
Rousseau, Jean-Jacques 90–1
rules of warfare in non-European settings 57–8

'Sakina affair,' the 44
Salisbury, Lord 111, 118
Sarkozy, Nicolas 125
savages and barbarians 54–5, 56, 59, 60
scapegoat theory and warfare 97–8
Self and the Other and the hero-protector narrative 93
self-consciousness and recognition 1
self-realisation through speech and action 25–6
self-recognition 42, 93
'semantic bridge' between emotion and identity 23
shame and vulnerability to misrecognition 6, 14, 15, 18, 20–3, 30–1
Sino-American relations 68, 78, 86, 95–6
Smith, Adam 91, 94
social culture of East Asia 67
social recognition, analysing 17–18; and disrespect 18, 34, 70–3, 79
social respect as an attitude 68–9
social stigmatisation 21
solidarity 18, 19, 23, 24 see also merit-based recognition
sovereignty and international law 53, 54, 60
special gestures to convey respect 77
speech and action as self-realisation 25–6
state institutions and the propagation of national narratives 71–2
statistics and quantifying dead enemies 128–9, 136
statuary non-recognition in warfare 97–8
status mismatches 105, 113; in Asian nations 66–7, 85–6 see also Anglo-German relations; Bundesrath-Affäre, the

# INDEX

status recognition 66, 69; in International Relations 1–2, 7–8, 9, 104–5
storytelling and narrative as form of disclosure 27
strategic dimension of warfare 88
*Struggle for Recognition, The* (book) 14
struggles for recognition 5, 50–1; and disclosure 13, 14–15, 24–7; and shame 6, 20–3 *see also* research study of AM (Al-Muhajiroun) transformation to radical Islam

*Theory of Moral Sentiments, The* 91
thinking as speculative activity 26
Thucydides 86
Tirpitz, Adm. Alfred von 112, 113
traditional theory 16
Transvaal, the 2, 106, 108, 114n1, 118
Turkish admittance into international society 51, 59

*Ummah,* the 45n7
'ungrievable lives,' notion of 127–8, 136
United States foreign policy 67–8, 72, 76–7, 78–9, 86, 96
utilitarian models and the recognition of war 87–8

Wahhabism and Islam 38–9
warfare and international law 56, 121, 122 *see also* case study on the protection of cultural artifacts during war
war on terror discourses 39–40, 41, 92, 93, 95, 126, 137; 9/11 attacks, the 36–8, 44, 127
Western definitions of terrorism 39–40
Westlake, John 52
Wilhelm II, Kaiser 103–4, 109, 110, 111, 113, 114n4
*Wissenssoziologische Diskursanalyse* 35–6
'world hegemony' discourse 40